Advanced Rust

Exploring Power Features of Rust for Intermediate and Advanced Developers

Nouman Azam

Apress®

Advanced Rust: Exploring Power Features of Rust for Intermediate and Advanced Developers

Nouman Azam
National University of Computer and Emerging Sciences,
Peshawar, Pakistan

ISBN-13 (pbk): 979-8-8688-2991-8 ISBN-13 (electronic): 979-8-8688-2992-5
https://doi.org/10.1007/979-8-8688-2992-5

Managing Director, Apress Media LLC: Welmoed Spahr
Acquisitions Editor: Melissa Duffy
Editorial Assistant: Gryffin Winkler
Copy Editor: Kezia Endsley

Cover designed by eStudioCalamar

Cover image designed by Unsplash

Distributed to the book trade worldwide by Springer Science+Business Media New York, 1 New York Plaza, New York, NY 10004. Phone 1-800-SPRINGER, fax (201) 348-4505, e-mail orders-ny@springer-sbm.com, or visit www.springeronline.com. Apress Media, LLC is a Delaware LLC and the sole member (owner) is Springer Science + Business Media Finance Inc (SSBM Finance Inc). SSBM Finance Inc is a **Delaware** corporation.

For information on translations, please e-mail booktranslations@springernature.com; for reprint, paperback, or audio rights, please e-mail bookpermissions@springernature.com.

Apress titles may be purchased in bulk for academic, corporate, or promotional use. eBook versions and licenses are also available for most titles. For more information, reference our Print and eBook Bulk Sales web page at http://www.apress.com/bulk-sales.

Any source code or other supplementary material referenced by the author in this book is available to readers on GitHub. For more detailed information, please visit https://www.apress.com/gp/services/source-code.

If disposing of this product, please recycle the paper

To all programmers who refuse to stop at "working code" and continue striving for software that is more understandable, safe, efficient, and maintainable. This book is dedicated to the developers, educators, researchers, and students who embrace the challenge of learning complicated concepts to gain deeper insights into the underlying language principles and design choices. Rust represents more than a programming language; it reflects a mindset that values correctness, reliability, and craftsmanship. May this work help you push beyond the fundamentals, explore the advanced capabilities of Rust, and build software with greater confidence and precision.

Table of Contents

About the Author xi

About the Technical Reviewer xiii

Acknowledgments xv

Introduction xvii

Chapter 1: Error Handling 1

Rust Error Handling 2

Examples of Unrecoverable Errors 2

Examples of Recoverable Errors 4

Propagating Errors 6

Multiple Error Types 9

Handling Multiple Error Types 10

Chaining Question Marks 13

Layered Outcomes 18

Result Wrapping an Option 19

Option Wrapping a Result 21

Using *anyhow* 23

Using *thiserror* 29

Summary 32

Chapter 2: Debugging 35

Debugging Basics 36

The Debug Macro 36

Standard Error Stream 40

The *Debug* Trait 44

Deriving the *Debug* Trait 45

The Pretty-print Debug Formatter 47
Manual Implementation of *Debug* 48
The *Display* Trait 51
Debugging with Panics 52
Debugging Panics with Backtracing 53
Capturing Panics Programmatically 56
Debugging in VS Code 59
Logging with *log* and *env_logger* 64
Structured Logging and Tracing 69
Using *rustfmt* 75
Summary 77
Chapter 3: Beyond Basic References 79
Types of References 80
Casting and Assignment of References 83
Casting of References 83
Assignment of References 85
Reference Patterns in *Let* Bindings 86
Type Inference in Reference Bindings 88
Value Assignment in Reference Binding 88
Additional Examples 89
Partially Using Compound Types as References 91
References in Compound Data Types 94
Reference Constraints in Method Chaining 96
The Banking Example Setup 96
Types of Methods in the Context of Method Chaining 99
Summary 103
Chapter 4: Coercions 105
Coercion Basics 106
Deref Coercion 106
Deref Coercion in Custom Defined Types 108
Common *Deref* Coercions 110

Coercion Sites 111
Coercion Types 113
Reference Coercion 114
Function Item Coercion 117
Trait Object Coercion 119
Coercion in Generics 122
Transitivity in Coercion 124
Least Upper Bound Coercion 127
LUB Coercion in *If/Else* Branches 127
LUB Coercion in a Series of *match* Arms 130
LUB Coercion in Array Elements 131
Summary 132
Chapter 5: Combinators 133
Combinators 134
Map Combinator 134
The *and_then* Combinator 136
The *or* Combinator 139
The *or_else* Combinator 140
The *unwrap_or* and *unwrap_or_else* Combinators 141
The *filter* Combinator 143
Combinator Chains 145
Transform Validate Fetch 146
Multiple Fallible Steps, Followed by Transformation 147
Multiple Fallbacks, Followed by Value Extraction 148
Validate, Transform, and Fallback 149
Transformations on Vectors 150
Using Combinators on Collections 150
Mandatory Value Transformation 151
Cleaning Option Values 152
Filtering Out None While Preserving Some 153

Combinators for Processing Vectors 154

The *skip* Combinator 154

The *take* Combinator 155

The *enumerate* Combinator 155

The *fold* Combinator 156

The *reduce* Combinator 157

Debugging Iterator Pipelines 158

Debugging by Breaking Iterator Chains 158

Debugging with the *inspect* Combinator 160

Summary 161

Chapter 6: Relationships in Lifetimes 163

Background of Lifetime Topics 163

Concrete Lifetimes 164

Generic Lifetimes 166

The *'static* Lifetime 167

Lifetime Elision Rules 169

Lifetime Bounds and Subtyping 170

Basic Lifetime Bounds 170

Implied Bounds 172

Variance 175

Covariance 175

Contravariance 178

Invariance 182

Summary 186

Chapter 7: Trait Limitations, Object Safety, and the Orphan Rule 187

Trait Object Limitations 188

Multiple Traits 188

Associated Types 193

Methods with Generics 197

Generic Traits and Trait Objects 201

Functions without *self* Parameters 204

Size and Trait Objects 209
Implications of Size Constraints on Traits and Methods 209
Implications of Sized Methods for Trait Objects 212
A Use Case of Sized Methods (Partial Object Safety) 213
The Orphan Rule 216
Sealed Traits 220
Summary 223
Chapter 8: Downcasting 225
Downcasting Basics 225
The *Any* Trait 226
Immutable Conversion to *&dyn Any* 227
Mutable Conversion to *&mut dyn Any* 230
Removing the *as_any* and *as_mut_any* Methods 232
Downcasting Use Case 234
Downcasting for Converting Between Trait Objects 236
Checking Type Without Downcasting 239
Summary 241
Chapter 9: Drop Check 243
Drop Check Basics 244
Effects of Manually Implementing Drop 244
Addressing Drop Check Constraints 247
Drop and Partial Move 248
Drop Order 250
Exceptions to Reverse Drop Order 252
Drop Order and Self-Referential Structs 256
Example of Self-Referential Structs 257
Self-Referential Stack Allocated Copy Types 258
Avoiding Drop 259
Use Case of *forget* in Benchmarking 261
Manually Dropping Data 262

Panic Safety 263
What Happens When Programs Panic 263
Understanding Double Panics 265
Handling Panics Using *catch_unwind()* 266
Handling Double Panics with *catch_unwind()* 268
Summary 269

Index 271

About the Author

Dr. Nouman Azam is a professor of computer science at the National University of Computer and Emerging Sciences (NUCES) in Peshawar, Pakistan. He earned his PhD in computer science from the University of Regina, Canada, and has since cultivated a strong academic and teaching career in traditional and online settings.

Dr. Azam teaches more than 60,000 students through online courses. His expertise in Rust programming is reflected in his popular course: Rust Programming Course: From Beginner to Expert 2.0. He is also the author of the book, *Rust: The Practical Guide* by Rheinwerk Computing.

About the Technical Reviewer

Yogendra Sharma is a senior solution architect at Intelizign Engineering Services GmbH and a seasoned full-stack Java developer with deep expertise in Python, backend engineering, and cloud-native microservices. Holding a B.S. in computer science, he leads development teams and architects developing scalable, polyglot solutions for enterprise PLM implementations across AECO/EPCMI digitalization initiatives. His work focuses on unifying BIM workflows, engineering processes, and lifecycle data management into cohesive, platform-driven ecosystems. With a strong passion for emerging technologies and real-world software architecture, Yogendra brings hands-on industry experience.

Acknowledgments

This book would not have been possible without the support, encouragement, and contributions of many individuals and communities.

First and foremost, I would like to express my gratitude to the Rust community for creating an ecosystem that continuously promotes learning, collaboration, and technical excellence. The collective efforts of language designers, library maintainers, educators, open-source contributors, and developers around the world have made Rust one of the most influential programming languages of modern software development.

I am deeply thankful to my students and learners from around the world. Through their questions, discussions, feedback, and curiosity, they have consistently inspired me to explore Rust from multiple perspectives and explain complex concepts in a more accessible manner. Many of the explanations and examples presented in this book were refined through years of teaching and interaction with learners.

I would also like to express my sincere gratitude to my family for their patience, understanding, and unwavering support throughout the development of this manuscript. Their encouragement during the many hours of research, writing, and revision was invaluable. Last but not least, I extend my special thanks to the Department of Computer Science at the National University of Computer and Emerging Sciences for providing the necessary support and resources whenever required throughout this endeavor.

Introduction

Rust has become one of the most influential system programming languages in modern software development. It combines high performance with strong memory safety guarantees, without requiring a garbage collector. While many developers learn the fundamentals of ownership, borrowing, and pattern matching, mastering Rust requires a deeper understanding of the language's advanced features and compiler internal rules.

This book, *Advanced Rust: Exploring Power Features of Rust for Intermediate and Advanced Developers*, is written for readers who already have a basic foundation in Rust. Rather than revisiting introductory concepts, the book focuses on advanced topics that enable developers to write safer, more flexible, and maintainable software. The book is intended for a broad audience, including students, self-learners, software developers, educators, and professionals who wish to deepen their understanding of the language. It is particularly well suited for readers who have completed an introductory Rust course or have experience working on small to medium-sized Rust projects and are now looking to further develop their skills and advance their expertise.

The book begins with Rust's error-handling system. We explore recoverable and unrecoverable errors, error propagation, layered outcomes, and techniques for handling multiple error types. We also cover the popular `anyhow` and `thiserror` crates, which simplify error management in real-world applications.

The next chapter focuses on debugging and diagnostics. Topics include the `Debug` and `Display` traits, panic handling, backtraces, structured logging, tracing, and debugging tools. These features help developers understand program behavior and diagnose problems more effectively.

We then examine advanced aspects of surrounding references. The discussion covers casting and assignments of references, reference patterns, reference constraints in method chaining, and the behavior of references in different contexts. These concepts provide a deeper understanding of how Rust manages access to data.

The book also explores various types of coercions in Rust. We study deref coercion, trait object coercion, reference coercion, functional item coercion, and least upper bound coercion. Understanding different types of coercions helps in developing an understanding of how Rust performs type conversions automatically while preserving safety.

Another major topic is combinators. We examine common combinators used with `Option`, `Result`, and iterators. Chapter 5 demonstrates how combinators can simplify data transformation, error handling, and collection processing. We also discuss techniques for debugging complex iterator pipelines.

A dedicated chapter focuses on lifetime relationships. We begin with lifetime fundamentals and then move to lifetime bounds, subtyping, and variance. Special attention is given to covariance, contravariance, and invariance. These topics are somewhat misunderstood and less covered in typical Rust literature.

The book also investigates the limitations of trait objects and object safety. Topics include associated types, generic methods, the orphan rule, and sealed traits. These concepts explain many of the design decisions behind Rust's trait system and library ecosystem.

Building on trait objects, we explore runtime type identification and downcasting. Readers learn how the `Any` trait works, how downcasting is performed, and when it can be useful in application design.

The final chapter examines drop checking and destruction semantics. We discuss drop order, partial moves, self-referential structures, panic safety, and unwind handling. These topics provide valuable insight into Rust's resource management model and compiler safety checks.

By the end of this book, readers will have a stronger understanding of Rust's advanced language features. They will be better equipped to reason about lifetimes, trait systems, type relationships, error handling, and runtime behavior. More importantly, they will gain the confidence needed to tackle complex Rust code and write it effectively.

CHAPTER 1

Error Handling

In any real-world program, things inevitably go wrong, whether a file refuses to open, a network call times out, or an unexpected state appears without warning. Rust's approach to error handling turns these uncertainties into structured, reliable outcomes, giving developers the tools to write code that gracefully anticipates and manages failure.

This chapter provides an in-depth exploration of error handling in Rust, one of the language's most powerful systems for ensuring safety and reliability without sacrificing performance. It begins by introducing Rust's approach to error handling, distinguishing between recoverable and unrecoverable errors and explaining how the `Result` and `Option` types form the foundation of Rust's error model. The discussion then moves to error propagation, illustrating how errors can be passed up the call stack efficiently and safely.

This chapter explores multiple error types, demonstrating how to manage diverse error sources within a unified interface. The concept of chaining question marks (`?`) is then introduced, showing how this process simplifies error flow and reduces boilerplate code. The chapter continues with a two-part discussion of layered outcomes, where we examine how `Result` and `Option` can be combined or nested to represent complex program states.

The topic then turns to popular error-handling libraries, starting with `anyhow`, which simplifies dynamic error management for application-level code, followed by `thiserror`, a crate designed to make custom error definitions clear and maintainable. By the end of this chapter, you will have a thorough understanding of Rust's error-handling philosophy, from the core mechanisms provided by the standard library to modern idiomatic patterns for writing robust and expressive error-handling code.

N. Azam, *Advanced Rust*, https://doi.org/10.1007/979-8-8688-2992-5_1

Rust Error Handling

Rust takes a unique and explicit approach to error handling. Unlike many languages that use exceptions, Rust encourages handling errors as part of the normal program flow. This makes errors more predictable and avoids hidden control flow. Rust categorizes errors into two main types: unrecoverable and recoverable.

- **Unrecoverable errors:** Errors that indicate a serious problem and require the program to stop (e.g., accessing an invalid memory location). These are typically handled using the `panic!` macro.
- **Recoverable errors:** Errors that can be handled gracefully (e.g., a file not found). These are typically represented using the `Result` type.

This section goes over some examples of unrecoverable and recoverable errors. This will set up the foundation for learning more advance topics in the sections that follow. The next section starts with examples of unrecoverable errors.

Examples of Unrecoverable Errors

The simplest example of an unrecoverable error occurs when the program reaches a section of code that has not been implemented yet. Consider the function in Listing 1-1.

Listing 1-1. Unimplemented Feature

```
fn unimplemented_feature() {
    panic!("This feature is not implemented yet");
}
```

The `panic!` macro is Rust's built-in mechanism for signaling unrecoverable errors. When it is encountered, the program immediately stops its normal flow, starts unwinding the stack, and displays an error message describing the issue. The function in Listing 1-1 may be part of project or software in which code is developed incrementally. During development, some of the functionality may not be currently implemented and therefore not available for use. Attempting to access the unimplemented code may lead to an unrecoverable error.

A program can enter into an unrecoverable error state when it reaches an invalid state or a value that it cannot handle. For instance, consider the value-processing function shown in Listing 1-2.

Listing 1-2. A Value-Processing Function

```
fn value_processing(value: i32) {
    match value {
        1 => println!("One"),
        2 => println!("Two"),
        _ => panic!("unexpected value: {}", value),
    }
}
```

The function takes in an integer and prints a message for certain expected values, but triggers a panic when it encounters any value outside those cases. Such situations are common in programs that require that the inputs conform to certain formats and ranges. Deviations from the predefined formats or ranges are treated as bugs that cannot be handled gracefully, resulting in the program entering an unrecoverable state.

Another example of an unrecoverable error appears in situations where a program must enforce strict conditions within its logic or test cases. Consider the function in Listing 1-3, which should only operate when the provided value is strictly positive.

Listing 1-3. A Function That Checks the Input

```
fn must_be_positive(n: i32) {
    assert!(n > 0, "Value must be positive, got {}", n);
}
```

The `assert!` macro will panic if the condition fails. A panic inside such functions indicates an unrecoverable error and signals a violation of expected behavior. These panics are intentional and serve as clear markers that the program logic is incorrect and needs to be fixed.

A program may also encounter an unrecoverable error during execution if it attempts to access an array index that is out of bounds, as depicted in this code:

```
let v = vec![1, 2, 3];
println!("{}", v[5]);
```

In such cases, Rust immediately triggers a panic to prevent accessing invalid memory, ensuring safety by stopping the program before undefined behavior can occur.

These examples illustrate some common scenarios of unrecoverable errors in Rust. The next section explains recoverable errors, which allow programs to handle failure gracefully and continue execution.

Examples of Recoverable Errors

Recoverable errors in Rust are typically handled using the Result enum. To provide a complete understanding, this section first reviews the basic structure and usage of the Result enum. The Result enum definition in Rust's standard library is depicted in Listing 1-4.

Listing 1-4. Definition of the Result Enum in the Standard Library

```
enum Result<T, E> {
    Ok(T),
    Err(E),
}
```

Here, T represents the type of the successful value, while E represents the type of the error. When a function returns Result, it can either return Ok(value), indicating success, or Err(error), indicating failure. This explicit representation ensures that recoverable errors are part of the program's normal flow and must be addressed before proceeding.

Now we'll go over some examples of recoverable errors in Rust using the Result enum. Consider an example of opening a file, shown in Listing 1-5.

Listing 1-5. A File Opening Function

```
use std::fs::File;
fn main() {
    let file = File::open("missing.txt");
    match file {
        Ok(f) => println!("File opened successfully: {:?}", f),
        Err(e) => println!("Failed to open file: {}", e),
    }
}
```

The open function in the fs file module is used to open a textual file. The open function returns a Result. When the file is successfully opened, Result returns an instance of the file. If it fails, Result returns an error variant. The code then handles the Result using a match. If it's successful, a suitable message is printed; otherwise, the error is handled by printing an error message.

When you're building a production-ready Rust app, you should add more actions to both cases. For instance, in the case of a success, you might add to the file or copy its contents to some other file. Similarly, in the case of a failure, you can guide the users with more options and actions to take.

Listing 1-6 shows another example involving a recoverable error, this time when parsing an integer. The function in Listing 1-6 accepts a string and parses it to an integer.

Listing 1-6. An Integer Parsing Function

```
fn parse_input_to_int(input: &str) -> Result<i32,
std::num::ParseIntError> {
    input.trim().parse::<i32>()
}
```

The `parse` method attempts to convert the given string into an integer. If the parsing is successful, an integer is returned; otherwise, an error is returned. The `trim` method removes all leading and trailing whitespace characters from a string, including spaces, tabs, and newlines. This is a recoverable error because you are gracefully handling the possibility that the input string might not be a valid integer, allowing the program to respond appropriately without crashing.

Listing 1-7 shows how the function in Listing 1-6 can be used in `main` with invalid inputs and handle its output using a `match` expression.

Listing 1-7. Using the Function in Listing 1-6 in `main`

```
fn main() {
    let user_input = "42a";
    match parse_input_to_int(user_input) {
        Ok(n) => println!("Parsed number: {}", n),
        Err(e) => println!("Invalid input: {}", e),
    }
}
```

This example can be useful for detecting faulty inputs to the system. If you could execute it, you would see the program handle the error without crashing.

Propagating Errors

Error propagation refers to the process of passing an error from one part of a program to a higher-level caller function, instead of handling it immediately where it occurs. This approach allows errors to be managed at an appropriate level in the program's logic, promoting cleaner and more maintainable code. In Rust, error propagation is commonly achieved using the ? operator, which is a shorthand for matching on a `Result` and returning the error if one occurs. The ? operator can also be used with the `Option` type, which is discussed later in this section.

The following example illustrates the basic usage and syntax. Consider the `read_number` function in Listing 1-8; it either returns a `Result` containing an i32 value or `parseinterror`.

Listing 1-8. A Function for Reading an Integer from a String

```
use std::num::ParseIntError;
fn read_number(input: &str) -> Result<i32, ParseIntError> {
    match input.trim().parse::<i32>() {
        Ok(num) => Ok(num),
        Err(e) => Err(e),
    }
}
```

The function matches on the input by first trimming any spaces using the `trim` method, and then tries to parse it into an i32 value, which returns a `Result` using the `parse` method. The `match` arms handle the output of the `parse` method.

Listing 1-8 works, but you can simplify it and make it more precise using the question mark ? operator. For instance, Listing 1-9 shows a simplified version of the code.

Listing 1-9. Simplifying the Code in Listing 1-8 Using the Question Mark Operator

```
use std::num::ParseIntError;
fn read_number(input: &str) -> Result<i32, ParseIntError> {
    let num = input.trim().parse::<i32>()?;
    Ok(num)
}
```

Using the question mark ? at the end of the statement returning a Result will unwrap the value in the case of an Ok variant and will allow the remaining code to execute afterward. If there is an error, it will stop the function execution and return early from the function with an error. The question mark in this case is somewhat equivalent to the code shown in Listing 1-10.

Listing 1-10. Definition of the read_number Function

```
fn read_number(input: &str) -> Result<i32, ParseIntError> {
    let num = input.trim().parse::<i32>()?;
    Ok(num)

    /* Equivalent Code
    let num = match input.trim().parse::<i32>() {
        Ok(n) => n,
        Err(e) => return Err(e),
    };
    */
}
```

Listing 1-10 means that the code returns the value inside the result in the case of an Ok variant and returns an error variant in the case of an error.

The question mark operator can be used multiple times inside a function. For instance, consider a function that extracts a username from a given email. You must first determine the position of the @ symbol in the string, since all the text in the email that comes before the @ symbol is the username. Listing 1-11 shows how this can be done.

Listing 1-11. Function for Extracting a Username from an Email

```
fn extract_username(email: &str) -> Option<&str> { // Error
    let at_pos = email.find('@')?;
}
```

The find method returns an Option enum. The Option enum in Rust represents a value that may or may not be present. It is commonly used to handle cases where a value could be missing, providing a safe alternative to null values. The Option enum is defined in the standard library, as shown in Listing 1-12.

Listing 1-12. Definition of the `Option` Enum in the Standard Library

```
enum Option<T> {
    Some(T),
    None,
}
```

Here, Some(T) contains a value of type T, while None represents the absence of a value.

Coming back to the function in Listing 1-11, the `find` method, when applied to a string, searches for a specified pattern and returns a Some variant, wrapping the index of the first occurrence if found, or None if the pattern is not present. The point to note is that when the question mark is applied to the end of the statement returning an option, the function will rename the function (in the case of a Some variant) or will return with a None variant.

Currently, the function in Listing 1-11 is not returning something meaningful; it is giving an error. You can complete the function by extracting out all the text before the `at_position` to obtain the username. Listing 1-13 shows the completed version of the function.

Listing 1-13. Updated Version of the Function in Listing 1-11

```
fn extract_username(email: &str) -> Option<&str> {

    let at_pos = email.find('@')?;
    let username = email.get(0..at_pos)?;
    Some(username)
}
```

The `get` method in this function extracts a substring from the string based on the specified range. It returns Some valid string if the range is valid, or None if the range is out of bounds. The second question mark allows the execution of the remaining function if this statement returns the Some variant; otherwise, it will return early with None.

Generally, when there are multiple ? operators in a function, each one is evaluated in sequence, passing control to the next only if the current value is valid. If any of them returns None (or an `Err` in the case of the `Result` enum), the function exits early and returns None immediately. At the end of the function, it returns the information of interest, which is the username.

Multiple Error Types

Working with the ? operator can sometimes be challenging, especially when multiple error types are involved. When the ? operator is used multiple times in a function, all the returned errors must have the same type. This section explores how to overcome this limitation and handle multiple types of errors effectively.

Consider a scenario where a system receives temperature readings from sensors in Celsius and converts them to Fahrenheit. The system is implemented using a few functions. The first function, which handles the temperature readings from the sensors, is defined in Listing 1-14.

Listing 1-14. Function that Obtains the Temperature from a Sensor

```
fn temperature_from_sensor(sensor_id: u32) -> Result<f64, u8> {
    match sensor_id {
        1 => Ok(25.0),
        2 => Ok(30.5),
        _ => Err(42),
    }
}
```

The function in Listing 1-14 accepts `sensor_id` and returns a result containing either a valid temperature or an error value, indicating an invalid `sensor_id`. If the sensor ID is not correct, the function returns an error with a value of 42, which indicates an invalid `sensor_id`. In any other case, the appropriate temperature readings are returned.

The system also consists of a function for converting Celsius to Fahrenheit. Listing 1-15 contains that function.

Listing 1-15. Function for Converting Celsius to Fahrenheit

```
fn convert_to_fahrenheit(celsius: f64) -> Result<f64, String> {
    if celsius < -100.0 || celsius > 100.0 {
        Err(String::from("Out of range"))
    } else {
        Ok(celsius * 1.8 + 32.0)
    }
}
```

This function accepts temperature in Celsius and either returns a valid temperature in Fahrenheit or an error, if the temperature in not in a valid range.

Finally, you have a sort of coordination function, which basically calls the two functions defined in sequence. The function takes in a `sensor_id` and returns the temperature in Fahrenheit. Listing 1-16 contains the definition of the function.

Listing 1-16. Definition of the Coordination Function

```
fn get_temperature_fahrenheit(sensor_id: u32) -> Result<f64, _> {
    let temp_celsius = temperature_from_sensor(sensor_id)?;
    let temp_fahrenheit = convert_to_fahrenheit(temp_celsius)?;
    Ok(temp_fahrenheit) // Error
}
```

Note that this discussion intentionally ignores the error in the returned `Result` enum for now; I will address it shortly. The function first obtains the temperature from the sensor by calling `temperature_from_sensor`. The ? operator at the end of this function call ensures that the function will proceed to convert the received temperature to Fahrenheit only if `sensor_id` is valid. In other words, if `sensor_id` is incorrect, the function will exit early and return an error.

Next, if the `sensor_id` is valid, the temperature value is passed to the `convert_to_fahrenheit` function. Notice the second use of the ? operator in the same function. This guarantees that the function will exit early with an error if the conversion fails, such as when the temperature is out of the allowed range. Finally, if all steps succeed, the function returns a valid Fahrenheit temperature.

The code in Listing 1-16 does not compile. The reason being that the error returned from the two functions used in the `get_temperature_fahrenheit` are of different types. The `temperate_from_ sensor` function uses u8, while `convert_to_fahrenheit` uses a string type for the error variant. To fix this, you can use two approaches, discussed next.

Handling Multiple Error Types

The first approach is to use the `map_err` method. This method transforms the error value of a `Result` while leaving the successful value unchanged. Listing 1-17 illustrates how you can use it to solve the problem in Listing 1-16 (i.e., handling multiple error types).

To use `map_err`, I need to introduce an enum called `TemperatureError`, shown in Listing 1-17.

Listing 1-17. Definition of the TemperatureError Enum

```
enum TemperatureError {
    Sensor(u8),
    Conversion(String),
}
```

The enum has two types of errors as its variants. In the coordinator function, we set the returning error to be of TemperatureError enum type and call the map_err, as depicted in Listing 1-18.

Listing 1-18. Revised Definition of the Function in Listing 1-16 with the map_error Method

```
fn get_temperature_fahrenheit(sensor_id: u32) -> Result<f64,
TemperatureError> {
    let temp_celsius = temperature_from_sensor(sensor_id).map_err(Temperatu
    reError::Sensor)?;
    let temp_fahrenheit =
        convert_to_fahrenheit(temp_celsius).map_err(TemperatureError::Con
        version)?;
    Ok(temp_fahrenheit)
}
```

The call to map_err, after the function calls, maps the error received from the call to the respective function to the appropriate enum variant. The function now works because there is one consistent custom error type in the returning Result enum.

An alternative solution is to change the returning error values from the two functions to TemperatureError type. To apply this solution, we need to change the definition of the two functions, as shown in Listing 1-19.

Listing 1-19. Revised Definitions of the Functions in Listings 1-14 and 1-15 with TemperatureError

```
fn temperature_from_sensor(sensor_id: u32) -> Result<f64, TemperatureError>
{ // Returning error type changed
    match sensor_id {
        1 => Ok(25.0),
```

```
        2 => Ok(30.5),
        _ => Err(TemperatureError::Sensor(42)), // changed
    }
}

fn convert_to_fahrenheit(celsius: f64) -> Result<f64, TemperatureError> {
// Returning error type changed
    if celsius < -100.0 || celsius > 100.0 {
        Err(TemperatureError::Conversion(String::from("Out of range")))
// changed
    } else {
        Ok(celsius * 1.8 + 32.0)
    }
}
```

Notice that the returning error values in the two functions are updated to make sure that they match the returning error type.

You don't have to use the `map_err` function in the coordinator function anymore. The updated function definition is shown in Listing 1-20.

Listing 1-20. Revised Definitions of the Function in Listing 1-16 Without the `map_err` Method

```
fn get_temperature_fahrenheit(sensor_id: u32) -> Result<f64,
TemperatureError> {
    let temp_celsius = temperature_from_sensor(sensor_id)?;
    let temp_fahrenheit = convert_to_fahrenheit(temp_celsius)?;
    Ok(temp_fahrenheit)
}
```

The second approach integrates the error handling directly into each function, returning a unified error type from the start. Generally speaking, use the first approach with `map_err` when the existing functions return different error types and you want to convert them to a common error type, without changing the original functions. Use the second approach when you can define a single error type from the beginning for all related functions, which makes the code simpler and easier to read.

You will revisit handling multiple error types when you explore the `anyhow` crate later in this chapter, as it offers a convenient way to work with diverse errors while reducing boilerplate and simplifying error propagation. The next section turns attention to another fundamental concept—chaining question marks.

Chaining Question Marks

The previous section explored how working with multiple error types can affect the use of the question mark operator and how different techniques help manage those variations. Building on that foundation, this section turns to an equally important concept of chaining multiple question mark operators. This section explains how several ? operators can be used in sequence to create clean, readable, and efficient flows for propagating errors through multiple steps of a function.

Chaining with the ? operator in Rust is similar to method chaining (see the note). It allows you to write concise and readable code by linking multiple operations together. Just like method calls are chained using the dot operator, the ? operator lets you chain fallible operations by automatically propagating errors and continuing only if each step succeeds. It helps to understand this topic with an example.

Note Method chaining is a style of writing code where multiple method calls are linked together in a single continuous expression, because each method returns a value that the next method can operate on. For example, a chain like `object.method1().method2().method3()` works only when each method provides a compatible form of `self` that allows the next method in the sequence to be called. In Rust, `self` can appear in three forms: owned (`self`), immutable reference (`&self`), and mutable reference (`&mut self`).

A chain is valid only when the output form of `self` from one method is compatible with the input requirement of the next. An owned `self` can flow into any method, a `&mut self` can flow into methods requiring `&mut self` or `&self`, and a `&self` can only flow into methods that also require `&self`.

Assume a code module responsible for handling e-commerce order processing, where each order holds essential details like the number of items, the price per item, the available balance, and whether the transaction is completed. All this information is stored in a `struct`, which is defined in Listing 1-21.

Listing 1-21. Definition of the `Order` struct

```
struct Order {
    item_count: i32,
    price_per_item: f64,
    balance: f64,
    completed: bool,
}
```

To complement the `Order` struct in this e-commerce order processing module, we define an `OrderError` enum in Listing 1-22.

Listing 1-22. Definition of the `OrderError` Enum

```
#{derive(Debug)]
enum OrderError {
    InvalidOrder,
    PaymentFailed,
    ShippingError,
}
```

This enum represents potential issues that may arise during the order lifecycle, such as `InvalidOrder` (due to incorrect details), a `PaymentFailed` scenario from an insufficient balance, or a `ShippingError` during delivery. This allows us to handle and propagate errors in a structured and meaningful way throughout the order processing flow.

Next, we add a few methods to the implementation block of `order`. First we add a `validate` method to validate the payment. Listing 1-23 shows the implementation of `Order` containing a `validate` method.

Listing 1-23. Definition of the `validate` Method

```
impl Order {
    fn validate(&self) -> Result<&Self, OrderError> {
        if self.item_count == 0 {
            Err(OrderError::InvalidOrder)
        } else {
            Ok(self)
        }
    }
}
```

According to the method, an order is considered to be valid if the `item_count` is non-zero. Next, we add a `process_payment` method. The code is shown in Listing 1-24.

Listing 1-24. Definition of the `process_payment` Method

```
impl Order {
    ...
    fn process_payment(&mut self) -> Result<&mut Self, OrderError> {
        let total_price = self.item_count as f64 * self.price_per_item;
        if self.balance < total_price {
            Err(OrderError::PaymentFailed)
        } else {
            self.balance -= total_price;
            Ok(self)
        }
    }
}
```

This method computes the total price of the order. It also determines if the available balance is less than the total price. If the available balance is less, it will return the appropriate error. In any other case, it will update the balance and return an updated `self` wrapped inside an `Ok` variant.

We now add one more function, called `ship_order`, shown in Listing 1-25.

Listing 1-25. Definition of the `ship_order` Method

```
impl Order {
    ...
    fn ship_order(&mut self) -> Result<&mut Self, OrderError> {
        if self.item_count > 10 {
            Err(OrderError::ShippingError)
        } else {
            self.completed = true;
            Ok(self)
        }
    }
}
```

This function returns an error if the number of items exceeds 10; otherwise, it will succeed and return an updated `self`. Notice that all the methods in Listings 1-23 through 1-25 return a `Result`; therefore, we can use question mark operators on the call to these methods.

We now add one coordinator method, which basically uses the methods in the implementation. This method is shown in Listing 1-26.

Listing 1-26. Definition of the `complete_order` Method

```
impl Order {
    ...
    fn complete_order(&mut self) -> Result<(), OrderError> {
        self.validate()?;
        self.process_payment()?;
        self.ship_order()?;
        Ok(())
    }
}
```

The method in this listing first validates the order by calling the `validate` method. If the order is valid, it processes the payment and ships the order.

The code in Listing 1-26 works. However, instead of calling the methods one by one, we can chain the methods, as shown in Listing 1-27.

Listing 1-27. Refining the Method in Listing 1-26 by Chaining the Methods

```
impl Order {
    ...
    fn complete_order(&mut self) -> Result<(), OrderError> {
        self.validate()?;
        self.process_payment()?.ship_order()?;
        Ok(())
    }
}
```

Note that the `validate` method cannot be chained with `process_payment` and `ship_order`. This is because the definition of the `validate_method` in Listing 1-23 returns a `&self`. However, the `process_payment` and `ship_order` methods in Listings 1-24 and 1-25 require a `&mut self` as input. A method returning `&self` cannot be chained with a method requiring a `&mut self`, so we cannot chain the `validate` method with the remaining two methods.

Chaining with the ? operator, as shown in the previous example, simplifies error handling by allowing sequential fallible operations to be written in a clean and compact manner. It also streamlines multi-step workflows, such as validating an order, processing payment, and then shipping, while automatically propagating any errors that occur at any stage.

The code in Listing 1-28 shows how the implementation in Listing 1-27 can be used inside the `main` function.

Listing 1-28. Using the Implementation of `Order` in `main`

```
fn main() {
    let mut order = Order {
        item_count: 5,
        price_per_item: 20.0,
        balance: 200.0,
        completed: false,
    };
```

```
    match order.complete_order() {
        Ok(_) => println!("Order completed successfully"),
        Err(e) => println!("Order processing failed: {:?}", e),
    }
}
```

In Listing 1-28, we first created an instance of the order and then match on the call to `complete_order`. If the order is completed successfully, meaning all the method calls inside the `complete_order` method are successful, we print a success message. If any of the method calls fail, we print an order processing failure message.

In summary, chaining with the question mark operator allows you to write concise and more readable code. It greatly simplifies complex control flows in functions that involve multiple fallible operations, making the overall logic easier to follow and maintain.

Layered Outcomes

In Rust, the `Option` and `Result` enums each model two possible outcomes. An `Option` represents either `Some` value or `None`, while `Result` captures success or failure. In real-world applications, however, outcomes are often more complex than just two choices. A function might succeed but return no meaningful value or it might fail for different reasons. By layering `Option` and `Result` together, Rust allows you to go beyond simple binary outcomes and express richer, more nuanced states in a clean and type-safe way.

This section explores two of the most expressive and commonly encountered layered patterns involving `Option` and `Result`: an `Option` wrapped inside a `Result`, and a `Result` wrapped inside an `Option`. These patterns highlight how Rust lets you precisely represent different combinations of success, failure, and the absence of values, adding clarity and structure to complex control flows. Here are the two patterns along with their common usage:

- `Result<Option<T>, E>`: A fallible operation that may or may not yield a value.
- `Option<Result<T, E>>`: An optional operation, which, if performed, may succeed or fail.

Although these types may appear structurally similar, they convey semantically distinct intents, and choosing between them depends on what you're trying to express in your program's logic. The next section covers the process of a `Result` wrapping an `Option`.

Result Wrapping an Option

A `Result` wrapping an `Option` type (i.e., `Result<Option<T>, E>`) expresses a three-way outcome:

- The operation is successful with a valid value.
- The operation is successful but has no value.
- The operation is unsuccessful with an error.

This is useful when the absence of a value is not an error but is part of the valid logic. The following example shows a sample use case of when this can be useful.

Suppose you intend to write a function that queries a database for a product based on the product ID. The query itself may fail, for instance, due to a database connection error. Even if the query is successful, the product itself might not exist in the database. To model this scenario, we first define a `Product` struct along with an enum to represent possible database connection errors, as shown in Listing 1-29.

Listing 1-29. Definition of the `Product` Struct and the `DBError` Enum

```
struct Product {
    id: u32,
    name: String,
}
enum DBError {
    ConnectionFailed,
}
```

Next, we define the `find_product` function, which takes a `u32` ID and returns a `Result` that wraps an `Option`. This signifies that the operation may fail and, if it succeeds, the product might not be present. The function is given in Listing 1-30.

Listing 1-30. Definition of `find_product`

```
fn find_product(id: u32) -> Result<Option<Product>, DBError> {
    db_connection()?;
    match id {
        0..=100 => Ok(Some(Product {
            id,
            name: "Laptop".to_string(),
        })),
        _ => Ok(None),
    }
}
```

Before learning about `find_product`, take a look at the simulated database connection function it depends on, which is shown in Listing 1-31.

Listing 1-31. Definition of `db_connection`

```
use rand::Rng;
fn db_connection() -> Result<(), DBError> {
    let mut rng = rand::thread_rng();
    if rng.gen_range(0.0..1.0) < 0.1 {
        Err(DBError::ConnectionFailed)
    } else {
        Ok(())
    }
}
```

The function is using the `rand` crate, so we will also need to add to the `cargo.toml` file (version 0.8 in this case). This function simulates a database connection attempt using randomness. The call to `thread_rng()` creates a fast, thread-local random number generator. The `gen_range` method on an `rng` produces a floating-point number within the given range. If this number is less than 0.1, the function returns `Err(DBError::ConnectionFailed)`, representing a failed connection. Otherwise, it returns `Ok(())`, indicating a successful connection without any meaningful return value.

Returning to the `find_product` function in Listing 1-30, the function first attempts to establish a database connection. If the connection fails, the error is immediately propagated because of the ? operator. If the connection succeeds, the function then simulates a database lookup using a `match` expression. For this example, we assume that valid products exist only for IDs between 1 and 100. If the ID falls within this range, the function returns `Ok(Some(Product { ... }))`. Otherwise, it returns `Ok(None)`, meaning the query succeeded but no product was found. In both match branches, the operation itself is successful, so both operations return an `Ok` variant.

In summary, the layered outcomes in this case clearly distinguish between three outcomes:

- The query failed (due to a database connection error).
- The query succeeded with a valid product (the product exists in the database).
- The query succeeded but there was no valid product (the product does not exist in the database).

The next section covers `Option` wrapping a `Result`.

Option Wrapping a Result

The `Option` wrapping a result type (i.e., `Option<Result<T, E>>`) conveys a two-stage process:

- In the first stage, we try to attempt an operation. The outer `Option` conveys this. It attempts to determine whether the operation was attempted.
- In the second stage, we try to determine whether the attempt succeeded or failed. The inner `Results` conveys this.

This approach is ideal when an operation is optional, such as user input fields that may or may not be provided. Let us go over an example where this type can be used.

Consider a user registration form where age is optional. If the user enters an age, we want to validate it as a number. If they don't provide one, we skip validation without an error. To code for this, we define a function called `handle_user_registration` with a name and an optional age as inputs, as shown in Listing 1-32.

Listing 1-32. Definition of `handle_user_registration`

```
use std::num::ParseIntError
fn handle_user_registration(
    name: &str,
    age_input: Option<&str>,
) -> Option<Result<u32, ParseIntError>> {
    println!("Registering user: {}", name);
    age_input.map(|s| s.parse::<u32>())
}
```

The function returns an `Option` wrapping a `Result` containing either a valid u32 age or `ParseIntError` if the `age_input` cannot be parsed into a u32 integer.

Inside the function, a user registration message is first displayed. Next, it uses a `map` method on the `age_input`. Inside the map, we call the `parse` method to convert the age into an unsigned integer. The mapping is applied only to the value contained within the `Option`. If the `Option` is `None`, there is no value to transform, so `None` is returned unchanged. If the `Option` is a some variant, the map applies the provided function, in this case `parse`, to the inner value. Since `parse` itself returns a `Result`, the inner value of Some will be converted into either an `Ok` variant (if parsing succeeds) or an `Err` variant (if parsing fails).

In summary, the execution of the function in Listing 1-32 may result in one of the following outputs:

- None (operation not attempted)
- `Some(Ok(valid_age))` (operation attempted and successful)
- `Some(Err(ParseIntError))` (operation attempted but failed)

The first output represents the first stage, where an operation was not attempted. The second and third cases represent a situation where the operation was attempted, which is either successful or not.

Listing 1-33 shows how Listing 1-32 can be used in `main`.

Listing 1-33. Using the Code in Listing 1-32 in `main`

```
fn main() {
    match handle_user_registration("Alice", Some("25")) {
        None => println!("Age not provided, continuing without age"),
```

```
        Some(Ok(age)) => println!("User age is valid: {}", age),
        Some(Err(e)) => println!("Invalid age input: {}", e),
    }
}
```

We first call the function with a valid name and an optional age and handle the possibilities inside a `match` arm.

Using *anyhow*

Building on the discussion of handling multiple error types introduced earlier in this chapter, this section introduces the anyhow crate, which provides a convenient and flexible way to work with different kinds of errors.

Error handling in Rust can often become verbose when dealing with multiple error types or complex control flows. The anyhow crate simplifies application-level error handling by providing a single, dynamic error type. Unlike strongly typed error enums commonly used in libraries, anyhow can wrap and propagate almost any error that implements the standard `Error` trait.

This section walks through an example to illustrate the basic usage and application of the crate. We begin by outlining the motivation behind using it and then move on to explaining how the crate is used in practice. Consider a simple function which reads in a file and then parses the contents to obtain an integer. Listing 1-34 shows the function definition.

Listing 1-34. Definition of the `read_and_parse_number` Function

```
use std::{fs::File, io::Error, io::Read, num::ParseIntError};
fn read_and_parse_number(file_path: String) -> Result<i32, _> { // Error
    let mut file = File::open(file_path)?;

    let mut contents = String::new();
    file.read_to_string(&mut contents)?;

    let number = contents
        .trim()
        .parse::<i32>()?;
    Ok(number)
}
```

The function accepts a file path and returns a `Result` enum containing an i32 value or an error. We have not mentioned anything for the error part for now since this function may return errors of different type.

First, we open the file using the `open` function. Notice the ? operator after the `open` function. This means that we will proceed with the remaining of the function only if this call is successful. In that case, we read in the contents into a string variable using the `read_to_string` method. The `read_to_string` method reads in the contents of the file and stores the contents in the `contents` variable. If this also happens successfully (as indicated by the ? operator at the end of the statement), then we will we parse the contents into an i32 value. If everything works fine, we return the number stored in a file by wrapping it inside an `Ok` variant.

The errors returned from function and method calls in Listing 1-34 are of different types. In particular, the `parse` function may return a `ParseIntError` while the `read_to_string` and `open` functions may return an IO error. For this reason, we did not mentioned the returning error type in the `Result` enum in Listing 1-34. You have already seen a couple of ways to handle error in such functions. One of the approaches was to manually implement the functionality of converting the error into the desired type and the second approach was to use the `map_err` method. This example looks at the manual implementation approach.

We define an enum called `AppError` with the two variants shown in Listing 1-35.

Listing 1-35. Definition of the `AppError` Enum

```
enum AppError {
    Io(Error),
    Parse(ParseIntError),
}
```

Next, we convert the expected errors types from the function and method calls in the function in Listing 1-34 (i.e., `ParseIntError`) and IO error (generally referred to as `Error` in Rust) into appropriate `AppError` type variants using the `From` trait. This is shown in Listing 1-36.

Listing 1-36. Enum AppError Definition

```
impl From<Error> for AppError {
    fn from(value: Error) -> Self {
```

```
        Self::Io(value)
    }
}

impl From<ParseIntError> for AppError {
    fn from(value: ParseIntError) -> Self {
        Self::Parse(value)
    }
}
```

The From trait in Rust defines how one type can be converted into another in a simple and consistent way. It contains a single from method, which takes a value of one type as input and returns a value of another type as output, allowing for type conversion. Listing 1-36 converts Error and ParseIntError to the AppError type.

In the read_and_parse_number function in Listing 1-34, we can now update its signature by mentioning the AppError for the error part in the Result enum. We do not need to alter the code in the body of the function. The updated function definition signature is depicted in Listing 1-37.

Listing 1-37. Revised Function Signature of read_and_parse_number

```
fn read_and_parse_number(file_path: String) -> Result<i32, AppError> {
   let mut file = File::open(file_path)?;

    let mut contents = String::new();
    file.read_to_string(&mut contents)?;

    let number = contents
        .trim()
        .parse::<i32>()?;
    Ok(number)

}
```

The appropriate from methods are automatically invoked to convert the error types whenever they are required. For instance, on this line:

```
let mut file = File::open(file_path)?;
```

The returning error is of type Error, which is converted using the appropriate from method to an AppError type.

Note that the conversion between error types can also be done using map_err, which requires less setup and does not need From implementations. However, we demonstrate the use of the from method in this case to show an alternative approach you might consider in similar scenarios. In Rust, map_err and from are both idiomatic ways for error conversions and you will see both in practice. It is therefore good to be aware of both.

Listing 1-38 shows how to use the function in Listing 1-37 in main.

Listing 1-38. Using the Function in Listing 1-37 in main

```
fn main() {
    let file = String::from("number.txt");
    match read_and_parse_number(file) {
        Ok(number) => println!("File contains number: {}", number),
        Err(e) => println!("Cannot process: {:?}", e),
    }
}
```

In this listing, we match on the call to the read_and_parse_number with a file path. The function may either successfully read and parse the number or it may fail. The code in Listing 1-37 compiles and is working. However, it can be improved using the anyhow error crate. To see the details, we will first add the anyhow crate to cargo.toml.

With the anyhow crate, you do not need to manually define the AppError enum. Additionally, you do not need conversions using the From implementations. The revised definition of the read_and_parse_number with the anyhow crate is shown in Listing 1-39.

Listing 1-39. Updated Definition of read_and_parse_number Using the anyhow Crate

```
use anyhow::Result;
fn read_and_parse_number(file_path: String) -> Result<i32> {
    let mut file = File::open(file_path)?;

    let mut contents = String::new();
    file.read_to_string(&mut contents)?;
```

```
    let number = contents
        .trim()
        .parse::<i32>()?;
    Ok(number)
}
```

Note that in the function signature, the returning result is simplified and does not require the error type. This is because this `Result` type is now the result defined in the anyhow crate, which we imported, and not the `Result` enum defined in the standard library, which requires an explicit error type. More concretely, the `Result` type in this case is somewhat equivalent to the following:

```
Result<i32> = Result<i32, anyhow::Error>
```

The `anyhow::Error` is a flexible, dynamic error type that allows you to wrap and represent any error implementing the `std::error::Error` trait. This makes it ideal for general-purpose application-level error handling, where the specific error types are not important. All the errors in the functions are now being wrapped by the `anyhow::Error` type.

Since all the errors are now wrapped in the general-purpose `anyhow::Error` type, some specific error details and type information may be lost in the process. The `context` method provided by the anyhow crate allows you to attach custom, human-readable messages to errors, making it easier to understand what went wrong and where. Listing 1-40 shows an updated function, which is created by adding context to the error, returned by the open function.

Listing 1-40. Updated Definition of `read_and_parse_number` with the `context` Method

```
use anyhow::{Context, Result};
fn read_and_parse_number(file_path: String) -> Result<i32> {
    let mut file = File::open(file_path).context("Failed to read file
    contents")?;
    ...
}
```

If you execute the code in main in Listing 1-40, the added context will be displayed if the file is not found. The context method is useful when the message is simple and does not require extra computation such as some sort of static message.

The anyhow also has another method called with_context. This method allows for generating error messages dynamically with attached contexts describing the cause of the errors. We can use it to update the definition of the function in Listing 1-40, by adding additional dynamic context to the parse method, as shown in Listing 1-41.

Listing 1-41. Updated Definition of read_and_parse_number with the with_context Method

```
use anyhow::{Context, Result};
fn read_and_parse_number(file_path: String) -> Result<i32> {
    let mut file = File::open(file_path).context("Failed to read file
    contents")?;

    let mut contents = String::new();
    file.read_to_string(&mut contents)?;

    let number = contents
        .trim()
        .parse::<i32>()
        .with_context(|| format!("Failed to parse integer from contents:
        {}", contents.trim()))?;
    Ok(number)
}
```

The information attached to with_context is now not a simple static message, but computes additional context dynamically, reflecting the cause of the error.

In summary, anyhow focuses on developer productivity, enabling concise error propagation through the ? operator, thus avoiding custom error types and boilerplate conversions. It also supports rich error messages, backtraces, and context addition via the context and with_context methods. The key characteristics of code, with and without anyhow, are summarized in Table 1-1.

Table 1-1. *Comparing Key Characteristics of Code with and without anyhow*

Aspect	**Without** anyhow	**With** anyhow
Custom error types	Must define custom error types when multiple error types are returned.	No need for custom error types. All errors use a single dynamic type.
Manual error conversion	May require manual conversion between error types.	No manual conversions needed.
Error type in Result	Result must explicitly specify a concrete error type.	No explicit error type needed and uses `anyhow::Error`.
Error propagation	Simple propagation using ?.	Propagation enriched with context via `context` and `with_context`.

Using *thiserror*

The `thiserror` crate is another very useful crate for handling errors in Rust. It simplifies the implementation of the standard `Error` trait for custom error types. More precisely, it provides a convenient way to define `error` enums with automatic trait implementations. Unlike `anyhow::Error`, which is used for flexible, type-erased error handling at the application level, `thiserror::Error` is ideal for defining precise, well-typed errors in libraries where clarity and structure are essential.

The following example highlights some of the strengths of `thiserror`. It uses the same enum defined in Listing 1-35 and given again in Listing 1-42.

Listing 1-42. Enum `AppError` Defined Earlier in Listing 1-35

```
enum AppError {
    Io(Error),
    Parse(ParseIntError),
}
```

The `Display` trait in Rust is used to control how a type is formatted when printed using the `println` macro, typically for user-friendly and readable output. It is common to implement it for error types to provide clear and descriptive error messages. The code in Listing 1-43 shows an implementation of `Display` for the `AppError`.

Listing 1-43. Display Trait Implementation for AppError

```
use std::fmt;
impl fmt::Display for AppError {
    fn fmt(&self, f: &mut std::fmt::Formatter<'_>) -> std::fmt::Result {
       match self {
            AppError::Io(e) => write!(f, "I/O Error: {}", e),
            AppError::Parse(e) => write!(f, "Parse Error: {}", e),
        }
    }
}
```

The display trait contains a single function of fmt, which dictates how an instance of the type should be formatted when it's printed. In this implementation, it will define how each variant of the AppError enum is displayed. The function takes two inputs—a reference to self and a mutable reference to an instance of the Formatter struct, which provides formatting capabilities, like writing to the output stream (such as console). The method fmt returns an fmt::Result type, which is an alias for the Result enum returning a unit type in the case of success or an format error (i.e., Result<(), fmt::Error>).

Inside the function, we match on self and write to a formatter instance to properly display the error. The write macro is similar to the format macro; it enables you to write a formatted string to the Formatter instance, which may be successful or may fail with an fmt::Error.

The implementation in Listing 1-43 defines how each AppError variant will be converted into a human-readable message, allowing us to control exactly what the error looks like when it appears on the console or in logs. This implementation works, but we can simplify it using the thiserror crate. More precisely, with thiserror, we do not need to have custom implementations for the Display trait. In addition, it do not require manual implementations of the From and Debug traits. To use thiserror in the code, we first need to add it to cargo.toml.

To automatically implement the Display for the AppError enum in Listing 1-42, we can use the error attribute defined in the thiserror crate. The code in Listing 1-44 defines the updated definition of the AppError enum with the error attribute.

Listing 1-44. Updated Definition of AppError using the [error] Attribute

```
use thiserror::Error;

#[derive(Debug, Error)]
enum AppError {
    #[error("I/O Error:")]
    Io(std::io::Error),

    #[error("Parse Error:")]
    Parse(ParseIntError),
}
```

In Listing 1-44, the #[error(...)] attribute will automatically implement the Display trait for each AppError, defining how the error will be formatted when printed with the associated error message, which is given in double quotes.

Note The Debug trait provides a developer-focused way to inspect values. Types that implement Debug can be printed using {:?} for a compact representation or {:#?} for a more readable, pretty-printed format. This makes it useful for debugging and understanding program state.

To automatically implement the From implementations for the enum variants, we can use the [from] attribute, as shown in Listing 1-45.

Listing 1-45. Updated Definition of AppError Using the [from] Attribute

```
use thiserror::Error;

#[derive(Debug, Error)]
enum AppError {
    #[error("I/O Error:")]
    Io(#[from] std::io::Error),

    #[error("Parse Error:")]
    Parse(#[from] ParseIntError),
}
```

The IO variant is converted to an `std::io::Error` while the `Parse` variant is converted into a `ParseIntError`. Note that we use the full path to the `std::io::Error` in the attribute to avoid confusing the error provided by `thiserror` crate (given by `this::error`).

The key advantage of `thiserror` in comparison to `anyhow` is that with `anyhow`, error types are erased into a general-purpose error container, which means you lose the ability to distinguish and act on specific error variants. In contrast, using the `thiserror` crate preserves the concrete error types, allowing you to match on different error cases and handle each one appropriately. This means you can further expand the possible actions of each error type and carry out appropriate tasks. The comparison of `anyhow` and `thiserror` is summarized in Table 1-2.

Table 1-2. *Comparing `anyhow` and `thiserror`*

`anyhow`	`thiserror`
Application-level error handling	Library-level error definitions
Single catch-all (`anyhow::Error`)	Custom typed errors (usually enum)
Cannot match on specific types after wrapping	Matching on specific error types is possible
Provides `context()` and `with_context()` to add information dynamically at runtime	Attributes attachment using `#[error("...")]`

Summary

This chapter introduced Rust's structured approach to error handling by distinguishing between unrecoverable errors, which are handled with `panic!`, and recoverable errors, which are represented using the `Result` and `Option` enums. Through multiple examples, you saw how Rust encourages explicit error management, enabling programs to gracefully respond to failures such as invalid input, missing files, or failed operations. The chapter also explained error propagation using the ? operator, showing how it simplifies control flow by automatically returning errors while keeping the code concise. The chapter explored how to manage multiple error types using techniques like `map_err`, common custom error enums, and layered outcomes such as `Result<Option<T>, E>` and `Option<Result<T, E>>`. The concept of chaining multiple ? operators was discussed to illustrate how fallible operations can be linked cleanly in multi-step workflows.

The chapter further highlighted the use of community crates, such as `anyhow` for flexible, application-level error handling and `thiserror` for creating structured, typed error definitions in libraries. Overall, this chapter provides a strong foundation for writing reliable and expressive Rust programs that anticipate and respond to failure effectively.

As you move to the next chapter on debugging, you will see how Rust's tools and techniques help identify, inspect, and resolve the issues that surface during development.

CHAPTER 2

Debugging

Even in carefully written programs, behavior does not always match expectations. The values may change unexpectedly, logic paths diverge, or execution fails silently. Debugging in Rust provides a disciplined set of tools and practices that help developers observe program behavior, isolate faults, and reason about failures with precision, ultimately turning opaque problems into understandable and fixable causes.

This chapter provides a comprehensive look at debugging in Rust, equipping you with both foundational and advanced techniques to identify and resolve issues effectively. It begins with the `dbg!` macro, a simple yet powerful tool for inspecting values during development without disrupting code flow. The discussion then turns to the standard error stream, explaining how Rust separates normal output from diagnostic messages for cleaner debugging. We next explore the `Debug` trait, which provides structured and human-readable representations of data for inspection.

The chapter continues with debugging through panics, showing how to interpret panic messages and backtraces to trace errors to their root causes. It also covers how to capture panics programmatically, enabling controlled error recovery and safer testing. Practical debugging techniques are then demonstrated using VS Code, one of the most popular Rust development environments.

The next sections focus on logging with `log` and `env_logger`, followed by structured logging and tracing, which introduce more sophisticated ways to monitor and analyze runtime behavior. Finally, we conclude with `rustfmt.toml`, highlighting how consistent formatting supports readability and debugging efficiency. By the end of this chapter, you will be more confident in applying Rust's debugging tools and best practices to build more reliable, maintainable, and production-ready applications.

N. Azam, *Advanced Rust*, https://doi.org/10.1007/979-8-8688-2992-5_2

Debugging Basics

Debugging is the systematic process of identifying, analyzing, and fixing issues in a program so that it behaves as intended. It is an essential skill because even code that appears correct can hide logical flaws, performance bottlenecks, or unexpected behaviors that only surface during execution.

Before diving in, it is important to distinguish between errors and debugging.

- **Errors:** Symptoms—such as compilation failures, runtime crashes, or incorrect outputs—that indicate something is wrong in the program.
- **Debugging:** The systematic process of tracing issues to their root causes, analyzing their behavior, and correcting them so that the program functions as intended.

This section begins with basic debugging techniques in Rust and gradually moves to more advanced topics.

The Debug Macro

The dbg! macro is a quick and convenient tool for debugging in Rust. It prints the value of an expression along with its filename and line number, and then returns the value unchanged, allowing you to continue using it in code without interruption.

How *dbg!* Works

Consider the code in Listing 2-1.

Listing 2-1. Simple Code for Finding the Maximum Value in a Vector

```
fn main() {
    let scores = vec![72, 85, 90, 67, 95, 88];
    let mut max_score = 0;
    for score in scores {
        if score > max_score {
            max_score = score;
         }
    }
}
```

The code defines a vector and contains simple logic for finding the maximum value in the vector by iterating through all the elements. During each iteration, the maximum score is updated whenever the current score in the vector is greater than the previously recorded maximum. Although the code in Listing 2-1 is correct and straightforward, in real-world scenarios you often encounter programs with hidden logical issues where intermediate computations need to be checked.

At the start of each iteration, we would like to inspect the value of the `score` variable and the value of `max_score`, inside the `if` statement, to check the correctness of our logic. Listing 2-2 shows how the `dbg!` macro can be used to view the value of the `max_score`.

Listing 2-2. Using the `dbg!` Macro to Display the Variables of `score` and `max_score`

```
fn main() {
    ...

    for score in scores {
        dbg!(score);
        if score > max_score {
    dbg!(max_score);
            max_score = score;
    }
}
```

Executing this program leads to the following output:

```
[src\main.rs:5:9] score = 72
[src\main.rs:8:13] max_score = 0
[src\main.rs:5:9] score = 85
[src\main.rs:8:13] max_score = 72
[src\main.rs:5:9] score = 90
[src\main.rs:8:13] max_score = 85
[src\main.rs:5:9] score = 67
[src\main.rs:5:9] score = 95
[src\main.rs:8:13] max_score = 90
[src\main.rs:5:9] score = 88
```

The dbg! macro prints the following four pieces of information in a single line for easy tracing.

- The filename
- The line number
- The exact expression being debugged
- The evaluated value

The dbg! macro writes to the standard err stream. A Rust program uses the following two main streams:

- **Standard output (stdout),** which is used to display normal program results.
- **Standard error(stderr),** which is used to display error messages.

This distinction helps separate the error messages from the regular output. This chapter returns to the details of standard error stream in a later section.

Additional Uses and Properties

Sometimes it may be more useful to print multiple values at the same time instead of separately printing them using the dbg! macro. Listing 2-3 shows how you can print both the variables of score and max_score at the same time.

Listing 2-3. Displaying score and max_score at the Same Time

```
fn main() {
    ...
    for score in scores {
        if score > max_score {
            dbg!(score, max_score);
            max_score = score;
        }
    }
}
```

This will generate more or less the same output as the code in Listing 2-2.

The dbg! macro can also be used to directly print the value of some computation. For instance, check out the code in Listing 2-4.

Listing 2-4. Displaying an Expression with dbg!

```
fn main() {
    ...
    for score in scores {
        if score > max_score {
           dbg!(max_score = score);
        }
    }
}
```

This will generate the following output multiple times:

```
[src\main.rs:8:13] max_score = score = ()
```

When an expression is provided to dbg!, it not only prints the expression, but also prints the computed expression. Since this is an assignment statement, it returns no value. This is indicated in Rust by a unit value (()).

Note In Rust, an *expression* is any piece of code that evaluates to a valid value.

When the debug macro is executed, it will return the value of the expression passed to it. For instance, consider the code in Listing 2-5.

Listing 2-5. Returning a Value from a dbg!

```
fn main() {
    let x = 5;
    let y = dbg!(x + 4);
    println!("{y}");
}
```

The code in Listing 2-6 defines a variable and passes it to the debug while adding four to it. The variable y stores the returning value of the dbg!. Executing the code will result in a value of 9 for variable y. This suggests that the dbg! returns the computed value from the expression passed to it.

The debug macro also takes ownership of something passed to it. The code in Listing 2-6 shows this.

Listing 2-6. Returning Value from a dbg!

```
fn main() {
    let x = String::from("5")
    dbg!(x);
    println!("{x}"); // Error
}
```

We first define a String variable x and pass it to the dbg!. Since the dbg! consumes the value of x, it is no longer available in the print statement and therefore the program does not compile. To fix the code, you may consider passing in a reference instead, as shown in Listing 2-7.

Listing 2-7. Fixing the Code in Listing 2-6

```
fn main() {
    let x = String::from("5")
    dbg!(&x);
    println!("{x}");

}
```

Standard Error Stream

As briefly introduced in the previous section, programs produce two types of output: standard output (stdout), which is used for normal program results, and standard error (stderr), which is reserved for error messages and warnings. Separating these streams ensures that errors do not mix with normal output, allowing each to be handled or redirected independently. Although this topic may seem slightly tangential, understanding standard output and error streams is crucial for debugging, as keeping normal output separate from error messages makes it easier to identify, trace, and resolve issues in a program. This section explores how to work with and separate these two streams in Rust.

We start by providing motivation for the two types of output streams in Listing 2-8.

Listing 2-8. A Simple Program for Explaining the Motivation for Two Types of Output

```
fn main() {
    println!("Program output");
    let x: Option<i32> = None;
    x.unwrap();
}
```

Listing 2-8 prints to the screen, defines an `Option`, and calls an `unwrap` on it. Executing the code in Listing 2-9 will produce the output shown in Listing 2-9.

Listing 2-9. Output of the Program in Listing 2-8

```
Program output

thread 'main' (36484) panicked at src\main.rs:21:7:
called 'Option::unwrap()' on a 'None' value
note: run with 'RUST_BACKTRACE=1' environment variable to display a
backtrace
error: process didn't exit successfully: 'target\debug\rust_debugging.exe'
(exit code: 101)
```

The program output and the error message are residing in the same place, which does not look good visually.

You can redirect the error messages to a separate file and keep the program output on the terminal. This can be done using the following command on the terminal:

```
cargo run 2> error_log.txt
```

Executing this command will create a separate file that contains only the error messages or, more accurately, the error stream. The program's regular output stream, without the error messages, will remain visible in the terminal. You can find the `error_log.txt` file in the same directory from which you executed the command, which is typically the root of your project.

Alternatively, you can redirect the standard output stream to a file and keep the error stream on the terminal using the following command.

```
cargo run > stdouput.txt
```

Again, as in the previous case, the `estdoutput.txt` file is in the same directory from which you executed the command.

The two commands can be executed at the same time using the following command:

```
cargo run > stdoutput.txt 2> error.txt.
```

Typically, the `print!` and `println!` macros are used to write to the standard output stream. To write to the error stream, Rust provides the `eprint!` and `eprintln!` macros. The following lines will write to the error stream.

```
eprint!("Error 1: Error Message 1");
eprintln!("Error 2: Error Message 2");
```

The text in quotes will be added to the error stream. This is useful when you intend to manually add error or debug information to standard error without mixing it with normal program output.

Note The dbg! macro discussed in the previous section also writes to the error stream.

Unlike the standard output, the standard error stream is typically not buffered. To illustrate this distinction, consider the code in Listing 2-10.

Listing 2-10. Buffering of Standard Output Stream and Standard Error Stream

```
fn main() {
    print!("This is standard output (stdout)");
    eprint!("This is standard error (stderr)   ");
}
```

In the code in Listing 2-10, one would expect the `print!` macro to write first to the terminal and the `eprint!` to do so later; however, executing it displays:

```
This is standard error (stderr)  This is standard output (stdout)
```

The error is written first to the terminal and then the `print` is written later.

It is important to note that standard output is line buffered. So as long as the line end has not been reached, the information will be stored in the buffer. However, as soon as the line end is reached, the buffered information will be released and displayed on the terminal. For instance, consider a next line character or `println` macro, as shown in Listing 2-11.

Listing 2-11. Using the `println!` Macro Will Immediately Write to the Terminal

```
fn main() {
    println!("This is standard output (stdout)");
    eprint!("This is standard error (stderr)");
}
```

The text in the `println!` macro will be immediately displayed in the code in Listing 2-11 and will not be buffered. Executing the code in Listing 2-11 will therefore produce the following output.

```
This is standard output (stdout)
This is standard error (stderr)
```

Table 2-1 summarizes the key differences between the standard output and standard error streams.

Table 2-1. *Key Differences Between the Standard Output and Standard Error Streams*

Feature	Standard Output (`stdout`)	Standard Error (`stderr`)
Primary purpose	Normal program output	Error and debugging messages
Buffering behavior	Line-buffered (flushes at end of a line)	Typically unbuffered (messages appear immediately)
Redirection syntax	`> file` or `1> file`	`2> file`

The *Debug* Trait

The Debug trait in Rust is a fundamental tool for inspecting and understanding the internal state of variables during development. While basic types can be printed directly, custom structs, enums, and other complex data types require the Debug trait to reveal their contents. By implementing or deriving this trait, Rust enables developers to obtain a structured, human-readable representation of their data, which is invaluable when tracing program flow, identifying incorrect values, or verifying assumptions during debugging. This section explores how the Debug trait works, how to enable it for custom types, and how it contributes to clearer and more effective debugging. First you'll walk through some examples to see it in action.

Consider the Point struct defined in Listing 2-12.

Listing 2-12. Definition of a Point Struct

```
struct Point {
    x: i32,
    y: i32,
}
```

In main, we will create a vector of points, as shown in Listing 2-13.

Listing 2-13. Vector of Points

```
fn main() {
    let points: Vec<Point> = vec![
        Point { x: 1, y: 2 },
        Point { x: -3, y: 4 },
        Point { x: 5, y: 6 },
    ];
}
```

To print the fields of the individual Point instances in the vector, you can iterate through the points, printing their x and y values, as shown in Listing 2-14.

Listing 2-14. Printing the Fields of the Point Instances in the Vector

```
fn main() {
    ...
```

```
    for point in &points {
        println!("Point with coordinates ({}, {})", point.x, point.y);
    }
}
```

The Point struct in Listing 2-14 is quite compact. In real projects, however, custom types can be much bigger. Manually printing their internal values with a println! statement can be tedious and time-consuming. Fortunately, the Debug trait makes this process much easier, smoother, and more efficient.

Deriving the *Debug* Trait

To add an implementation of Debug for the point, you can derive it for the Point, as shown in Listing 2-15.

Listing 2-15. Deriving the Debug for Point

```
#[derive(Debug)]
struct Point {
    x: i32,
    y: i32,
}
```

This will generate an implementation of the Debug for Point. In main now, instead of looping through the point instances of the vector, you can use the debug formatter ({:?}) to print all the points in the vector. This is shown in Listing 2-16.

Listing 2-16. Using the debug formatter to Print the Point Instances in the Vector

```
fn main() {
    let points: Vec<Point> = vec![
        Point { x: 1, y: 2},
        Point { x: -3, y: 4},
        Point { x: 5, y: 6},
    ];

    println!("{:?}", points);
}
```

Executing this code will print the points in a formatted way, as shown here:

```
[Point { x: 1, y: 2 }, Point { x: -3, y: 4 }, Point { x: 5, y: 6 }]
```

The Debug trait, although useful for simple types, may not be very effective when types are nested and complex. As an example, consider the line struct in Listing 2-17, which defines a line by start and end fields, which are Points.

Listing 2-17. Definition of Line struct

```
#[derive(Debug)]
struct Line {
    start: Point,
    end: Point,
}
```

In main now, we create a couple of points and use them to define a line, as shown in Listing 2-18.

Listing 2-18. Defining an Instance of the Line Struct in Main

```
fn main() {
    let p = Point { x: 3, y: 4 };
    let q = Point { x: 5, y: 7 };

    let l = Line { start: p, end: q };
    println!("{:?}", l);
}
```

Executing the code in Listing 2-18 will generate the following output:

```
Line { start: Point { x: 3, y: 4 }, end: Point { x: 5, y: 7 } }
```

This displays the information but it's a bit hard to read and follow. In particular, it prints the internal structure of the Line and Point structs in a raw, nested format, showing all field names and values without any formatting or simplification. This can be overwhelming for complex or deeply nested data. The pretty-print debug formatter can be quite handy and useful in this regard.

The Pretty-print Debug Formatter

The pretty-print debug formatter ({:#?}) can be used to better visualize the internal state. It also uses the Debug trait but formats the output in a multi-line, indented, and human-readable style, which is useful for complex or nested data structures. The code in Listing 2-19 shows how to use it.

Listing 2-19. Updating the Code in Listing 2-18 with Pretty-Print Debug Formatter

```
fn main() {
    ...
    let l = Line { start: p, end: q };
    println!("{:#?}", l);
}
```

The code in Listing 2-19 will generate the output shown in Listing 2-20.

Listing 2-20. Output of the Program in Listing 2-19

```
Line {
    start: Point {
        x: 3,
        y: 4,
    },
    end: Point {
        x: 5,
        y: 7,
    },
}
```

The internal state of the line instance is now formatted and visually easy to read.

Manual Implementation of *Debug*

Sometimes, you may want more control than what the derived Debug trait implementation provides. In such cases, implementing Debug manually allows you to decide exactly what information is displayed and how it is formatted. As an example, consider the Color struct defined in Listing 2-21.

Listing 2-21. Definition of the Color Struct

```
#[derive(Debug)]
struct Color {
    red: u8,
    green: u8,
    blue: u8,
}
```

In Listing 2-21, we derived the Debug trait for Color, which allows us to print its values. In main, we can use the debug formatter to display an instance of Color, as shown in Listing 2-22.

Listing 2-22. Creating and Displaying an Instance of Color Using the Debug Formatter

```
fn main() {
    let magenta = Color {
        red: 255,
        green: 0,
        blue: 255,
    };
    println!("{:?}", magenta);
}
```

If you execute the code in the Listing 2-22, it will display the Color instance as follows:

```
Color { red: 255, green: 0, blue: 255 }.
```

However, assume that your development team finds it more useful to work with the hex codes corresponding to the colors during debugging. You can manually implement the debug to achieve this. Listing 2-23 shows the manual implementation of the Debug for Color.

Listing 2-23. Manual Implementation of Debug for Color

```
use std::fmt::{self, Debug};
impl Debug for Color {
    fn fmt(&self, f: &mut fmt::Formatter) -> fmt::Result {
        write!(f, "Color (#{:X}{:X}{:X})", self.red, self.green, self.blue)
    }
}
```

The Debug trait contains a mandatory method called fmt, which takes a reference to self and a mutable reference to a Formatter struct. The write! macro allows us to write our custom-defined string to the Formatter struct instance, instead of printing it directly. The method returns a Result to indicate whether writing to the Formatter succeeded or failed. The {:X} syntax formats each value in uppercase hexadecimal. You don't have to derive the Debug (#[derive(Debug)]) in the code in Listing 2-21 any longer. Note that the same method was discussed in Chapter 1. We obtain the desired output of Color (#FF0FF) when we execute the method in Listing 2-23.

The fmt method for the Debug trait can be redefined to control how an instance is displayed, including support for the pretty-print debug format specifier. In doing so, the alternate method on the Formatter can be used to adjust the output accordingly. The code in Listing 2-24 shows how to do this.

Listing 2-24. Using the Alternate Method to Add Support for Pretty-Print Debug

```
impl Debug for Color {
    fn fmt(&self, f: &mut fmt::Formatter) -> fmt::Result {
        if f.alternate() {
            write!(
                f,
                "Color {{hex: \"#{:X}{:X}{:X}\",
                red: {},
                green: {},
```

```
                blue: {}
        }}",
                self.red, self.green, self.blue, self.red, self.green,
                self.blue
            )
        } else {
            write!(f, "Color (#{:X}{:X}{:X})", self.red, self.green,
            self.blue)
        }
    }
}
```

The alternate() method detects whether the pretty-print form ({:#?}) was requested, allowing the formatter to choose between the expanded output in the if branch and the compact output in the else branch. In particular, when the pretty-print specifier is used, the formatter executes the code in the if block; otherwise, it falls back to the standard debug format in the else block. In main, we use the implementation shown in Listing 2-25.

Listing 2-25. Using the Implementation in Listing 2-24 in main

```
fn main() {
    let magenta = Color {
        red: 255,
        green: 0,
        blue: 255,
    };
    println!("{:?}", magenta);
    println!("{:#?}", magenta);
}
```

The printing with the debug formatter ({:?}) will display the instance as Color (#FF0FF). On the other hand, the printing with the pretty-print formatter ({:#?}) will generate the following output:

```
Color {hex: "#FF0FF",
                red: 255,
```

```
            green: 0,
            blue: 255
    }
```

The *Display* Trait

The Display trait is closely related to Debug. Unlike Debug, which is intended for developer-facing, detailed, and diagnostic output, the Display trait is meant for clean, user-facing presentation. In other words, Display focuses on formatting values in a readable, polished way for end users, while Debug emphasizes exposing internal state for troubleshooting.

The Display trait, unlike Debug, cannot be derived for types. For instance, this is not valid #[derive(Display)] and will generate an error if you add it before some type. You can however manually implement it for your types. Listing 2-26 shows an implementation of the display for the Color struct defined in Listing 2-21.

Listing 2-26. Implementation of Display for Color

```
use std::fmt;
impl fmt::Display for Color {
    fn fmt(&self, f: &mut fmt::Formatter) -> fmt::Result {
        write!(
            f,
            "RGB({}, {}, {}) - hex: #{:X}{:X}{:X}",
            self.red, self.green, self.blue, self.red, self.green,
            self.blue
        )
    }
}
```

Similar to Debug, the Display trait also contains an fmt method with more or less the same details. The interesting aspect of this implementation is that it is automatically called by the print statement to fill in the corresponding placeholder.

The code in Listing 2-27 shows how this implementation can be used in main.

Listing 2-27. Using the Implementation in Listing 2-26 in `main`

```
fn main() {
    let magenta = Color {
        red: 255,
        green: 0,
        blue: 255,
    };
    println!("{}", magenta); // use either this style
    println!("{magenta}"); // or this one
}
```

As shown Listing 2-27, with the manual implementation of the `Display` trait for `Color`, you can print the `magenta` instance either by using a placeholder `{}` or by directly including its name inside the braces `{magenta}`. Both syntaxes work because `Display` defines how the instance is formatted for printing. Table 2-2 summarizes the differences between the two traits.

Table 2-2. *The Differences between the Debug and Display Traits*

Feature	Debug Trait	Display Trait
Audience	Developer-facing, diagnostic details	User-facing, clean, and polished output
Format specifier	`{:?}` or `{:#?}` (pretty-print)	`{}` (simple placeholder)
Implementation	Can be derived automatically (`#[derive(Debug)]`)	Must be implemented manually

Debugging with Panics

When a panic occurs in Rust, the program by default either unwinds or aborts without providing much structured context, which can make analyzing recurring or complex failures difficult. By enabling backtraces and using panic hooks, developers can trace the exact location and cause of a failure, making debugging more structured and controlled. This section explores techniques for debugging with panics in Rust.

Debugging Panics with Backtracing

In Rust, backtracing records the sequence of function calls leading to a panic, providing a detailed roadmap of the program's execution. It is useful for pinpointing the exact location and cause of errors, making debugging complex or layered code much more efficient. This section illustrates the workings of backtracing with the help of an example.

Consider the set of functions defined in Listing 2-28.

Listing 2-28. Definitions of Functions for Handling User Login Requests

```
fn handle_request() {
    println!("Handling login request...");
    process_login("alice", "");
}

fn process_login(username: &str, password: &str) {
    println!("Processing login for user: {}", username);
    check_credentials(username, password);
}

fn check_credentials(username: &str, password: &str) {
    println!("Checking credentials for {}", username);
    let hashed = hash_password(password);
    println!("Hashed password: {}", hashed);
}

fn hash_password(password: &str) -> String {
    if password.is_empty() {
        panic!("Password cannot be empty!");
    }
    format!("hashed_{}", password)
}
```

Listing 2-28 contains a `handle_request` function, which simulates handling a login request by printing a message and then calling `process_login` with a username and password, effectively initiating the flow of checking user credentials. The `process_login` function accepts a username and password, prints a message indicating which user is being processed, and then calls the `check_credentials` function with the same information. The check_credentials function prints a message showing which user's credentials are being verified and then calls hash_password to simulate hashing the password. In this example, the hash_password function simply simulates a hashing process by prefixing the password with hashed_ instead of performing real encryption. Note that if the password is empty, the function will panic. These functions are called sequentially, one after the other, starting with handle_request. You can initiate this sequence of calls from the main function by simply calling handle_request, as shown here:

```
fn main() {
    handle_request();
}
```

Calling handle_request will lead to the following function calls: handle_request() → process_login("alice", "") → check_credentials("alice", "") → hash_password("") → panic!("Password cannot be empty!")

In this program, the panic occurs deep in the call hierarchy inside the hash_password function, which is several layers below the initial handle_request function. If you execute the call to handle_request, the error message may not be detailed enough to tell you exactly where the problem occurred. Debugging errors in such cases, where panics are several layers deep in the call hierarchy, can be tricky, because all you see is the panic message without knowing which sequence of function calls led there.

To address this, backtracing can be used. A backtrace records the exact chain of function calls that led to a panic or error, allowing developers to see not just where the program failed but how it got there. More precisely, it works by unwinding the call stack at runtime and listing each frame in order, providing a roadmap to trace and fix the root cause efficiently.

Note The *call stack* is a data structure used by the program to keep track of active function calls. Each time a function is called, information about that call is pushed onto the stack, and when the function returns, that information is removed. This allows the program to know where to resume execution after a function finishes.

A *frame* is an entry in the call stack that represents a single function call. It typically contains information such as the function's local variables, parameters, and the location in the code where execution should return once the function completes. In a backtrace, each frame shows a step in the sequence of calls that led to the panic.

We can enable the backtraces in Rust by setting up the environment variable, as shown in Listing 2-29.

Listing 2-29. Enabling Backtraces by Setting Up Environment Variables

```
fn main() {
   unsafe {std::env::set_var("RUST_BACKTRACE", "1")};
    handle_request();
}
```

Note that it is unsafe to set up backtraces in Rust. Executing the code in Listing 2-29 will generate detailed output, as shown in Listing 2-30.

Listing 2-30. Complete Stack Backtrace for the Code in Listing 2-29

```
stack backtrace:
   0: std::panicking::panic_handler
             at /rustc/25d319a0f656ee8faa7a534da299e76e96068a40/library\
             std\src\panicking.rs:690
   1: core::panicking::panic_fmt
             at /rustc/25d319a0f656ee8faa7a534da299e76e96068a40/library\
             core\src\panicking.rs:80
   2: rust_debugging::hash_password
             at .\src\main.rs:30
   3: rust_debugging::check_credentials
             at .\src\main.rs:24
   4: rust_debugging::process_login
             at .\src\main.rs:19
   5: rust_debugging::handle_request
             at .\src\main.rs:14
   6: rust_debugging::main
             at .\src\main.rs:38
```

```
  7: core::ops::function::FnOnce::call_once<void (*)(),tuple$<> >
            at C:\Users\Dr. Nouman Azam\.rustup\toolchains\nightly-x86_64-
            pc-windows-msvc\lib\rustlib\src\rust\library\core\src\ops\
            function.rs:250
  8: core::hint::black_box
            at C:\Users\Dr. Nouman Azam\.rustup\toolchains\nightly-x86_64-
            pc-windows-msvc\lib\rustlib\src\rust\library\core\src\
            hint.rs:473
```

We intentionally condensed the output to focus on explaining the structure and the flow of function calls. The stack backtrace in the output consists of functions calls, which are ordered as numbers from 1 through 8 in the output. Reading the stack backtrace from the bottom to top, we first see the functions `black_box` and `call_once` at numbers 8 and 7. We will revisit these shortly. Above them, the `main` function appears, which calls `handle_request`, which in turn calls `process_login`, then `check_credentials`, and finally `hash_password`, where the panic occurs.

The functions numbered at 0, 1, 7, and 8 are internal functions from Rust's standard library and runtime. These are automatically inserted during compilation to manage panics and low-level execution. They are not part of the code but appear in the backtrace as part of the full call stack. Currently, there is no way to suppress these internal standard library functions from appearing in the Rust panic backtrace. However, they are always located at the start and end of the stack.

Despite the presence of these internal functions, the information that matters (i.e., the sequence of our own function calls leading to the panic) is clearly visible. The backtrace in this case allows us to precisely trace the chain of function calls and determine the exact site in the call hierarchy that caused the panic.

You should now understand how panics occur and how backtraces help trace the sequence of function calls leading to a panic. The next section explains panic hooks, which allow you to customize the behavior of the program when a panic occurs.

Capturing Panics Programmatically

Rust's default panic output is limited because it only prints a message. Moreover, the panic does not allow any custom actions when a panic occurs. By using custom panic hooks, you can log detailed information and format the output or trigger actions like cleanup and alerts whenever a panic happens.

Listing 2-31 shows how to custom define a panic hook using the `set_hook` function.

Listing 2-31. Defining a Custom Panic Hook Using the `set_hook` Function

```
use std::panic::set_hook;
fn main() {
    set_hook(Box::new(|info| {
        eprintln!("Custom Panic: {}", info);
        if let Some(location) = info.location() {
            eprintln!(
                "Occurred in file '{}' at line {}",
                location.file(),
                location.line(),
            );
        }
    }));

    panic!("Main fn panicked!");
}
```

The `set_hook` function allows the code to register a *custom panic handler*. It takes a boxed closure as an argument, and this closure receives a parameter called `info`, which contains details about the panic, including the error message and the location where it occurred. Inside the closure, we define custom behavior to execute when a panic happens. For example, printing a message, logging details, or performing other actions. Listing 2-31 prints a custom panic message to the error stream and then displays the file and line number where the panic occurred. Calling `info.location()` returns the location of the panic, which you can further inspect using the `file` and `line` methods.

Finally, by adding a `panic!` to the end of `main`, you can trigger the panic and see the custom messages printed to the terminal. The execution of Listing 2-31 will produce the following output on the terminal:

```
Custom Panic: panicked at src\main.rs:51:5:
Main fn panicked!
Occurred in file 'src\main.rs' at line 51
error: process didn't exit successfully: 'target\debug\rust_debugging.exe'
(exit code: 101)
```

Note that the definition of the set_hook must appear before any panic in the code to take effect. If you move the panic before the set_hook, the compiler will give a warning of "unreachable statement".

At any given time, only one panic hook is active. If multiple hooks are defined in the code, the one that is defined just before the panic occurs will be invoked. If, however, you want to handle different types of panics differently, you may inspect the payload contained in the panic info. Listing 2-32 shows how this can be done.

Listing 2-32. Handling Panics Differently

```
fn main() {
    set_hook(Box::new(|info| {
        let message = info.payload().downcast_ref::<&str>();

        match message {
            Some(&"Database error") => {
                println!("Handling DB error specifically");
            }
            Some(&"Config missing") => {
                println!("Handling config error");
            }
            Some(msg) => {
                println!("General panic: {}", msg);
            }
            None => {
                println!("Unknown panic payload");
            }
        }
    }));
    panic!("Some Error");
}
```

We first inspect the payload of info by calling the payload method. The payload is the message that you attach to the panic, when calling a panic. The downcast_ref method converts a trait object into a concrete type (in this case a reference to a String type). I explain this in detail in Chapter 8. Next, we match on the message of the panic and take different actions based on the payload message. The call to panic! at the end of main will trigger this output:

```
General panic: Some Error
```

Since it matches the second-to-last arm of the match, it is a panic with an arbitrary message.

In summary, by handling panics in this way, you can inspect the panic's payload, differentiate between types of errors, and take customized actions depending on the situation. This approach allows Rust programs to respond more intelligently to failures, rather than simply aborting, providing developers with greater control and flexibility when managing unexpected conditions.

Debugging in VS Code

When code is unclear or behaves unexpectedly, it helps to break it down step by step. By examining what each part does and what data flows through it, you can confirm the logic or spot mistakes. This stepwise reasoning is a key debugging practice for understanding unfamiliar or faulty code.

In VS Code, you can analyze the code step by step using VS Code's built-in debugger. It makes analysis easier by letting you pause execution, inspect variables, and follow the flow to confirm logic or spot mistakes. Consider the code in Listing 2-33.

Listing 2-33. Sample Code for Debugging

```
fn main() {
    let numbers = vec![10, 20, 30, 40, 50];
    let target = 70;
    let mut sum = 0;
    for (i, num) in numbers.iter().enumerate() {
        sum += num;
        if sum == target {
            println!("Found target at index: {}", i);
            break;
        }
    }
    println!("Final sum: {}", sum);
}
```

This code iterates through the `numbers` vector and keeps adding the values one by one, until the sum reaches 70. The `enumerate` method returns a tuple corresponding to each entry of the vector containing an index of the entry and its value. If you execute this code, it does not find the target sum of 70. Assuming that you expected the target sum of 70, you are not able to obtain it from the given vector.

Let's analyze this code using the VS Code build in the debugger. First we will install the extension of `CodeLLDB`, which will enable interactive debugging for Rust programs. To install the `CodeLLDB`, open VS Code and then click the extensions icon in the activity bar on the left side (or press Ctrl+Shift+X). In the search bar, type `CodeLLDB`. You will see something similar to Figure 2-1.

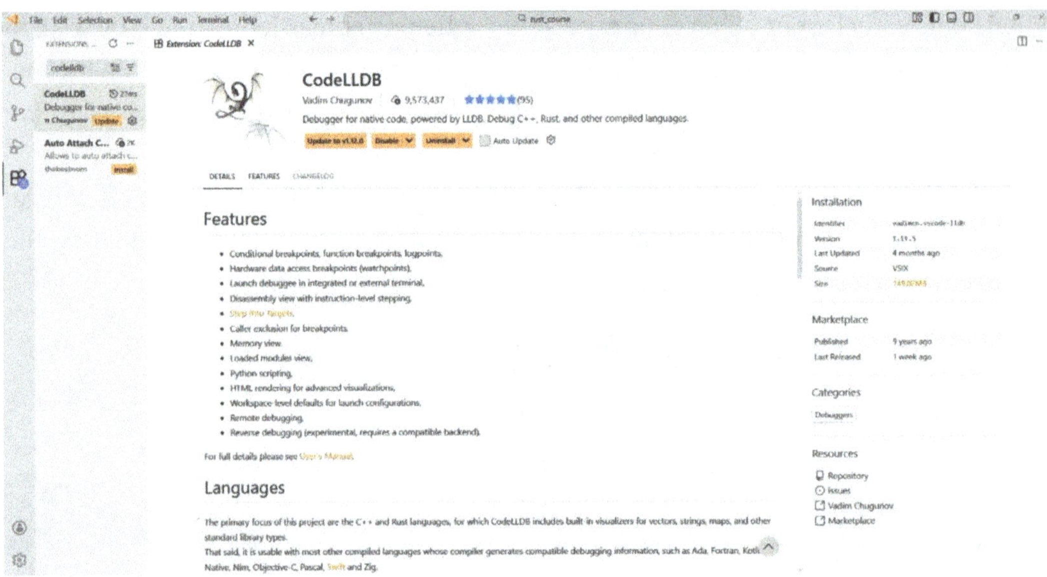

Figure 2-1. *Installing* `CodeLLDB`

Click the Install button next to the extension named `CodeLLDB`. Once it's installed, you should see `CodeLLDB` in your list of installed extensions. The installation of `CodeLLDB` enables interactive debugging for Rust programs.

Next open the code file containing the code, such as `main.rs`. From the right activity bar on the left side of VS Code, select the Run and Debug mode (or press Ctrl+Shift+D). You can now add breakpoints to the code. Breakpoints are markers you place in your code that tell the debugger to pause program execution at a specific line. When the program stops at a breakpoint, you can inspect variable values, watch how data changes, and step through the code one line at a time.

To add a breakpoint to the code, go to the left side of the editor and click in the gutter next to the line number where you want the program to pause. This places a red dot, indicating an active breakpoint, and you can add as many breakpoints as needed throughout your code. Figure 2-2 shows a breakpoint on Line 8 of the code.

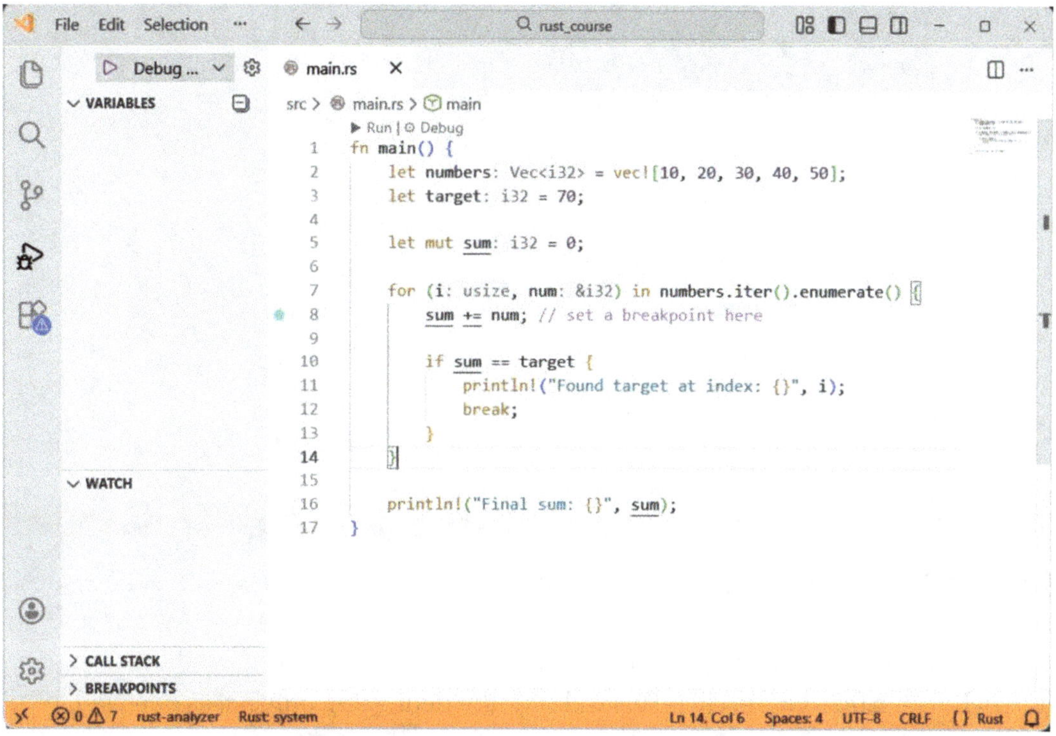

***Figure 2-2.** Setting a breakpoint at Line 8*

In Figure 2-2, we added a breakpoint at Line 8 since we would like to inspect the `sum` and `num` variables. To start debugging, select the debug executable by clicking Debug, as shown in Figure 2-3.

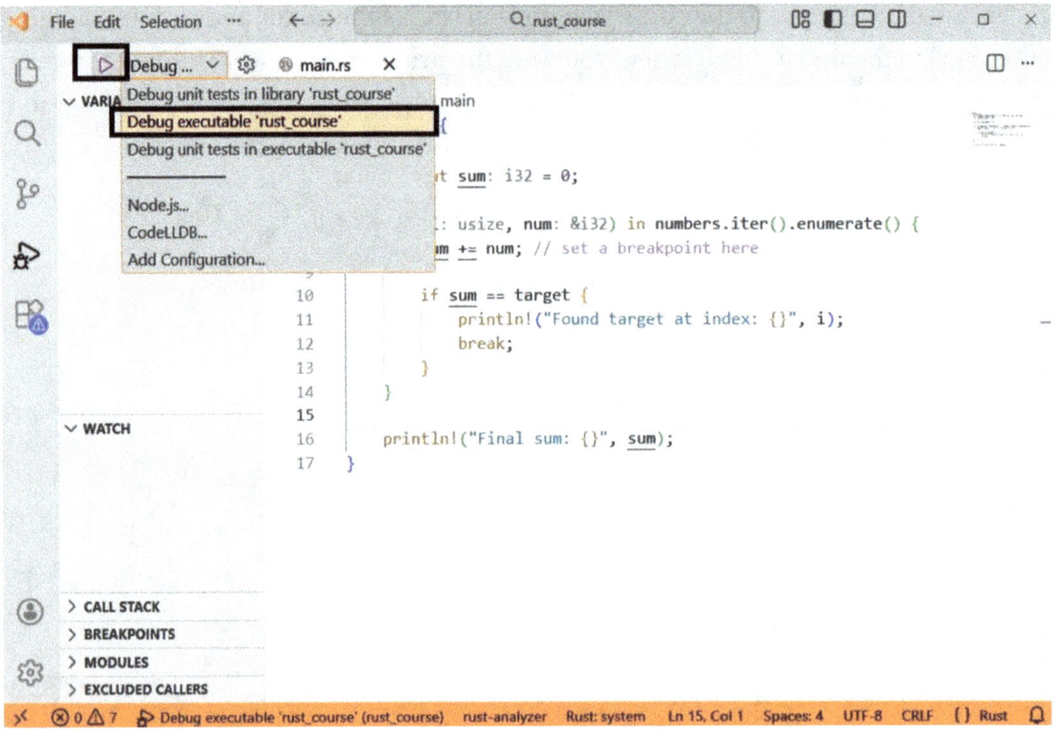

Figure 2-3. *Starting the debugging process*

After you select the Debug executable, you click the small play green button to start debugging (see Figure 2-3). This will start the debugging process, as depicted in Figure 2-4.

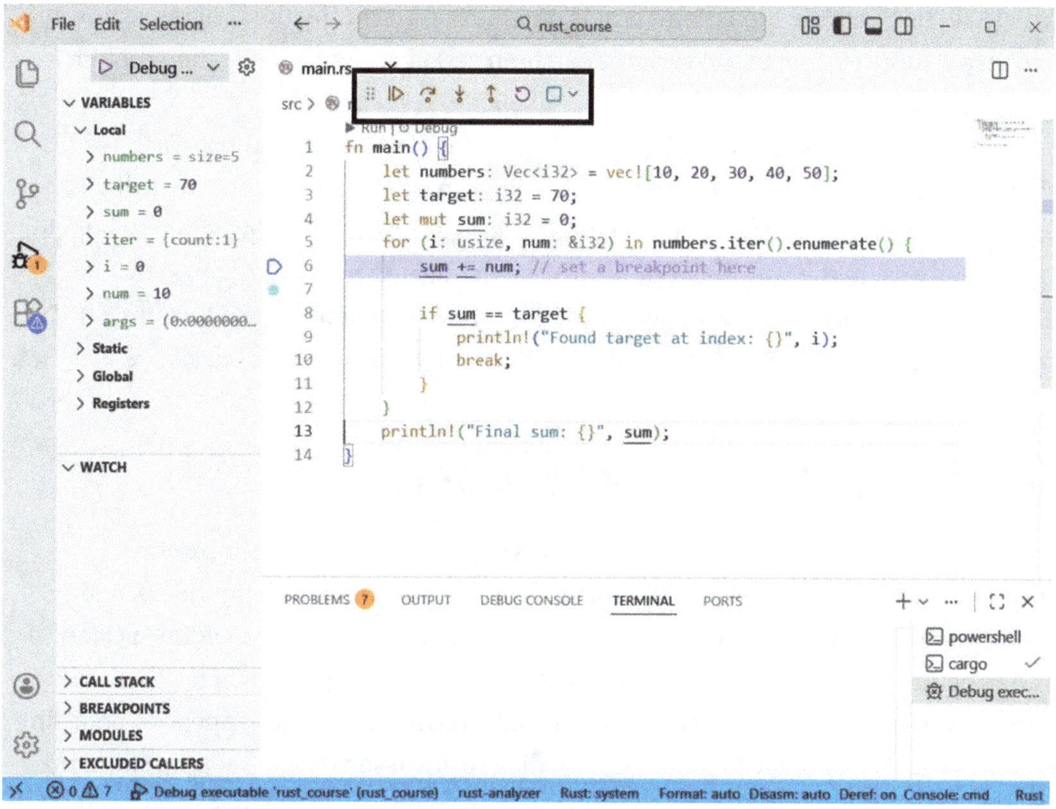

Figure 2-4. *Showing the debugging options after debugging is initiated*

On the left side of the view, VS Code provides several panels, including Variables, Call Stack, Breakpoints, Modules, and more. For now, our focus is on inspecting variables. The Variables panel is divided into sections such as Local, Static, Global, and Registers. The Local section shows all variables that belong to the currently executing function, which in this case is the `main` function.

When you start debugging a program, the program by default will execute statements until it reaches a breakpoint. The statement corresponding to the breakpoint is not executed. This is why we note a value of 70 stored in the target variable, while the sum still has a value of 0 (see the variable on the left side under the Variables panel in Figure 2-4).

The debugging comes with many other options, which are indicated in Figure 2-4 by the white rectangular box. Pressing the continue button (blue colored play button) will force the program to execute until the next breakpoint. This means that the code in the loop body will execute and the program will stop again on the next breakpoint, which will be the same breakpoint that is on Line 8. Continuing the program this way and inspecting the state of the variable can help you figure out exactly the problem in the code.

The other options indicated in the white rectangular box in Figure 2-4 are useful when you are debugging at very fine level, close to hardware, because they will take you to the internal Rust code and to registers. For general-purpose program debugging, I prefer only using the continue option. To exit debugging mode, you can select disconnect, which is red square box inside the white rectangular box in Figure 2-4. This style of debugging is very useful, especially when checking for logic bugs.

Logging with *log* and *env_logger*

In real applications, debugging often requires capturing useful runtime details such as warnings, errors, or trace messages, without mixing them into the normal program output. The `log` and `env_logger` crates help with this by providing a clean and structured way to record such information. They offer logging macros that write messages to the error stream, and you can control which messages appear by choosing a log level. This makes it easier to focus on diagnosing issues while keeping standard output clear and uncluttered. This section looks into the details of these two crates.

The two crates work together but serve different purposes. The `log` crate offers different macros for logging information. The `env_logger` crate is used to process and handle the logs provided by the `log` crate. To use them in code, first make sure that they are included the `cargo.toml` file.

Listing 2-34 defines a `login` function that logs different kinds of information using the logging macros provided by the `log` crate.

Listing 2-34. Using the `log` Crate to Log Information Using Different Macros

```
use log::{ LevelFilter, debug, error, info, warn};
fn login(username: &str, password: &str) {
    debug!("Trying to authenticate user: {}", username);

    if username.is_empty() || password.is_empty() {
        error!("Empty username or password");
        return;
    }
```

```
    if username == "admin" && password == "secret" {
        info!("Admin login successful");
    } else {
        warn!("Login failed for user: {}", username);
    }
}
```

The log crate offers different macros for logging information, summarized here:

- **error!:** Logs errors, indicating that the program has encountered a failure or cannot continue.
- **warn!:** Logs warnings, which are potentially problematic situations that are not fatal but should be reviewed.
- **info!:** Logs general information, which are typically high-level informational messages about the normal flow of the application.
- **debug!:** Logs detailed diagnostic messages, which are useful for debugging and tracing the internal flow of the program.
- **trace!:** Logs very fine-grained information, which is used for step-by-step tracing of execution.

Listing 2-34 first tries to authenticate a user. If the username or password is empty, the function logs an error using `error!` and returns. If the username and password matches the record, it logs the information using `info!` about a successful login. Otherwise, it logs a warning using `warn!`.

You can now use the `env_logger` crate to process the log messages generated using the `log` crate. Listing 2-35 shows how to do this.

Listing 2-35. Using the `env_logger` Crate to Process the Logging Messages

```
use env_logger;
fn main() {
    env_logger::init();

    login("admin", "secret");
}
```

We first initialize the `env_logger` and then make a call to the `login` function. This code will not produce any output. This is because, by default, only errors logged using `error!` are shown in the output. If you call the function with some incorrect information such as `login("guest", "")`, this function call will now produce the following output:

```
[2025-12-09T10:15:39Z ERROR rust_debugging] Empty username or password
```

The logging framework internally relies on priority levels to decide which level of logging information to display. Table 2-3 shows the logging levels and their respective priorities.

Table 2-3. *Priority Levels of Logging Messages*

Level	Priority	Use Case Example
Error	5	Critical failures
Warn	4	Recoverable issues or unexpected behavior
Info	3	Normal runtime events
Debug	2	Developer-level debugging
Trace	1	Extremely detailed, fine-grained diagnostics

In Table 2-3, the numbers with higher values represent a higher priority level. Errors have the highest priority followed by warnings, then infos, then debugs, and finally traces, which have the least priority. The messages shown on the terminal depend on the logger filtering based on priority level, which by default is set to `Error`.

The code in Listing 2-36 shows how to change the default filtering level.

Listing 2-36. Changing the Default Filtering Level Based on the Priority of the Logging Messages

```
use log::{LevelFilter, debug, error, info, warn};
use env_logger::Builder;

fn main() {
    Builder::new().filter_level(LevelFilter::Trace).init();
    login("admin", "secret");
}
```

This code begins by creating a new logger configuration using the `Builder::new()` constructor. We then set the global log filter to `LevelFilter::Trace`, which is the lowest-priority level. This will allow all types of log messages to be displayed. Finally, calling `init()` completes the configuration and activates the logger. As a result, every log statement in the program will now be displayed when the program is executed. The program in Listing 2-36 will generate the following output:

```
[2025-12-09T10:37:20Z DEBUG rust_debugging] Trying to authenticate
user: admin
[2025-12-09T10:37:20Z INFO  rust_debugging] Admin login successful
```

The logging information can be set for individual modules. To see an example of this, consider the `security` module in Listing 2-37.

Listing 2-37. Definition of the `security` Module

```
mod security {
    use log::{debug, info, trace};

    pub fn check_access(user: &str) {
        debug!("Checking access rights for: {}", user);
        trace!("Performing low-level permission check for: {}", user);

        if user == "admin" {
            info!("Access granted to admin.");
        } else {
            info!("Limited access for user: {}", user);
        }
    }
}
```

The `security` module contains the `check_access` function, which logs a sequence of diagnostic messages at different log levels to illustrate how access control decisions are traced within the `security` module. It performs a simple check on the provided username and reports whether full or limited access is granted, using debug, trace, and info to distinguish the granularity of each log event. Listing 2-38 shows how you can set the filtering level on a module basis.

Listing 2-38. Setting a Filtering Level Based on a Module

```
use env_logger::Builder;
use log::{LevelFilter};
fn main() {
    Builder::new()
        .filter_module("rust_debugging::security", LevelFilter::Trace)
        .init();

    security::check_access("admin");
}
```

In main now, we use the filter_module method instead of filter_level used in Listing 2-36 to set the filtering level on a per-module basis. Note that rust_debugging is the top-level module, while the security is the submodule. Executing the code in Listing 2-38 produces the following output:

```
[2025-12-11T03:16:44Z DEBUG rust_debugging::security] Checking access
rights for: admin
[2025-12-11T03:16:44Z TRACE rust_debugging::security] Performing low-level
permission check for: admin
[2025-12-11T03:16:44Z INFO  rust__debugging::security] Access granted to admin.
```

The logging information for the module is displayed as per the defined filtering level. Moreover, the module information is appended with the logging information.

You can modify the code in Listing 2-38 to define difference levels for functions belonging to different modules. Listing 2-39 shows how this can be done.

Listing 2-39. Setting Filtering Levels for Different Modules

```
use env_logger::Builder;
use log::LevelFilter;
fn main() {
    Builder::new()
        .filter_module("rust_debugging", LevelFilter::Debug)
        .filter_module("rust_debugging::security", LevelFilter::Trace)
        .init();

    security::check_access("admin");
}
```

The rust_debugging module now has different filtering levels compared to the rust_debugging::security module.

Structured Logging and Tracing

The log and env_logger crates provide a simple logging system that records logging messages with levels. They are good but not sufficient for capturing detailed context and event details.

The tracing and tracing-subscriber crates can handle structured, event-based diagnostics. They add the ability to record events and follow asynchronous or concurrent flows across tasks. This makes them much better for modern, complex Rust applications, where you need to see not just what happened, but also where and in which context it happened.

Let's go through an example to see more details.[1] We start by adding the following dependencies to the cargo.toml file.

```
[dependencies]
tokio = {version = "1.46.1", features = ["full"]}
tracing = "0.1.41"
tracing-subscriber = "0.3.19"
```

The version numbers may change if updated versions become available. The tracing crate is similar to the log crate used earlier with env_logger. It provides core logging macros such as debug, error, and info. It also adds support for structured, context-rich instrumentation. Likewise, the tracing-subscriber crate plays a role similar to env_logger. It receives the emitted events and then filters and formats them. It also manages how and where they are recorded.

To see an application of the two crates, consider an online store that needs to process user requests. The processing or user requests are done in three steps—authenticating the user, validating the order, and saving the order to a database. Listing 2-40 shows the structure of process_request, which we will refine soon.

[1] The example in this section is based on Async code. It is therefore advisable to go through the key concepts of Async code before starting this section.

Listing 2-40. Structure of `process_request`

```
async fn process_request(user_id: u32, order_id: u32) {
    // Step 1: call authenticate_user

    // Step 2: call validate_order

    // Step 3: call save_to_db
}
```

The `process_request` function will complete the processing in three steps. The code in Listing 2-41 shows the code of the `authenticate` that's required to complete Step 1.

Listing 2-41. Definition of `authenticate` function

```
use tokio::time::{Duration, sleep};
use tracing::{debug, error, info};

async fn authenticate(user_id: u32) {
    debug!(%user_id, "Authenticating user");
    sleep(Duration::from_millis(50)).await;
    info!(%user_id, "Authentication successful");
}
```

The function in the previous listing logs a debugging message using the `debug!` macro. It then simulates the authentication computation by putting the task to sleep with the `sleep` function. After the simulated work reflecting authentication logic completes, it logs a final informational message using the `info!` macro to indicate that the authentication was successful.

The `process_request` function validates the order. Listing 2-42 shows the implementation of the `validate_order` function.

Listing 2-42. Definition of the `validate_order` Function

```
use tokio::time::{Duration, sleep};
use tracing::{debug, error, info};

async fn validate_order(order_id: u32) -> Result<(), &'static str> {
    debug!(%order_id, "Validating order");
```

```
    sleep(Duration::from_millis(80)).await;

    if order_id % 2 == 0 {
        Ok(())
    } else {
        Err("Invalid order quantity")
    }
}
```

The validate_order function begins by logging a debugging message following simulation of validation work by sleeping for a short duration. After that, it applies a simple check on order_id. Even IDs are treated as valid and return Ok(()). Odd IDs return an error message. This allows the example to demonstrate both successful and failing validation cases.

The last step in the process_request function in Listing 2-40 is to save it to the database. Listing 2-43 shows the definition of the save_to_DB function.

Listing 2-43. Definition of the save_to_DB Function

```
use tokio::time::{Duration, sleep};
use tracing::{debug, error, info};

async fn save_to_db(order_id: u32) -> Result<(), &'static str> {
    debug!(%order_id, "Saving order to database");
    sleep(Duration::from_millis(100)).await;
    Ok(())
}
```

The function starts by logging a debugging message using the debug! macro, indicating which order_id is being saved. It then simulates the database operation by sleeping for a short duration with sleep. After the simulated delay, the function returns Ok(()) to indicate a successful save.

We can now use the definitions of the functions in Listings 2-41–2-43 to update the process_request function in Listing 2-40. Listing 2-44 shows the updated code.

Listing 2-44. Updated Definition of process_request in Listing 2-40

```
use tracing::{debug, error, info};
```

```
async fn process_request(user_id: u32, order_id: u32) {
    authenticate(user_id).await;

    if validate_order(order_id).await.is_err() {
        error!(%order_id, %user_id, "Validation failed");
        return;
    }

    match save_to_db(order_id).await {
        Ok(_) => info!(%order_id, "Order saved successfully"),
        Err(e) => error!(%order_id, error = %e, "DB save failed"),
    }
}
```

The process_request function coordinates the full request workflow. It first calls authenticate to verify the user, then validates the order using validate_order. If validation fails, it logs an error and returns early. Otherwise, it attempts to save the order to the database and logs either a success or an error message based on the result.

The code in Listings 2-41–2-44 use various macros for logging information. In main, you can now use the tracing_subscriber crate to perform structured logging. Listing 2-45 shows the code in main.

Listing 2-45. Using tracing_subscriber in main for Structured Logging

```
use tokio::time::{Duration, sleep};
use tracing::{debug, error, info};
use tracing_subscriber;

#[tokio::main]
async fn main() {
    let subscriber = tracing_subscriber::FmtSubscriber::builder()
        .with_max_level(tracing::Level::DEBUG)
        .finish();

    tracing::subscriber::set_global_default(subscriber).expect("Setting
    tracing subscriber failed");
```

```
    let task1 = tokio::spawn(process_request(1, 42)); // valid order
    let task2 = tokio::spawn(process_request(2, 43)); // invalid order

    let _ = tokio::join!(task1, task2);
}
```

This code first creates an instance of a tracing subscriber using `tracing_subscriber::FmtSubscriber::builder`. The formatting subscriber (`FmtSubscriber`) is responsible for collecting tracing events, applying filtering rules, formatting them, and outputting them to the console. You can configure the maximum log level by calling `with_max_level(tracing::Level::DEBUG)`. This works similarly to how we configured log levels with `env_logger` in the previous tutorial. Finally, we call `finish` to complete the subscriber setup.

Next, we register the subscriber as the global default using `tracing::subscriber::set_global_default`. This enables structured logging across the entire application. After the logging setup, we create two asynchronous tasks with `tokio::spawn`. Each task calls `process_request` to handle a specific order. The first task processes a valid order, while the second simulates an invalid order. Finally, we use `tokio::join!` to wait for both tasks to complete before the program exits. This ensures that all logs are produced and that the asynchronous workflow finishes properly. We obtain the following output by executing the code in Listing 2-45.

Listing 2-46. Output of the Code in Listing 2-45

```
2025-12-11T04:56:13.234598Z DEBUG rust_debugging: Authenticating user
user_id=2
2025-12-11T04:56:13.234576Z DEBUG rust_debugging: Authenticating user
user_id=1
2025-12-11T04:56:13.302742Z  INFO rust_debugging: Authentication successful
user_id=1
...
```

The output includes debugging information, similar to what was previously provided by the `log` and `env_logger` crates. However, to capture more detailed, function-level information, you can annotate each function with `#[instrument]`. This will essentially add automatic tracing of function calls and their parameters, giving deeper insights into the program's execution flow. Listing 2-47 shows how to annotate the `process_request` function with `#[instrument]`.

Listing 2-47. Annotating the Function with `#[instrument]`

```
use tracing::{debug, error, info};

#[instrument]
async fn process_request(user_id: u32, order_id: u32) {
    ...
}
```

In the same way, you can annotate `#[instrument]` to the functions in Listings 2-41–2-43. If you execute the code in `main` again, you will obtain the output shown in Listing 2-48.

Listing 2-48. Output after Annotating the `#[instrument]`

```
2025-12-11T04:57:08.464863Z DEBUG process_request{user_id=2 order_
id=43}:authenticate{user_id=2}: rust_debugging: Authenticating user
user_id=2
2025-12-11T04:57:08.464873Z DEBUG process_request{user_id=1 order_
id=42}:authenticate{user_id=1}: rust_debugging: Authenticating user
user_id=1
...
```

We now see much more detailed information compared to what was provided by the `log` and `env_logger` crates. The log includes both function names and the input values that led to a specific event. For example, looking at the first output in Listing 2-46, the log entry for authenticating `user_id=2` shows that it occurred inside the `authenticate` function, which was called from `process_request` with `user_id=2` and `order_id=43`. This makes it easy to trace the flow of execution and understand the context of each log message.

In summary, building on the discussion from the previous section, you can see that `log` and `env_logger` are useful for general debugging at the module level, but they do not provide detailed function-level insights. On the other hand, `tracing` and `tracing-subscriber` offer richer, structured logging that captures function calls, parameters, and execution flow, making them especially effective for asynchronous applications.

Using *rustfmt*

When discussing debugging in Rust, one often overlooked factor is how code formatting impacts the debugging process. Poorly formatted code, whether inconsistent, cluttered, or difficult to read, can make even small bugs harder to spot, as your attention is drawn to irregular spacing, misaligned indentation, or long, unreadable lines. This is precisely where `rustfmt` becomes invaluable.

`rustfmt` is the official Rust code formatter. It automatically ensures a consistent style across your entire project. Instead of every developer writing in their own style, `rustfmt` enforces a unified style so that when you open a file to debug, your eyes immediately recognize the structure of the code rather than having to mentally parse the formatting. This reduces the cognitive load during debugging and makes it easier to quickly spot a missing brace, a wrong function call, or misplaced logic.

To customize how `rustfmt` formats your code, you can use the configuration file named `rustfmt.toml`. This file is placed at the root of your project and specifies your preferred formatting rules. To add it to your project, simply create a file named `rustfmt.toml` in the project root. The file can now be recognized using the `cargo fmt` command.

We added some contents to the `rustfmt.toml` file in Listing 2-49.

Listing 2-49. Annotating the Function with `#[instrument]`

```
max_width = 100
reorder_imports = true
comment_width = 100
```

The configuration in Listing 2-49 will format code to a maximum line width of 100 characters, automatically reorder `imports` statements alphabetically, and wrap comments at 100 characters, thereby breaking long comment lines into shorter lines.

There are many interesting and useful configuration options that you can set. For instance, adding `use_field_init_shorthand = true` will automatically simplify struct initialization. Consider the code in Listing 2-50.

Listing 2-50. Initializing the `Foo` Struct in `main` Using Variables with Matching Field Names

```
struct Foo {
    x: u32,
```

```
    y: u32,
    z: u32,
}

fn main() {
    let x = 1;
    let y = 2;
    let z = 3;

    let a = Foo {
        x: x,
        y: y,
        z: z,
    };
}
```

When this code is saved, you may notice that the struct instance is simplified to the field names only and looks like this:

```
let a = Foo { x, y, z };
```

There are numerous other options available, which you can explore in detail on the `rustfmt` documentation page.[2] It is searchable and provides complete information on each option, including visual examples showing how different values affect formatting.

While `rustfmt` doesn't detect bugs directly, it creates a clean and consistent code environment that greatly aids debugging. By standardizing code structure, it reduces visual clutter, helps you spot errors faster, and makes team debugging sessions more efficient.

Once your `rustfmt.toml` is configured to your preference, you can apply the formatting by running `cargo fmt` in the terminal. Alternatively, in VS Code, you can set it to format automatically on save. In short, `rustfmt` and its configuration file are more than just tools for tidy code. They help you focus on program logic instead of deciphering messy, inconsistent formatting.

[2] https://rust-lang.github.io/rustfmt/

Summary

This chapter delved into debugging techniques that helped developers identify, analyze, and resolve issues effectively. It began with the `dbg!` macro for quick runtime inspection, followed by an exploration of standard output and error streams that separate normal results from diagnostic messages. The chapter then covered the `Debug` and `Display` traits, demonstrating how to implement and customize them for developer-facing or user-facing outputs. It explained panics, backtracing, and custom panic hooks for controlled error handling. Practical debugging was illustrated using VS Code, including breakpoints and variable inspection. Logging with `log` and `env_logger` was discussed, progressing to structured, function-level tracing using `tracing` and `tracing-subscriber`. Finally, the chapter emphasized the role of `rustfmt.toml` in maintaining consistent code formatting, which supports readability and debugging efficiency. Together, these tools equip you to write more reliable and maintainable Rust programs.

The next chapter covers advanced topics in references.

CHAPTER 3

Beyond Basic References

As programs grow in complexity, simple borrowing patterns are often no longer sufficient to model real-world relationships between data. Going beyond basic references, Rust introduces more advanced ownership and reference mechanisms that enable flexible yet safe data sharing, allowing developers to express complex lifetimes and aliasing scenarios without sacrificing the guarantees that make Rust reliable.

This chapter takes a deeper look into references in Rust, moving beyond the basics to explore their full expressive power and subtle behaviors. It begins by examining the different types of references, clarifying the distinctions between immutable and mutable references and how they interact with ownership and borrowing rules. Next, it studies binding referenced variables and how they allow flexible yet controlled access to data.

The chapter then delves into destructuring references, revealing how references can be broken down within patterns to access nested or composite data structures. The chapter continues by exploring references in compound data types, such as tuples, arrays, and structs, emphasizing how borrowing works in these contexts. The section on pattern matching shows how references integrate naturally with Rust's pattern syntax, including their use in destructured struct parameters.

The chapter also covers casting and assignment of references, discussing type compatibility and how implicit and explicit reference conversions occur. Finally, it explores reference constraints in method chaining, demonstrating how lifetimes and borrowing rules influence chained method calls. By the end of this chapter, you will have a thorough understanding of how references operate in complex Rust code, enabling you to write more efficient, expressive, and safe programs.

N. Azam, *Advanced Rust*, https://doi.org/10.1007/979-8-8688-2992-5_3

Types of References

We usually distinguish between two primary kinds of references in Rust: mutable and immutable. An immutable reference cannot be reassigned to point to a different value. Consider the example in Listing 3-1.

Listing 3-1. Updating an Immutable Reference

```
fn main() {
    let mut string_1 = String::from("Hello");
    let mut string_2 = String::from("World");
    let reference = &string_1;
    reference = &string_2; // Error
}
```

This code does not compile because the reference called `reference` is bound immutably, and it therefore cannot be redirected to refer to `string_2`. In other words, the code is attempting to modify an immutable reference, which Rust prevents.

To permit reassignment, the reference itself must be mutable, as shown in Listing 3-2.

Listing 3-2. Allowing Reassignment by Making the Reference Mutable

```
fn main() {
    let mut string_1 = String::from("Hello");
    let mut string_2 = String::from("World");
    let mut reference = &string_1;
    reference = &string_2;
}
```

Once the binding is declared to be mutable, we can change which string the variable reference points to. In summary, based on the binding of a variable to a reference, for a given type T and binding variable `ref`, there are two types:

- Type 1: Immutable binding of an immutable reference (i.e., `ref: &T`)
- Type 2: Mutable binding of an immutable reference (i.e., `mut ref: &T`)

Note In Rust, *binding* refers to the act of associating a name with a value, reference, or resource. It is done with the `let` statement.

In Listings 3-1 and 3-2, the references to data (or Strings) are immutable (i.e., `&String` types). However, references to data can also be mutable, such as `&mut String` type.

Similar to how immutable references behave, we observe the same principles when working with mutable references. Listing 3-3 illustrates this behavior.

Listing 3-3. Immutable Binding Holding a Mutable Reference

```
fn main() {
    let mut string_1 = String::from("Hello");
    let mut string_2 = String::from("World");
    let reference = &mut string_1;
    reference.push_str("!");
    reference = &mut string_2; // Error
}
```

Here, the `reference` variable is immutable, but the data it points to is mutable. You may use the reference to modify `string_1`, yet you cannot redirect it to `string_2`. As before, marking the binding mutable resolves this restriction, as seen in Listing 3-4.

Listing 3-4. Mutable Binding of a Mutable Reference

```
fn main() {
    let mut string_1 = String::from("Hello");
    let mut string_2 = String::from("World");
    let mut reference = &mut string_1;
    reference.push_str("!");
    reference = &mut string_2;
}
```

This leads to two additional types of references for a given type T and a binding of `ref`:

- Type 3: Immutable binding of a mutable reference (i.e., `ref: &mut T`)
- Type 4: Mutable binding of a mutable reference (i.e., `mut ref: &mut T`)

Beyond these common forms and types of references, Rust also allows more nested reference types, such as a mutable reference to an immutable reference. Listing 3-5 illustrates this concept.

Listing 3-5. Immutable Binding of a Mutable Reference to an Immutable Reference

```
fn main() {
    let mut string_1 = String::from("Hello");
    let mut string_2 = String::from("World");
    let reference = &mut &string_1;
    *reference = &mut &string_2;
}
```

Although the syntax `&mut &string_1` may appear somewhat intricate, it follows predictable semantics. In the `&mut &String` expression, the inner `&String` represents an immutable reference to a `String` value. Wrapping this inner `&String` inside an outer `&mut` produces a `&mut &String`, which is a mutable reference to an immutable reference. This distinction is essential: the outer `&mut` allows you to modify the inner binding, meaning you can change which `&String` the `&mut &String` points to. However, because the inner reference is still an immutable `&String`, the underlying `String` data cannot be mutated through this structure. Consequently, a `&mut &String` permits reassignment of the referenced `&String`, but it never grants permission to mutate the actual `String` itself. As a result, even though the binding `reference` itself is not mutable, the inner reference can still be reassigned via dereferencing, as shown by the last statement in Listing 3-5. If you also make the binding mutable, you get yet another type of reference, shown in Listing 3-6.

Listing 3-6. Mutable Binding of a Mutable Reference to an Immutable Reference

```
fn main() {
    let mut string_1 = String::from("Hello");
    let mut string_2 = String::from("World");
    let mut reference = &mut &string_1;
    reference = &mut &string_2;
}
```

Here, reassignment occurs without dereferencing because the binding itself permits mutation. Based on Listings 3-5 and 3-6, we have two more types of references:

- Type 5: Immutable binding of a mutable reference to an immutable reference (i.e., `ref: &mut &T`)
- Type 6: Mutable binding of a mutable reference to an immutable reference (i.e., `mut ref: &mut &T`)

On a practical note, the first four types are more than sufficient for general programming in Rust. The remaining two occur infrequently but are useful for understanding advance topics such as variance (covered in Chapter 6).

Casting and Assignment of References

Before exploring more advanced interactions with references, it is useful to understand how Rust treats casting and assignment operations at the reference level. These operations determine not only whether a value can be reassigned or transformed, but also how bindings, reference types, and mutability propagate through an expression. By examining casting and assignment in this context, you gain a more structured view of how Rust enforces safety and consistency in its reference semantics. The next section starts with casting.

Casting of References

Casting in Rust allows the conversion of one type to another type. The casting of an i32 value to an f32 is shown in Listing 3-7.

Listing 3-7. Casting an i32 Value to an f32 Value

```
fn main() {
    let x = 5;
    let y = x as f32;
}
```

Casting between references however is not very simple and must be done carefully. An immutable reference cannot be casted to a mutable reference. The code in Listing 3-8 explains this.

Listing 3-8. Casting an Immutable Reference to a Mutable Reference

```
fn main() {
    let data = 42;
    let immutable_ref = &data;
    let mutable_ref = immutable_ref as &mut i32; // Error
}
```

In this code, we define variable data and create an immutable reference to it. Finally, we try to convert the immutable reference to a mutable reference, which results in an error "`trying to cast to a mutable reference type`". This is not allowed due to borrowing rules, which provide guarantees that as long as immutable reference exists, there will no mutable access to the data. Doing a cast from immutable reference to mutable reference may break this guarantee. In this case, you may think that we are not breaking the borrowing rules, as the immutable and mutable do not coexist. That is, the immutable reference is limited to one line only, and the mutable reference is limited to another line. However, in larger codebases, there is a chance of someone doing this accidently, thereby breaking the borrowing rules. To avoid any potential issues, Rust does not allow it by default.

Casting from a mutable reference to immutable reference is however allowed. Listing 3-9 provides an example of this.

Listing 3-9. Casting a Mutable Reference to an Immutable Reference

```
fn main() {
    let mut data = 42;
    let mutable_ref = &mut data;
    let immutable_ref = mutable_ref as &i32;
}
```

The last line in this listing casts the immutable reference to a mutable reference. This code compiles and is in conformity with the rule borrowing rules.

A mutable reference ensures exclusive access, meaning no other references (mutable or immutable) can exist at the same time. When a mutable reference is converted to an immutable one, it effectively surrenders its ability to mutate the value, ensuring that only read access remains. This transition is safe because no other references were allowed while the mutable reference existed, preventing any possibility of data races or unexpected modifications.

Assignment of References

Before diving deeper into references, it is important to understand how Rust handles casting and assignment. These operations govern how bindings, reference types, and mutability interact, providing a clearer view of Rust's safety and consistency rules for references.

The first thing to note is that immutable references, when assigned to a variable, are copied. This is explained in Listing 3-10.

Listing 3-10. Assignment of an Immutable Reference Leads to a Copy

```
fn main() {
    let mut str = String::from("");
    let ref_str_1 = &str;
    let ref_str_2 = &ref_str_1;
    println!("{ref_str_1}");
}
```

In this listing, a `String` variable `str` is first defined. An immutable reference to `str` is then created and assigned to `ref_str_1`. Next, `ref_str_1` itself is referenced and assigned to `ref_str_2`. Finally, the original `str` is accessed in the `println!` macro. The code compiles successfully, demonstrating that assigning a reference to another variable does not move the original value. Instead, the reference is copied, leaving the original variable `str` fully accessible. This is because references are stack allocated, and therefore they are copied and not moved.

The mutable references however behave differently. Consider the code in Listing 3-11.

Listing 3-11. Assignment of a Mutable Reference Leads to a Copy

```
fn main() {
    let mut str = String::from("");
    let ref_str_1 = &mut str; // this line changed
    let ref_str_2 = ref_str_1;
    println!("{ref_str_1}"); // Error
}
```

This listing assigns the mutable reference `ref_str_1` to `ref_str_2` and tries to access `ref_str_1` afterwards, which leads to an error of "`borrow of moved value: 'ref_str_1'`".

The reason behind this behavior is rooted in Rust's borrowing rules. If mutable references were allowed to be copied, it would enable multiple mutable references to coexist simultaneously, which violates Rust's rule that only one mutable reference to a value is allowed at a time. According to the borrowing rules, this restriction ensures safe, data-race-free mutation. On the other hand, copying an immutable reference simply creates additional immutable references. Rust allows any number of immutable references to coexist because they do not permit mutation, so no violation of the borrowing rules occurs in this case.

Reference Patterns in *Let* Bindings

A generalized form of declaring a variable along with its type is expressed as `variable: SomeType`. The identifier on the left represents the variable name and may also encode information about its mutability, while the right side specifies the variable's type. This form has been used consistently throughout the chapter and was also central to the previous section, which examined different kinds of references.

For convenience, the following list summarizes the reference forms discussed earlier:

- `ref: &SomeType`
- `mut ref: &SomeType`
- `ref: &mut SomeType`
- `mut ref: &mut SomeType`

- `ref: &mut &SomeType`
- `mut ref: &mut &SomeType`

In all of these cases, the left side of the colon represents a variable binding, which may be either mutable or immutable, while the right side represents a reference type that determines how the underlying data can be accessed. The `variable: SomeType` pattern is the most common and idiomatic way of expressing typed bindings in Rust.

However, Rust also permits alternative syntactic forms such as:

- `&variable: SomeType`
- `&mut variable: SomeType`

These forms are syntactically valid and tend to appear in specific contexts, most notably in function parameters or in pattern-based bindings. These types of bindings are typically referred to as *reference patterns* (or borrowed patterns)[1] in `let` bindings. Although they are less common in everyday variable declarations, they are perfectly normal Rust syntax. What makes these forms particularly interesting is how the Rust compiler determines, or resolves, the actual type of the variable being bound. To understand this behavior, examine the concrete example shown in Listing 3-12.

Listing 3-12. Understanding How Variable Types Are Resolved

```
fn main() {
    let mut x = 42;
    let y = &mut x;
    let &mut z = y;
}
```

The code first defines a mutable variable `x` and then creates a mutable reference `y` to it. The final line introduces a new binding using the pattern `let &mut z = y;`. At first glance, this may appear to create another mutable reference, but that is not what happens. If you are using an editor such as VS Code, you may notice that the compiler automatically infers and annotates the type of `z` as `i32`. This raises an important question: how did the compiler arrive at this conclusion? This is explored in the next section.

[1] Also sometimes referred to as *destructing references.*

Type Inference in Reference Bindings

In reference (or borrowed) bindings where a reference appears on the left side of a binding pattern, such as `&variable: SomeType` or `&mut variable: SomeType`, Rust applies pattern matching to determine the concrete type of the variable being introduced. Rather than directly assigning a reference, the compiler attempts to match the structure of the pattern on the left with the value provided on the right.

Considering the code line `let &mut z = y`, on the left side, we have a pattern that expects a mutable reference. To resolve the type of `z`, Rust examines the type of `y`, which is being assigned to `z`. In this example, `y` has the type `&mut i32` because it is a mutable reference to `x`, and `x` is an `i32` value.

Conceptually, this assignment can be viewed as `&mut z = &mut i32`. At this point, pattern matching takes place. The mutable reference on the left side (`&mut z`) is matched against the mutable reference on the right side (`&mut i32`). Once the reference layer is matched and removed, what remains is the underlying type. That remaining type, which is an `i32`, is assigned to `z`. The type of `z` is therefore inferred to be an i32 value or `z = i32`.

The variable `z` is not a reference at all. It is a plain `i32` value obtained by destructuring the mutable reference `y`. This mechanism explains how Rust infers the type of `z` and highlights the role of pattern matching in resolving variable types when references appear directly in binding patterns. Having established how the type of `z` is inferred, the next key point to understand is how the actual assignment to `z` takes place. This is covered in the next section.

Value Assignment in Reference Binding

After inferring the type of `z`, the compiler proceeds to evaluate the assignment expressed in the final line of Listing 3-12. It determines that the value for `z` must be derived from `y`. However, based on the earlier pattern-matching step in the previous section, the compiler already knows that `z` expects an owned value, not a reference. Since `y` itself is a reference, the compiler implicitly follows that reference to reach the underlying value, which is `x`.

At this point, the compiler observes that `x` is of type i32, which implements the Copy trait. Because i32 is a copy type, Rust makes a copy of the value stored in `x` and assigns that copied value to `z`. No ownership is transferred, and no borrowing rules are violated in the process. This behavior is subtle but important. This distinction becomes especially significant when reasoning about similar patterns involving heap-allocated, non-Copy types, where copying is not implicit and ownership semantics differ. We revisit this contrast later in the same section when discussing heap allocated types within the same context.

In summary, these two statements are equivalent in the context of code in Listing 3-12:

```
let &mut z = y;
let z = *y;
```

The value of z is obtained by dereferencing y and producing an owned value.

Additional Examples

This section looks at some additional examples to solidify your understanding. Consider the code in Listing 3-13.

Listing 3-13. Type Inference in Immutable Reference Binding

```
fn main() {
    let mut x = 42;
    let y = &x;
    let &z = y; // let z = *y;
}
```

The code in Listing 3-13 is similar to the code in Listing 3-12. However, y is now an immutable reference and z is also an immutable reference binding. As in the previous case, the type of z will be inferred based on the type of the variable y, which is a simple reference. So from the type's context, we have the following:

```
&z = &i32.
```

The two references on the left and right sides will match and therefore z will be inferred to be an i32 type. The assignment to z will next take place, which will be a copy of value pointed by y, which is basically the copy of x.

Listing 3-14 is an example involving nested references.

Listing 3-14. Type Inference When y Is a Nested Reference

```
fn main() {
    let mut x = 42;
    let y = &&x;
    let &z = y;
}
```

In this case, z will be inferred based on the type of y as follows:

```
&z = &&y
```

The single reference on the left side matches the reference on the right side, and as a result, the type of z is inferred to be `&i32`. The variable z will therefore be assigned a reference to x. This means that in the code Listing 3-14, we have now two references to x. In Listing 3-14, if we change the last line to let `&&z = y`, it will change the type of z to an i32 value.

Now we'll explore the behavior of non-copy types that are heap allocated, such as String in the context of reference binding. Consider the code in Listing 3-15.

Listing 3-15. Behavior of Heap Allocated Types in Case of Reference Bindings

```
fn main() {
    let mut x = String::from("");
    let y = &x;
    let &z = y; // Error
}
```

The code in Listing 3-15 is similar to the code in Listing 3-12, but x is now a `String` variable. This code will not compile. As explained earlier, the type of z will be inferred as an owned `String` and therefore assignment to z will take place through y. The compiler will follow the reference y which points to x. Since x is a heap-allocated type that cannot be copied, it gives an error.

You may think that assignment of heap-allocated types are allowed and in this case the statement must have been valid. The variable z will be the new owner in that case. However, if you look closely, z is assigned a value by following the reference y. Since y is a reference that does not own the data, we cannot change ownership through y. The compiled error message is also pointing toward this: "`cannot move out of '*y' which is behind a shared reference`".

The reference pattern can also appear in function signatures. For instance, consider this function signature:

```
fn some_fn_1(&x: &i32) {}
```

In this signature, the reference to `x` will match a reference to an i32 and therefore `x` is inferred to be an i32 value. Note that the function calls must provide the type specified in the signature (the `&i32` value).

In the same way, in this function signature,

```
fn some_fn_2(&mut x: &mut i32) {}
```

the mutable references to the left and right will match and `x` is inferred as an i32 value.

The patterns in the function signatures (i.e., accepting a reference from caller and using the actual value inside the functions) are common when the caller naturally deals with references, but the function logic benefits from having direct access to the underlying values.

Partially Using Compound Types as References

Sometimes you may be want to use some portion of a tuple or a struct as a reference while other parts as owned values. As an example, consider this tuple:

```
let tuple = (String::from("Nouman"), String::from("Azam"));
```

We would like to destructure the tuple such that we extract a reference to the first `String`, and take ownership of the second `String`. Destructing the tuple based on a reference to the tuple shown here will not work in this case.

```
let (first_name, last_name) = &tuple;
```

This will capture both the values as references, which is not what we intend. Using the tuple without a reference, as given here,

```
let (first_name, last_name) = tuple;
```

will also not solve this problem. In this case, both the values are not owned values.

The `ref` keyword can solve the problem in such cases. This code line shows how to use it:

```
let (ref first_name, last_name) = tuple;
```

The ref in this case creates a reference to a value, rather than moving or copying the value. More precisely, it forces a variable to use a reference, irrespective of what the value is, instead of an owned value. In the previous code line, the first_name variable, which was an owned value without the ref keyword, has been forced to use a reference to the value.

It is pertinent to note that the ref keyword does not behave like an ordinary reference. In the context of generalized syntax for variable declaration covered earlier (i.e., variable: SomeType), the ref can only be used to the left of the colon. This means that the following syntax is not valid:

```
let x =  ref 5;
```

Another important distinction of using ref is that it does not take part in the pattern matching like ordinary references. For instance, consider these code lines.

```
let &x = &5; x = &i32
let ref x = &5;  x = &&i32
```

In the first case, we use a simple reference and therefore pattern matching will occur as explained earlier. As a result, x will be inferred as an &i32 value.

In the second case, however, the ref has different semantics and therefore x is of a different type (i.e., &&i32). In particular, when a ref is used with a variable such as x in this case, it simply means that, whatever value is mentioned for x, use a reference to that value. Since x is a reference to an i32, ref x is a reference to a reference to an i32. If we remove the reference to the value 5, as shown here:

```
let ref x = &5;
```

x is now a simple reference to an i32.

Adding the type annotation to the variable x, such as let ref x: i32 = 5; does not change the semantics. The ref before x will convert the type of x to a reference to an i32 value.

It is also crucial to understand how functions behave when ref is used in their parameter patterns. Consider the following function signature:

```
fn some_fn(ref s: String) {}
```

In this example, the parameter s is declared with the ref keyword. This suggests that s should be treated as a reference to a String. You might therefore assume that since s has a type &String, the function will not take ownership of any String value passed to it. To see how this works in practice, we can call this function from main, as shown in Listing 3-16.

Listing 3-16. Calling the some_fn Function from main

```
fn main() {
    let str = String::from("");
    some_fn(str);
    println!("{str}"); // Error
}
```

At first glance, you might expect this code to compile without issues. Since the function parameter s is declared with ref, it appears that s should be of type &String, which would allow us to continue accessing the original variable str after the function call. However, the code does not compile, and the compiler produces an error: "borrow of moved value: str".

The reason for this behavior is subtle. Despite the presence of ref in the function signature, the function parameter s still takes ownership of the String passed to it. As a result, str is considered moved, and any attempt to access it after the function call is invalid. Generally speaking, when a variable is passed through ownership to function, irrespective of how the value is actually used, Rust transfers its ownership.

This highlights an important distinction. Using ref in a function parameter pattern does not automatically prevent ownership from being transferred; instead, it mainly affects how the variable is bound within the function. Understanding this behavior is essential when working with function parameters in Rust, particularly to avoid unintended moves or ownership issues.

Table 3-1 summarizes the differences between simple references and references created using ref.

Table 3-1. *Differences Between Simple References and References Created Using* `ref`

Aspect	Simple Reference (& / &mut)	References Created Using ref
Role in pattern matching	Takes part in pattern matching when used on the left side of variable declaration	The ref does not take part in pattern matching when used on the left side of variable declaration
Use	Preferred for creating explicit references to values	Used in special cases where regular syntax cannot achieve the desired behavior
Ownership in function signatures	Does not take ownership	The ref changes ownership

References in Compound Data Types

References can sometimes behave differently in various compound data types. This section explores their behavior in the context of tuples and vectors.

In tuples, borrowing rules are applied on per-element basis. Mutably borrowing one element does not stop mutably borrowing other elements. The code in Listing 3-17 demonstrates this.

Listing 3-17. Accessing Parts of Tuple Through Immutable and Mutable References

```
fn main() {
    let mut tuple = (String::from("Rust"), String::from("Lang"));
    let mut_ref1 = &mut tuple.0;
    let immut_ref1 = &tuple.1;
    println!("{} {}", mut_ref1, immut_ref1);
}
```

In this code, we have a tuple containing two `String` values. We create a mutable reference to the first element of the tuple (`tuple.0`) and an immutable reference to the second element (`tuple.1`). Lastly, we access the mutable and immutable reference at the same time. The access to both references on the last print line demonstrates that Rust allows simultaneous mutable and immutable references to parts of the same tuple as long as they refer to different parts of a tuple. In summary, the mutable access to one element does not stop an immutable access to the second element.

Vectors behave differently. The borrowing rules are not applied on a per-element basis. They are applied to the whole vector. This means that mutably borrowing any element of the vector will stop any further access to any element of the vector, either mutably or immutably. The code in Listing 3-18 demonstrates this.

Listing 3-18. Accessing Vector Through Immutable and Mutable References

```
fn main() {
    let mut data = vec![10, 20, 30, 40, 50, 60];
    let mut_ref1 = &mut data[2];
    let immut_ref1 = &mut data[4]; // Error
    println!("{} {}", mut_ref1, immut_ref1);
}
```

In this code, we try to access one element immutably and another mutably. Rust does not allow this and gives an error.

There is, however, a way to safely access multiple elements mutably at the same time in a vector using the `split_at_mut` method. This code line shows how the method can be used:

```
let (a, b) = data.split_at_mut(2);
```

This method divides the vector into two separate, non-overlapping mutable slices, enabling simultaneous mutable access to different parts of the vector while fully adhering to Rust's borrowing rules. The variables `a` and `b` are now of type `&mut [i32]`, which means they both have mutable access through mutable references. The input to the method is the index at which we want to split the vector. In this code line, the data will be split on the second index, which will split the vector `data` in Listing 3-18 into two parts, given by

```
a = [10, 20], and b = [30, 40, 50, 60].
```

We can now modify both parts independently without having any borrowing issues. For instance, the code in Listing 3-19 will update the first elements in each split and print the updated splits.

Listing 3-19. Accessing Different Parts of a Vector via Mutable References

```
fn main() {
    let mut data = vec![10, 20, 30, 40, 50, 60];

    let (a, b) = data.split_at_mut(2);
    a[0] += 1;
    b[0] += 1;
    println!("a: {:?}, b: {:?}", a, b);
}
```

If you want to divide a vector into more than two parts, you can call `split_at_mut` again on one of the resulting slices to create additional, finer-grained mutable splits.

Reference Constraints in Method Chaining

Method chaining is a powerful and expressive feature in Rust that allows consecutive method calls on the same instance of a type. Whether a chain is valid depends on how the `self` parameter is received and returned in each method. In particular, `self` may be taken by value, borrowed immutably, or borrowed mutably. The ability to continue chaining relies directly on Rust's borrowing rules: moving ownership, creating an immutable reference, or creating a mutable reference each impose different restrictions on which operations can follow in the chain. This topic is explained by using a banking example.

The Banking Example Setup

Listing 3-20 adds a definition of the `BankAccount` struct.

Listing 3-20. Definition of the BankAccount Struct

```
#[derive(Debug)]
struct BankAccount {
    balance: i32,
    owner: String,
}
```

The struct contains basic information regarding the balance and account holder name. Next we add some functionality to the implementation block of BankAccount. First, we add a new constructor function. The definition of the function is shown in Listing 3-21.

Listing 3-21. Definition of New Constructor Function for BankAccount

```
impl BankAccount {
    fn new(owner: String, initial_balance: i32) -> Self {
        println!("Account opened successfully");
        Self {
            balance: initial_balance,
            owner,
        }
    }
}
```

The function accepts an owner name and initial_balance and returns an instance of the BankAccount.

Let's add a few more methods to the implementation for some routine tasks, including changing owner, checking the balance, deposits, withdraws, and viewing the owner name. These methods are shown in Listing 3-22.

Listing 3-22. Definition of Methods for BankAccount

```
impl BankAccount {
    ...
  fn change_owner(mut self, new_owner: String) -> Self {
        self.owner = new_owner;
        self
```

```
    }

    fn check_balance(&self) {
        println!("{}'s balance: ${}", self.owner, self.balance);
    }

    fn deposit(&mut self, amount: i32) -> &mut Self {
        self.balance += amount;
        println!("Deposited ${} to {}'s account", amount, self.owner);
        self
    }

    fn withdraw(&mut self, amount: i32) -> &mut Self {
        if self.balance >= amount {
            self.balance -= amount;
            println!("Withdrew ${} from {}'s account", amount, self.owner);
        } else {
            println!(
                "Insufficient funds for withdrawal in {}'s account",
                self.owner
            );
        }
        self
    }

    fn view_owner(&self) -> &Self {
        println!("Account owner: {}", self.owner);
        self
    }
}
```

Let's go over the functions in Listing 3-22 briefly. Firstly, we have the `change_owner` method, which updates the account owner and returns the modified account to allow further use. The `check_balance` method borrows the account immutably and simply prints the current balance without changing any state. The `deposit` method borrows the account mutably, increases the balance by the specified amount, and returns a mutable reference to the instance. Similarly, the `withdraw` method also borrows the account mutably, conditionally reduces the balance if sufficient funds are available, and returns a mutable reference to the instance. Finally, the `view_owner` method borrows the account immutably, prints the owner's name, and returns an immutable reference to the account.

Notice that the methods in the implementation shown in Listing 3-22 collectively demonstrate all three ways in which `self` can be received as a method parameter. The following summary groups the methods based on how they accept `self`.

- Owned form (`self`): `change_owner`
- Reference to self (`&self`): `check_balance` and `view_owner`
- Mutable reference to self(`&mut self): self`, `deposit` and `withdraw`

Moreover, the methods in the implementation shown in Listing 3-22 also demonstrate all three ways in which `self` can appear as a return value. The following summary groups the methods based on how they return `self`.

- Owned form (`Self`): `change_owner`
- Reference to `self` (`&Self`): `view_owner`
- Mutable reference to `self` (`&mut Self`): `deposit` and `withdraw`

In Rust, methods can be called and chained one after another to create fluent and expressive code. However, whether such chaining is possible depends strictly on how each method receives and returns `self`. The next section covers this in detail.

Types of Methods in the Context of Method Chaining

Methods can be divided into four types from the viewpoint of method chaining:

- Methods returning nothing
- Methods returning a mutable reference to `self`
- Methods returning a reference to `self`
- Methods returning an owned type of `self`

The following sections go over each of these types one by one.

Methods Returning Nothing

This example creates an instance of BankAccount in main and then invokes the method to check its balance. Listing 3-23 illustrates this.

Listing 3-23. Creating an Instance of BankAccount and Checking the Balance

```
fn main() {
    let mut account = BankAccount::new("Micheal".to_string(), 4_000);

    account.check_balance();
}
```

The code creates a new BankAccount instance using the new constructor function and then calls the check_balance defined in Listing 3-22. The input to the check_balance is a reference to self. The check_balance however does not return anything. Methods that do not return anything cannot be chained further to other methods. For instance, you will get an error if you try to deposit something after checking the balance, as shown in this code line:

```
account.check_balance().deposit; // Error
```

This error happens because check_balance does not return any value, whereas the deposit method requires a mutable reference to self as its input. Since the required input for the deposit method is not available after the call to check_balance, the compiler reports an error.

Note When a method is invoked using dot notation, Rust automatically determines how self should be passed to the method based on the method's signature. Depending on whether the method expects self, &self, or &mut self, the compiler implicitly moves the value, borrows it immutably, or borrows it mutably, allowing method calls to remain concise while still enforcing ownership and borrowing rules. In Rust, an *expression* is any piece of code that evaluates to a valid value.

In general, methods that do not return anything cannot be chained further to extend or grow the chain. The next section covers the second type of methods.

Methods Returning a Mutable Reference to Self

This example shows how methods returning a mutable reference to `self` behave. Consider depositing some amount in the newly created account and then withdrawing some amount from it, as shown in Listing 3-24.

Listing 3-24. Depositing and Withdrawing from a Newly Created Account

```
fn main() {
    let mut account = BankAccount::new("Micheal".to_string(), 4_000);

    account.deposit(100).withdraw(50);
}
```

We first deposited 100 and then withdrew 50. The method chaining in Listing 3-24 works because the output from the `deposit`, which is a mutable reference, satisfies the input requirement for the `withdraw` method. Now the interesting part is that we can extend the chain by adding `view_owner`, as shown here:

```
account.deposit(100).withdraw(50).view_owner();
```

In this case, the `withdraw` method returns a mutable reference to `self`, while the `view_owner` method requires an immutable reference. Why does this work? This is because a mutable reference can be cast to an immutable reference. Specifically, the mutable reference returned by `withdraw` is automatically cast or changed into an immutable reference to satisfy the input requirement of `view_owner`.[2] This conversion is what makes the method chain valid.

Note however that we cannot chain it with a method, because that requires an owned type of `self`, such as `change_owner()`. This code line will give an error.

```
account.deposit(100).withdraw(50).change_owner(String::from(("new_
owner"))); // Error
```

This line gives an error since `withdraw` returns a mutable reference to `self`, while `change_owner` requires an owned type of `self`. Since with mutable reference, we do not have access to ownership, it gives an error.

[2] Note that when a type is implicitly converted into another type, it is more accurately referred to as coercion and not casting. In this case, it is more appropriate to say coercion rather than casting. Chapter 4 covers coercion in detail.

In general, a method returning a mutable reference can only be chained to another method accepting a mutable reference or to a method accepting an immutable reference.

Methods Returning a Reference to Self

The third type of method are those that return a reference to `self`. Such methods can only be chained with methods that return an immutable reference. For instance, the method of `view_owner` in Listing 3-22 can only be chained with `check_balance`. This is shown in this code line:

```
account.view_owner().check_balance();
```

If we attempt to chain it to a method, requiring a mutable reference such as the method of deposit, it will return an error. The following line of code will therefore not compile:

```
account.view_owner().check_balance().deposit(50); // Error
```

This is because an immutable reference cannot be converted (coerced) into a mutable reference. In the same way, we also cannot combine with methods that require an owned form of `self`.

Methods Returning an Owned Type of Self

Finally, we look at the method that returns an owned type of `self`. Such methods can be chained to all forms of `self`. For instance, consider the `change_owner` method in Listing 3-22. We can chain the method with itself, as shown in this code line:

```
account
        .change_owner("new_owner".to_string())
        .change_owner(String::from("another_owner"));
```

We can also chain it to a method that requires a mutable reference, such as `deposit`:

```
account.change_owner("new_owner".to_string()).deposit(50);
```

Additionally, it can also be chained with a method that requires an immutable form of `self`, such as `view_owner`:

```
account.change_owner("new_owner".to_string()).view_owner();
```

In summary, methods that return an owned form of `self` can be chained with methods accepting any of the three forms of `self`. Table 3-2 summarizes these chaining rules.

Table 3-2. *Method Chaining Rules*

Returning Form of `self`	Can Chain to `self`	Can Chain to `&self`	Can Chain to `&mut self`
`Self`	Yes	Yes	Yes
`&Self`	No	Yes	No
`&mut Self`	No	Yes	Yes

Summary

This chapter explored references in Rust beyond their basic use, focusing on their deeper semantics and practical implications. It examined different forms of references and bindings, including mutable, immutable, and nested references, and clarified how mutability and ownership interact at the reference level. The chapter explained casting and assignment of references, highlighting the safety rules enforced by Rust's borrowing model. It also introduced reference patterns in `let` bindings and function parameters, showing how pattern matching influences type inference and value assignment. The behavior of references in compound data types such as tuples and vectors was analyzed, including safe techniques like `split_at_mut` for vectors. Finally, the chapter demonstrated how references constrain works in method chaining. Using a detailed banking example, the chapter illustrated how different forms of `self` affect chaining behavior.

The next chapter builds on these concepts by introducing *coercion*, explaining how Rust automatically converts certain types in specific contexts to make code more ergonomic without compromising its strict safety guarantees.

CHAPTER 4

Coercions

As code evolves, explicit type conversions can quickly become repetitive and obscure their intent. Rust's coercion rules address this by allowing certain types to be implicitly adjusted in well-defined contexts, reducing syntactic noise while preserving strict type safety and making programs easier to read and reason about.

This chapter focuses on the concept of type coercion in Rust, a powerful mechanism that allows one type to be automatically converted into another when certain conditions are met. It begins by exploring the basics of coercion, including the widely used `deref` coercion, which enables seamless access between smart pointers, references, and owned types. The discussion then moves to various coercion sites, identifying where and how coercions occur in code.

The chapter continues with reference and function item coercions, explaining how Rust handles implicit conversions between related function types and reference levels. The chapter also covers trait object coercion and unsized coercion, revealing how dynamically sized types and trait objects fit into Rust's coercion model. Next, it examines coercion in generics, explaining how it interacts with type inference and generic constraints.

The concepts of transitivity and least upper bound coercion are then introduced, showing how Rust determines valid coercion paths and resolves type hierarchies safely. By the end of this chapter, you will understand how coercion simplifies Rust code, enhances flexibility, and integrates smoothly with the language's strict type system.

N. Azam, *Advanced Rust*, https://doi.org/10.1007/979-8-8688-2992-5_4

Coercion Basics

In Rust, *coercion* refers to the implicit transformation of one type into another compatible type without requiring an explicit cast. Coercion typically occurs in contexts where the compiler can confidently adjust types, such as function arguments, method calls, or variable assignments. Understanding when and how coercion happens is essential for writing idiomatic Rust code and for avoiding subtle type-related bugs.

In layman terms, coercion happens when one type is converted automatically by the compiler to another type without any programmer intervention. There are many types of coercions. The next section starts with the most basic and common type of coercion, called `Deref` coercion.

Deref Coercion

`Deref` coercion is a Rust feature that automatically converts a reference to a type into a reference to another type by calling the `deref` method of the `Deref` trait. The definition of the `Deref` trait is shown in Listing 4-1.

Listing 4-1. Definition of the `Deref` Trait

```
pub trait Deref {
    type Target: ?Sized;
    fn deref(&self) -> &Self::Target;
}
```

The `Deref` trait contains one method of `deref`, which converts a reference to a type, indicated by a reference to self (`&self`), into a reference to a target type, where the target type is optionally sized. Optionally sized types are discussed in detail in Chapter 10.[1]

The `deref` coercion happens from a `&T` to a `&U` if `T` implements the `Deref` trait that converts a reference to `T` into a reference to `U`. You can write this in short form as follows:

```
// Deref Coercion: &T -> &U
```

As an example, the code in Listing 4-2 shows the `Deref` implementation for the `String` type in the standard library.

---

[1] In Rust, an optionally sized type is one that may or may not have a known size at compile time, letting code handle both fixed-size and dynamically sized values safely.

Listing 4-2. Definition of the `Deref` Trait for `String` in the Standard Library

```
impl ops::Deref for String {
    type Target = str;

    fn deref(&self) -> &str {
        &self.as_str()
    }
}
```

This implementation of `Deref` converts a reference to self (`&self`) or String type (`&String`) to a reference to str (`&str`) type. This means that a reference to String can be coerced to a reference to `str` type.

Listing 4-3 shown an example of this.

Listing 4-3. Example of `deref` Coercion Using Strings

```
fn accept_str(s: &str) {
    println!("Received: {s}");
}
fn main() {
    let s = String::from("Some String");
    accept_str(&s); // accept_str(s.deref())
}
```

The code in Listing 4-3 defines a function called `accept_str` that takes a string slice (`&str`) and prints it. In `main`, a string is created and a reference to it is passed to `accept_str`, allowing the function to read its contents without taking ownership. Notice that although the function accepts a reference to `str` type (`&str`), we provided a reference to `String` type (`&String`) from `main` in the function call, and still the code compiles and does not give an error of mismatched types. This is due to `deref` coercion, which coerces a reference to `String` to a reference to `str` type. You may think of it as calling a `deref` method on the string and then passing it to the function. This means that the following two lines of code are equivalent in the context of Listing 4-3:

```
accept_str(&s);
accept_str(s.deref());
```

In summary, whenever Rust expects a &str, the compiler allows either a &str or a &String, and the code will compile successfully due to implementation of the Deref trait for String. The next section looks at deref coercion leveraged with custom defined types.

Deref Coercion in Custom Defined Types

Rust's Deref trait can also be leveraged in custom types, allowing references to your own types to be automatically converted to references of another type in certain contexts. Take a look at an example to develop an understanding.

The code in Listing 4-4 defines a custom defined type of HtmlText.

Listing 4-4. Definition of a Custom Defined Type of HtmlText

```
struct HtmlText {
    contents: String,
    is_escaped: bool,
}
```

The HtmlText struct defines a simple data type for representing HTML content. It has two fields: contents, a String that stores the actual text, and is_escaped, a bool that indicates whether the text has already been HTML-escaped. This structure can be used to manage HTML content safely and track whether it needs further processing.

Next we add an implementation of Deref for the HtmlText, as shown in Listing 4-5.

Listing 4-5. Implementation of Deref for HtmlText

```
impl Deref for HtmlText {
    type Target = String;

    fn deref(&self) -> &Self::Target {
        &self.contents
    }
}
```

This Deref implementation in Listing 4-5 allows HtmlText to be coerced to a reference to String. In particular, it will enable us to treat it like a String in contexts that expect a &String. By returning a reference to the contents field, it lets code work directly with the inner text of the HtmlText instance while still preserving the is_escaped information.

Next, we examine code that demonstrates the use of the Deref implementation from Listing 4-5 for HtmlText. The example in Listing 4-6 is provided for this purpose.

Listing 4-6. Using the Deref Implementation for HtmlText

```
fn print_length(s: &String) {
    println!("Length: {}", s.len());
}
fn main() {
    let html_input = HtmlText {
        contents: String::from("<b>Hello</b>"),
        is_escaped: false,
    };
    print_length(&html_input);
}
```

The code defines a function called print_length that prints the length of a given String. In main, an HtmlText instance is created with some HTML content and a flag is set to false. Finally, print_length is called with a reference to html_input to display the length of its contents.

Notice that even though the print_length function in Listing 4-6 expects a reference to a String, we were able to pass a reference to HtmlText and it still works. This is because HtmlText implements Deref, which converts a reference to HtmlText into a reference to String. On the line in main where we call print_length, a coercion from &HtmlText to &String occurs. Semantically, the code line in Listing 4-6 where we make a call to print_length is equivalent to the following:

```
print_length(&html_input.deref()
```

Another advantage of Deref implementation for HtmlText is now we can directly call String methods on an HtmlText instance. For instance, the following method call is valid for the html_input defined in Listing 4-6:

```
println!("Contains 'Hello'!{}", html_input.contains("Hello"));
```

Only string methods that accept a reference to `String` can be called in this context.

Some `deref` coercions are very common and frequently used compared to others. The next section covers the common ones.

Common *Deref* Coercions

In addition to coercing a reference to `String` into a reference to `str`, there are two other common types of coercions:

- Coercion of a reference to a `Vec<T>` to a slice (`&[T]`).
- Coercion a reference to a `Box<T>` to a reference to its inner value (`&T`).

This section looks at examples of both types of coercions. Consider the code in Listing 4-7.

Listing 4-7. Examples of Common Types of Coercions

```
fn main() {
    // &Vec<T> -> &[T]
    let array: &[i32];
    let vec = &vec![1, 2, 3];
    array = vec;

    // &Box<T> ->  &T
    let i: &i32;
    let value = Box::new(5);
    i = &value;
}
```

In this code, we first create an array slice and then define a reference to a vector. Finally, the reference given by the variable `vec` is assigned to a variable expecting a slice (`&[i32]`). Here, variable `vec` is of type `&Vec<i32>`, but `array` requires a slice having a type of (`&[i32]`). Rust automatically converts the `&Vec<i32>` into a slice `&[i32]`. This is because in the standard library, the `vec` implements the `Deref`, which converts a reference to vector to a reference to an array slice.

In the second example in Listing 4-7, a reference to a Box<i32>, is assigned to a variable expecting a reference to an i32. The variable value is a Box<i32>, while i expects a value of type &i32. Rust automatically dereferences the box when taking a reference, converting &Box<i32> into &i32. Again, this is possible due to the Deref implementation for Box in the Rust standard library.

Just like the Deref trait, which enables coercion for immutable references, Rust also provides the DerefMut trait to enable coercion for mutable references. For example, the three common coercions (i.e., &String → &str, &Vec<T> → &[T], and &Box<T> → &T) are also possible with mutable references.

As an example, the code in Listing 4-8 shows the DerefMut implementation for String in the standard library.

Listing 4-8. Implementation of DerefMut for String in the Standard Library

```
impl ops::DerefMut for String {
    #[inline]
    fn deref_mut(&mut self) -> &mut str {
        self.as_mut_str()
    }
}
```

The DerefMut contains a single method of deref_mut, which in Listing 4-8 converts a mutable reference to String (&mut String) into a mutable reference to str (&mut str). The rest of the behavior mirrors that of immutable reference coercion, so I have omitted a detailed explanation.

Now that you understand how coercion works and the rules that govern it, the chapter now shifts the focus to the places in code where coercion can occur. The next section examines coercion sites in detail, building directly on the concepts introduced here to understand how and where the compiler applies these conversions in practice.

Coercion Sites

Coercion sites in Rust refer to specific locations in the code where the compiler performs implicit type conversions through coercion (i.e., the exact places where Rust allows coercion to occur). Although this topic may seem slightly off track, it is necessary to cover it before moving forward. We return to the types of coercion in the following sections. To keep distractions to a minimum, this section is intentionally kept concise.

The first coercion site appears in a let binding. Consider the code in Listing 4-9.

Listing 4-9. Coercion in a let Binding

```
fn main() {
    let s: &str;
    s = &String::from("Some String");
}
```

The code declares a variable s type &str and later assigned a reference to a String to the same variable, s. As discussed earlier, a reference to String can be coerced into a reference to str. Therefore, this assignment is valid. In this case, the right side of the assignment serves as the coercion site, where the compiler performs the implicit conversion.

Another common coercion site occurs in function arguments. Consider the function definition and invocation shown in Listing 4-10.

Listing 4-10. Coercion at a Function Call Site

```
fn accepts_str(s: &str) {
    println!("Hi, {s}!");
}

fn main() {
    let s = String::from("Some String");
    accepts_str(&s);
}
```

The accepts_str function expects a reference to a string slice (&str), yet the call site provides a reference to a String. This works because Rust applies deref coercion to the argument at the point of the function call. Here, the coercion site is the argument position in the function invocation.

Coercion can also occur in function return positions. Listing 4-11 gives an example of this coercion site.

Listing 4-11. Coercion in Function Return Values

```
fn returns_str(s: &String) -> &str {
    println!("Returning, {s}!");
    s
}
```

The `returns_str` function accepts a reference to a String and returns the same reference back but declares it as `&str`. Rust applies coercion at the return position in this case, which is the final expression in the function body without a trailing semicolon. This final expression acts as the coercion site.

Another coercion site is the struct field initialization. Consider the struct definition and its usage shown in Listing 4-12.

Listing 4-12. Coercion During Struct Field Initialization

```
struct ContainsStr<'a> {
    s: &'a str,
}

fn main() {
    let container = ContainsStr {
        s: &String::from("Some String"),
    };
}
```

In this code, the field `s` of `ContainsStr` expects a reference to `str`, yet it is initialized with a reference to a `String`. Rust applies `deref` coercion at the point where the field is assigned, making the struct initialization valid. In this case, the field assignment itself is the coercion site.

Coercion Types

Having explored the concept of coercion and its various sites in the previous sections, the chapter now explains the different types of coercion in Rust. Understanding these types helps clarify how and when Rust performs automatic conversions between types. This section examines each coercion type in detail and shows how they facilitate more flexible and expressive code. It starts with the reference coercion.

Reference Coercion

In Rust, reference coercion refers to the compiler's ability to automatically convert a mutable reference into an immutable reference when required. This conversion is one-way in the sense that a mutable reference can be coerced into an immutable one; however, the reverse is never permitted.

Reference coercion is particularly useful in situations where a function expects an immutable reference, but the caller happens to hold a mutable one. To see this in action, consider the function shown in Listing 4-13.

Listing 4-13. A Function Accepting an Immutable Reference to String

```
fn accepts_str(s: &String) {
    println!("{s}");
}
```

This function takes an immutable reference to a `String` and prints its contents. There is no mutation involved inside the function.

We can also use the function in `main` by passing in a mutable reference, as shown in Listing 4-14.

Listing 4-14. Coercion from a Mutable Reference to an Immutable Reference

```
fn main() {
    let mut s = String::from("Some String");
    let mut_ref = &mut s;
    let s1 = accepts_str(mut_ref);
}
```

In this code, a mutable `String` is created, followed by a mutable reference `mut_ref`. This mutable reference is then passed to the `accepts_str` function. Although the function expects an immutable reference and a mutable one is provided, the code compiles successfully because Rust automatically coerces the `&mut String` into `&String` at the call site.

Reference coercion may sometimes seem to contradict Rust's borrowing rules. For instance, what if the mutable reference is used after the function call, as shown in Listing 4-15?

Listing 4-15. Code in Listing 4-14 Modified by Accessing the `mut_ref` After a Call to `accept_str`

```
fn main() {
    let mut s = String::from("Some String");
    let mut_ref = &mut s;
    let s1 = accepts_str(mut_ref);
    println!( "mut_ref: {}", mut_ref);
}
```

We expect the compiler to give an error because the mutable and immutable references should not coexist. The mutable reference `mut_ref` starts from the line on which it is defined and ends on the last print line. During this period, we should have no immutable borrow. However, on the line where we call the `accepts_str` function, we have an immutable borrow due to reference coercion. The code still compiles and this is due to Rust's non-lexical lifetimes (NLL). The non-lexical lifetimes allow the compiler to track the *actual usage* of borrows, not just their scope. In Listing 4-15, the immutable borrow is strictly limited to the line on which we call the `accept_str` function. Rust knows that once the function returns, the immutable borrow will be dropped and there is no mutation taking place during call to function, so therefore it is safe.

Note Non-lexical lifetimes in Rust refer to lifetimes of references that are determined by the actual usage of the reference in the code, rather than by the textual scope in which the reference appears.

The situation becomes even more interesting when the function returns the immutable reference back to main and we use the mutable and immutable reference at the same time. This is shown in Listing 4-16.

Listing 4-16. Updated Definition of `accept_str` and its Usage in `main`

```
fn accepts_str(s: &String) -> &String {
    println!("{s}");
    s
}
fn main() {
```

```
    let mut s = String::from("Some String");
    let mut_ref = &mut s;
    let s1 = accepts_str(mut_ref);

    println!("mut_ref: {}, immut_ref: {}", mut_ref, s1);
}
```

In this listing, both `mut_ref` and the returned immutable reference `s1` appear to coexist. From a conceptual standpoint, this might seem like a clear violation of borrowing rules. However, from the borrow checker's perspective, there is effectively still only one underlying mutable reference. However, Rust allows this because it knows that there is no mutation using the reference. The compiler will only complain if we try to update using the mutable reference, as shown in Listing 4-17.

Listing 4-17. Trying to Update Mutable Through Mutable Reference

```
fn main() {
    let mut s = String::from("Some String");
    let mut_ref = &mut s;
    let s1 = accepts_str(mut_ref);

    mut_ref.push('h');
    println!("mut_ref: {}, immut_ref: {}", mut_ref, s1); // Error
}
```

This code will not compile and will give an error of "`cannot borrow *mut_ref as mutable because it is also borrowed as immutable`".

To better understand why the code in Listing 4-16 is allowed, it helps to build a mental model from the borrow checker's perspective. From the compiler's point of view, there is effectively a single mutable reference, even though the code appears to contain two distinct references. This distinction becomes relevant to the borrow checker only when a mutation is attempted through the mutable reference.

In summary, the coercion from a mutable reference to an immutable reference will not create an issue as long as you do not update the value using the mutable reference (because the function might return an immutable reference).

Lastly, it's important to note that reference coercion is different from reference casting, which is covered in Chapter 3. Reference coercion is an automatic, compiler-driven adjustment. It follows strict rules enforced by the borrow checker. In contrast, reference casting (performed using a keyword) is a manual operation that may involve reinterpretation of types.

Function Item Coercion

In addition to reference coercion, Rust also supports other forms of coercion that operate on different language constructs. This section shifts the focus to function item coercion, which enables functions to be passed as arguments, stored in variables, or used in contexts that expect a function pointer, without requiring any explicit conversion by the programmer. To develop an understanding, we first explain what a function item is.

The code in Listing 4-18 defines a function and then assigns the function name to a variable.

Listing 4-18. Understanding a Function Item

```
fn some_fn(x: i32) {
    println!("{x}");
}

fn main() {
    let f = some_fn;
}
```

This code assigns the name of the function to variable `f`. If you inspect the type of the variable `f` in VS Code, it has a concrete type of `fn some_fn(i32)` that encodes the name of the function. In this case, the variable `f` is said to be a function item.

Now if we want intend to pass a function as a value, such as an argument to another function, Rust must coerce the function item into a function pointer type. As an example, consider the functions defined in Listing 4-19.

Listing 4-19. Definitions of the `email_notification` and `sms_notification` Functions

```
fn email_notification(user: &str) {
    println!("Sending email to {user}...");
```

```
}

fn sms_notification(user: &str) {
    println!("Sending SMS to {user}...");
}
```

The functions in Listing 4-19 simulate sending notification messages to a user, with one function mimicking the process of sending an email and the other mimicking the process of sending an SMS text message. Next, we consider a `notify_user` function, which uses these functions. The definition of the function is given in Listing 4-20.

Listing 4-20. Definition of the `notify_user` Function

```
fn notify_user(method: fn(&str), s: &str) {
    method(s);
}
```

This function takes a parameter method of type `fn(&str)`, which is a function pointer type and a user string. The variable method is a function pointer in this case. Generally speaking, a function pointer is a variable that stores the memory address of a function, allowing the function to be called indirectly through that variable. The `notify_user` function simply calls the provided function given by the variable `method` with the `user` as the argument.

The code in Listing 4-21 shows how the function in Listing 4-20 can be used in `main`.

Listing 4-21. Using the notify_user Function in `main`

```
fn main() {
    let notification_method = email_notification;
    notify_user(notification_method, "Alice");
}
```

This code first declares a variable of type functional item initialized from the `email_notification` function name having a type of fn `email_notification(&str)`. Next, the function item is passed to the function of `notify_user` as an argument. Note that the `notify_user` function expects the type `fn(&str)` while we provided the `fn email_notificaiton(&str)` type; yet, the code still compiles. This is due to function item coercion. In particular, the compiler converts the function item `fn email_notification(&str)` into a function pointer `fn(&str)`.

We can also directly pass a named function like `send_sms_notification` into `notify_user` without explicitly assigning it to a variable, as follows:

```
notify_user(sms_notification, "Alice");
```

Rust will again in coerce the function item into a function pointer.

Lastly, it is useful to highlight the key differences between a function item type and a functional pointer. First, a function item type is a concrete type of a specific function while a function pointer is a pointer to any function with a matching signature. Secondly, a function item type is unique for every function, while a function pointer is a common type that may be shared between multiple functions. Thirdly, a function item type is used where the exact function is known; however, function pointers are used for dynamic behavior such as passing arguments to functions that are resolved during execution. Lastly, a function item type can be coerced to a functional pointer but a function pointer cannot be coerced further. Table 4-1 summarizes the differences between the two.

***Table 4-1.** Differences Between a Function Item and a Function Pointer*

Function Item Type	Function Pointer
The concrete type of a specific function	A pointer to any function with a matching signature
Unique per function	Common type
Used where the exact function is known	Used for dynamic behavior, such as passing as arguments
Can coerce to a function pointer	Cannot coerce

Trait Object Coercion

Trait object coercion allows a reference to a type that implements a trait to be automatically converted into a trait object reference.[2] This enables calling trait methods on values without knowing their exact concrete type at compile time. Given a reference to some type T (i.e., &T), trait object coercion will convert it into the type dyn `Some_trait`, where T implements `Some_Trait`. In short, you can express this type of coercion as follows:

```
&T -> &dyn Trait // T implements Trait
```

[2] This discussion assumes that you are aware of trait object details.

The following example explains how trait coercion works. Consider the Command trait defined in Listing 4-22.

Listing 4-22. Definition of the Command trait

```
trait Command {
    fn execute(&self);
}
```

The trait contains a single method of execute, which takes in a reference to self. Next, we define a couple of types shown in Listing 4-23.

Listing 4-23. Definitions of TurnOnLight and AdjustThermostat Structs

```
struct TurnOnLight {
    room: String,
}

struct AdjustThermostat {
    temperature: f32,
}
```

TurnOnLight contains a room name and AdjustThermostat holds a temperature value. Next, we implement the Command trait for the two types depicted in Listing 4-24.

Listing 4-24. Implementations of the Command Trait for the TurnOnLight and AdjustThermostat Structs

```
impl Command for TurnOnLight {
    fn execute(&self) {
        println!("Turning on lights in the {}", self.room);
    }
}

impl Command for AdjustThermostat {
    fn execute(&self) {
        println!("Setting thermostat to {}C", self.temperature);
    }
}
```

Each implementation of execute in Listing 4-24 prints a message of either turning on the light or adjusting the temperature. Finally, we add a general-purpose execute_command function, given in Listing 4-25.

Listing 4-25. Definition of a General-Purpose execute_command Function

```
fn execute_command(command: &dyn Command) {
    command.execute();
}
```

The function accepts a reference to a trait object of type dyn Command. and calls execute on the command.

You can now use the code in Listings 4-22–4-24 in main. The code in Listing 4-26 depicts this.

Listing 4-26. Using the Code in Listings 4-22–4-24 in main

```
fn main() {
    let light_cmd = TurnOnLight {
        room: String::from("Living Room"),
    };

    let thermostat_cmd = AdjustThermostat { temperature: 22.5 };

    execute_command(&light_cmd);
    execute_command(&thermostat_cmd);
}
```

The code in Listing 4-26 creates instances of TurnOnLight and AdjustThermostat. Next, we call the execute_command with references to created instances. In particular, we call the execute_command with &light_cmd, and then with &thermostat_cmd. Notice that the function requires a reference to trait object of type &dyn Command; however, we provided references to concrete types (i.e., &light_cmd and &thermostat_cmd). However, Rust allows the code to compile. This is again due to coercion, more precisely due to trait object coercion. On the execute_command(&light_cmd); line, a reference to light_cmd is converted to a trait object dyn command (i.e., &light_cmd -> &dyn Command). On the next line, a reference to thermostat_cmd is coerced to the dyn command (i.e., &thermostat_cmd -> &dyn Command).

Trait object coercion enables polymorphic behavior, allowing different types to be treated uniformly via trait references. The same coercion also enables storing values of different types in a single vector. Consider this code line:

```
let commands_queue: Vec<&dyn Command> = vec![&light_cmd, &thermostat_cmd];
```

This line enables you to store the two command instances of different types in a single vector of type `dyn command` due to trait object coercion.

Trait object coercion is useful in at least two ways. First, it allows you to write more flexible functions that can accept different types of parameters rather than being limited to specific types. Second, it helps reduce code duplication. Without trait object coercion, you would need to write separate functions for each concrete type. With it, you can hide the concrete type and create more generic, reusable functions.

Coercion in Generics

In Rust, coercions like converting a mutable reference to an immutable reference typically happen in function calls and other coercion sites, allowing flexible use of references. However, when generics are involved with trait bounds, the compiler must resolve the exact type and ensure that it satisfies the trait before applying any coercion. As a result, coercible types may still fail to compile in generic contexts unless the trait is explicitly implemented for those specific forms. You can build a deeper understanding of this topic through some examples. Consider the code in Listing 4-27.

Listing 4-27. A Generic Function, Struct `A`, and its Usage in `main`

```
struct A;
fn generic_fn<T >(x: T) {}
fn main() {
    let mut a = A;
    generic_fn(&a);
    generic_fn(&mut a);
}
```

This code defines a type `A` and a generic function named `generic_fn`. In `main`, we create an instance of `A` and call the generic function with an immutable reference and a mutable reference.

To resolve the generics in the generic functions, a process of *monomorphization* is applied. When you call a generic function with a specific type, the compiler generates a separate, concrete version of that function for that type. This means that the compiler will first generate a function version for an immutable reference, which will look something like this:

```
fn generic_fn_immutable_ref(x: &A) {}
```

Now based on the generated function version shown previously, one may assume that since this version accepts an immutable reference, in the second call to the function, coercion may apply and the same implementation may be invoked by coercing a mutable reference to an immutable one. However, it is not the case and another version of the same function will be created based on the second call to the function in Listing 4-27. The second generated version of the function will look something like this:

```
fn generic_fn_mutable_ref(x: &mut A) {}
```

This code in Listing 4-27 works without involvement of any type of coercion.

Let's explore what happens when we introduce a trait bound on the generic `T` in `functiongeneric_fn` in Listing 4-27. The code in Listing 4-28 shows this.

Listing 4-28. Updated Version of Code in Listing 4-27 with `SomeTrait` and `trait` Bound for `T`

```
trait SomeTrait {}
struct A;
fn generic_fn<T: SomeTrait >(x: T) {}
fn main() {
    let mut a = A;
    generic_fn(&a); // Error
    generic_fn(&mut a); // Error
}
```

The code in Listing 4-28 is similar to the code in Listing 4-27 with an added trait of `SomeTrait`, which is also a trait bound on `T` in the `generic_fn` function.

The code now does not compile for both immutable and mutable references. If we look at the first error (pause), it says, "The trait bound reference to `A: SomeTrait` is not satisfied. The trait `Some_Trait` is not implemented for &A." We have similar message for the second call. This make sense because by adding a trait bound, the compiler requires any type `T` in the call to function `generic_fn`, which implements the `SomeTrait`.

Let's add an implementation of `SomeTrait` for a reference to `A`, as shown here:

```
impl SomeTrait for &A {}
```

This resolves one error in Listing 4-28. The compiler now knows that we have an implementation of reference to `A` for `SomeTrait`. However, one may expect that since a mutable reference can be coerced into an immutable reference, the same implementation may also be valid for a mutable reference. This is however not the case. The compiler still complains on the line in Listing 4-28:

```
generic_fn(&mut a); // Error
```

The error message is "the trait bound `&mut A: SomeTrait` is not satisfied. `SomeTrait` is implemented for `&A`, but not for `&mut A`". If we add an implementation for a mutable reference, as shown here, the code in Listing 4-28 will compile:

```
impl SomeTrait for &mut A {}
```

In summary, even though a mutable reference to `T` can coerce to an immutable reference to `T` in other contexts, such as when calling a function that takes `&T`, Rust does not perform such coercions for trait resolution in generics.

Transitivity in Coercion

This section explores *transitivity* in coercion, a powerful concept in Rust's type system. The idea is straightforward: if a value of type `A` can be coerced into type `B`, and `B` can in turn be coerced into type `C`, then Rust can automatically coerce `A` directly into `C`. This mechanism enhances code flexibility and expressiveness by eliminating the need for manual intermediate conversions. As a concrete example of this principle, consider the `Book` struct defined in Listing 4-29.

Listing 4-29. Definition of the Book Struct

```
struct Book {
    name: String,
    authors: String,
    publication_year: u32,
}
```

The Book struct stores basic information about the book, including the name of the book, the names of the authors, and the year it was published (publication_year). Next, we implement Deref for Book, as shown in Listing 4-30.

Listing 4-30. Implementation of Deref for Book

```
use std::ops::Deref;

impl Deref for Book {
    type Target = String;
    fn deref(&self) -> &Self::Target {
        &self.name
    }
}
```

The code in Listing 4-30 tells Rust how to dereference a Book instance. In this case, dereferencing a Book gives us a reference to its name field, which is a String. Next, we add a simple printing function, as depicted in Listing 4-31.

Listing 4-31. Definition of the print_str Function

```
fn print_str(s: &str) {
    println!("{}", s);
}
```

The function simply prints a given string. Let's now use the code in Listings 4-29–4-31 in main. Listing 4-32 shows the code in main.

Listing 4-32. Using the Code in Listings 4-29–4-31 in `main`

```
fn main() {
    let my_book = Book {
        name: String::from("Rust Programming"),
        authors: String::from("Nouman Azam"),
        publication_year: 2020,
    };

    print_str(&my_book);
}
```

This first creates an instance of Book and calls the `print_str` function with a reference to the `my_book` instance. Notice that the `print_str` function accepts a `&str` type and we provided a reference to a Book type; however, due to transitivity in coercion, the code compiled. The transitivity coercion chain looks like this:

```
&Book -> &String -> &str
```

Due to `Deref` implementation for the Book in Listing 4-30, a reference to Book is coerced to a reference to `String`, which is further coerced into a string slice `&str` (due to `Deref` coercion).

The first conversion, which is `&Book -> &String`, is somewhat similar to calling the `deref` on the Book instance (i.e., `my_book.deref()`), which results in a `&string` type. The next coercion (i.e., from `&String` to `&str`) happens automatically. Overall, the conversion from `&Book` to `&str` is semantically equivalent to calling the `deref` twice on the Book instance. The following line depicts this:

```
my_book.deref().deref() -> &str
```

In general, the chain may be longer than the one considered in the previous example. For instance, imagine that we change the call to the function in Listing 4-32 to the following line:

```
print_str(&Box::new(my_book));
```

In this case, the chain will look as follows:

```
&Box<Book> -> &Book -> &String -> &str
```

As covered earlier, a reference to `Box` with an inner value coerces to a reference to the inner value, which is a reference to `Book` in this case. The remaining coercions take effect, as discussed earlier.

In brief, the associativity in coercion allows types to be coerced step-by-step through a chain of compatible conversions, enabling more flexible code. This also reduces the need for explicit casts by allowing the compiler to apply multiple coercions transitively when resolving types.

Least Upper Bound Coercion

Least upper bound (LUB) coercion in Rust arises when multiple control-flow branches, such as those in an `if` or `match` expression, produce values of different types that must ultimately be treated as a single, unified type. In such situations, Rust attempts to determine a common *supertype* to which all branch results can be coerced, ensuring that the overall expression has a well-defined type. This process may require applying coercions at several points simultaneously, particularly when each branch yields a distinct but compatible type. Rust resolves this by selecting the most general type that satisfies all branches, known as the *least upper bound (LUB)*. LUB coercion plays a central role in maintaining type consistency across complex control-flow expressions.

Although LUB coercion may happen in many different cases, this chapter considers it in the following three situations:

- A series of `if/else` branches.
- A series of `match` arms.
- A series of array elements.

The following sections cover each of these cases in detail.

LUB Coercion in *If/Else* Branches

Least upper bound coercion commonly arises in `if/else` expressions, where each branch may yield a value of a different type, yet the overall expression must resolve to a single, unified type. You can see an example of this by considering a `JsonValue` struct in Listing 4-33.

Listing 4-33. Definition of the `JsonValue` struct

```
struct JsonValue {
    raw: String,
    is_parsed: bool,
}
```

The struct contains a raw string and information on whether the string is parsed or not. Next, we implement the `Deref` for `JsonValue`, which is shown in Listing 4-34.

Listing 4-34. Implementation of `Deref` for `JsonValue`

```
use std::ops::Deref;

impl Deref for JsonValue {
    type Target = String;

    fn deref(&self) -> &Self::Target {
        &self.raw
    }
}
```

The implementation in Listing 4-34 will convert a reference to `JsonValue` to a reference to a raw `String` field of the `JsonValue` struct.

Now in `main`, consider the example of LUB shown in Listing 4-35.

Listing 4-35. Using the Code from Listings 4-33 and 4-34 in `main`

```
fn main() {
    let condition = true;
    let result = if condition {
        &String::from("Hello")
    } else {
        &JsonValue {
            raw: r#"{"name": "Alice", "age": 30}"#.to_string(),
            is_parsed: false,
        }
    };
}
```

This code creates a bool variable and introduces a let if structure, which will either return a reference to String if the condition is true or a reference to JsonValue if the condition is false.

In Rust, all branches in if/else are required to evaluate to a single, common type. In Listing 4-35, however, the if branch and the else branch initially appear to return different types, yet the code compiles. This is due to least upper bound coercion. Conceptually, the Rust compiler analyzes the control-flow branches in sequence, examining the type produced by each arm. When it encounters a type that differs from those seen earlier, it checks whether the new type can be coerced into the previously established common type. If such a coercion is possible, the analysis proceeds. Otherwise, the compiler attempts to determine a more general type to which both the earlier and the current types can be coerced. The resulting type, once determined, becomes the type of the entire expression. In this example, the if branch returns a reference to String, while the else branch returns a reference to JsonValue. Since the latter type can be coerced into a reference to String due to implementation of Deref for JsonValue in Listing 4-34, the expression type resolves successfully and the code compiles.

The code will still work if we change the code in Listing 4-35 by annotating the type of &str to result, as shown in Listing 4-36.

Listing 4-36. Updated Code in Listing 4-35 with an Annotated Type for result

```
fn main() {
    let condition = true;
    let result: &str = if condition {
        &String::from("Hello")
    } else {
        &JsonValue {
            raw: r#"{"name": "Alice", "age": 30}"#.to_string(),
            is_parsed: false,
        }
    };
}
```

This code compiles due to LUB again. Since `result` is declared as `&str`, the compiler checks whether the value produced by each branch can be coerced into a string slice. In the first arm, `&String` is directly coerced to `&str`, while in the second arm, coercion transitivity in coercion is applied, where `&JsonValue` is first coerced to `&String` and then further coerced to `&str`. Because both branches ultimately resolve to the annotated type, the entire expression therefore compiles.

LUB Coercion in a Series of *match* Arms

The principle of LUB coercion also applies to `match` expressions, where all arms are required to produce values that can be coerced into a common type determined through least upper bound analysis. The code in Listing 4-37 provides an example in this regard.

Listing 4-37. Code Example of LUB in a `match` Expression

```
use std::any::Any;

struct A;
struct B;
struct C;

fn main() {
    let value = 3;
    let a = &A;
    let b = &B;
    let c = &C;

    let result = match value { // Error
        1 => a,
        2 => b,
        _ => c,
    };
}
```

We first imported the `Any` trait from the standard library and created three types: `A`, `B`, and `C`. The `Any` trait in Rust is implemented for almost all types. It is particularly useful for recovering the concrete type from a trait object. We explore this later in Chapter 8. For now, it is sufficient to know that the types `A`, `B`, and `C` have this trait due to auto-implementation provided by the compiler. In `main`, we define a value and create references of the three types. Finally, we match on value and return a reference to one of the three types depending on the value. This code does not compile. Just like with `if/else`, all the arms from the `match` expression must return the same type. However, we are returning different types in each arm.

The error in Listing 4-37 can be fixed using LUB. Since almost all types implement the `Any` trait, we can coerce them into a reference to `dyn Any`, as shown in Listing 4-38.

Listing 4-38. Fixing the Code in Listing 4-37 Using the `Any` Trait

```
fn main() {
    let value = 3;
    let a = &A;
    let b = &B;
    let c = &C;

    let result: &dyn Any = match value {
        1 => a,
        2 => b,
        _ => c,
    };
}
```

This compiles. Due to trait object coercion, a reference to the concrete types `A`, `B`, and `C` can be coerced to a reference to `dyn Any`. Since all the three types can be coerced to the same type, LUB coercion takes effect.

LUB Coercion in Array Elements

Least upper bound coercion also plays a role when constructing arrays. In Rust, all elements of an array must have the same type, and the code will compile if the compiler can determine a common type to which all elements can be coerced. Consider the code in Listing 4-39.

Listing 4-39. Code for Explaining LUB in Array Elements

```
fn main() {
    let string_array = vec![
```

```
        "Rust",
        &String::from("Rust"),
        &JsonValue {
            raw: r#"{"name": "Alice", "age": 30}"#.to_string(),
            is_parsed: false,
        },
    ];
}
```

This code defines a vector where the first element is of type `&str`, the second element is of type `&String`, and the last element is of type `&JsonValue`, which is defined in Listing 4-33. The code works because all three types can be coerced to the least common type, which is a `&str` in this case.

In summary, LUB coercion is useful when different control flow branches produce different types that share a common trait or supertype. Instead of manually unifying the types by restructuring the code, Rust attempts to find the closest shared supertype that multiple sites can coerce into.

Summary

This chapter explored the concept of coercion in Rust, starting from the fundamental principles and moving through specialized forms such as `deref` coercion and reference coercion. It examined how coercion applies to function items, trait objects, and generics, and how transitivity allows Rust to chain coercions across multiple types. The chapter also covered least upper bound (LUB) coercion, illustrating how Rust determines a common type in control-flow constructs like `if/else` branches, `match` arms, and array elements. Understanding these coercion mechanisms is essential for writing flexible and type-safe Rust code, as they enable smooth interoperability between related types while maintaining strict type safety.

The next chapter will delve into combinators, building on these concepts to show how iterator transformations and functional patterns can be applied efficiently in Rust.

CHAPTER 5

Combinators

Once data can be accessed and iterated over safely, the next challenge lies in transforming it expressively and concisely. Combinators build on Rust's iterator and option-based abstractions, enabling developers to compose complex operations from small, reusable building blocks without resorting to verbose control flow.

This chapter explores the use of combinators in Rust as elegant tools for transforming and managing data without explicit control flow. It begins by studying combinators on the `Option` type, showing how they help handle optional values concisely and safely. The discussion then extends to chaining combinators on `Option`, showing how multiple operations can be composed for clear and expressive code. The chapter further examine techniques for iterating over `Option`, bridging the gap between optional values and iterator-based processing.

The chapter continues with combinators on `Result`, highlighting their power in managing success and error cases without verbose branching. We then move to vector transformations, demonstrating how combinators can efficiently modify, filter, or map collections. The section on combinators for processing vectors deepens this understanding by showcasing real-world examples of data manipulation pipelines.

Finally, the chapter covers debugging iterator pipelines, introducing methods and tools to trace, inspect, and validate the flow of data through complex combinator chains. By the end of this chapter, you will be able to write cleaner, more functional Rust code that leverages combinators for clarity, safety, and performance.

N. Azam, *Advanced Rust*, https://doi.org/10.1007/979-8-8688-2992-5_5

Combinators

Combinators are powerful helper methods provided by Rust that allow developers to transform and chain values in a very expressive and concise way, without having to write repetitive conditional logic. They help you focus on *what* you want to do with a value, rather than *how* to handle every possible case manually. By using combinators, you can compose sequences of operations in a readable and fluid manner, making the code cleaner and less error-prone.

The following sections explore some of the most commonly used combinators, such as `map` and `and_then`. To keep things practical and easy to follow, we first focus on combinators in the context of the `Option` type. This is because `Option` is one of Rust's most frequently used built-in types and provides an excellent foundation for understanding how combinators work. Grasping these concepts with `Option` will make it easier to extend and apply them later to other types, such as vectors and more complex collections.

Map Combinator

The section explores the map combinator within the context of an `Option` enum. To properly set up the background, we briefly review the `Option` enum. Its definition in the Rust standard library is given in Listing 5-1.

Listing 5-1. Definition of the Option Enum

```
enum Option<T> {
    Some(T),
    None,
}
```

It represents the presence or absence of some value, `T`. If the value is present, it is wrapped in the `Some` variant, and if absent, it is represented as `None`.

The map combinator applies a transformation to the value inside a `Some` variant using a closure and returns the transformed value wrapped in `Some`. If the `Option` is `None`, it simply returns `None` without performing an operation. Listing 5-2 demonstrates the use of `map` on an `Option`.

Listing 5-2. Using map on an Option

```
fn main() {
    let name = Some("alice");
    let upper = name.map(|s| s.to_uppercase());
}
```

This example creates a name initialized from the Some variant. It then calls the map to transform the inner string slice of the Option into uppercase. The map function takes a closure, and the argument to this closure is the inner value of the Option. The body of the closure specifies how this value is transformed.

It is important to note that the input value provided to the closure is not wrapped in an Option. Additionally, the closure itself does not return an Option; it rather returns an owned String. Despite this, the result of calling map is automatically wrapped in a Some variant, because map always produces an Option as output.

Also notice that the input to the closure is a string slice (&str), while the output is an owned String. This difference arises from the behavior of the to_uppercase method. The signature of the to_lowercase for &str is given here:

```
fn to_lowercase(&self) -> String
```

This suggests that it returns the uppercase equivalent of the string slice as a new owned String. Consequently, even though the closure transforms a reference into an owned value, the map combinator ensures that the final result remains an Option enum containing the transformed value. The upper variable therefore has a type of Option<String>. We confirm the result by using an assert_eq! macro:

```
assert_eq!(upper, Some(String::from("ALICE")));
```

Note The assert_eq! macro in Rust is used to compare two values for equality during testing or debugging. If the values are equal, the program continues normally; if they are not equal, the macro causes a panic and prints both values.

The transformation will not take effect if we pass in a None variant, as shown in Listing 5-3.

Listing 5-3. `map` in the Case of a None Variant

```
fn main() {
    let name: Option<&str> = None;
    let upper = name.map(|s| s.to_uppercase());
    println!("{:?}", upper);
}
```

In this case, we must explicitly annotate the type of the `Option` for the variable `name`, because the compiler cannot infer the inner type when the `Option` is `None`. The variable `upper` will also contain `None`, since no transformation is applied when the original `Option` is `None`. Consequently, the `println!` statement outputs `None`.

The closure inside the map function does not run for a `None` variant. To explicitly observe this behavior, we add a `println!` statement inside the closure, as shown in Listing 5-4.

Listing 5-4. Updated Code from Listing 5-3 with a Closure Body Containing a Print Statement

```
fn main() {
    let name = Some("alice");
    let upper = name.map(|s| {
        s.to_uppercase();
        println!("This will not run");
    });
}
```

If we execute this code, no output appears on the terminal, indicating that the body of the closure was never executed. This demonstrates that for `None` cases, there is no execution overhead. This makes the map very efficient for working with optional values. It allows you to safely transform `Some` values while automatically skipping `None` cases without any additional checks.

The *and_then* Combinator

The `and_then` combinator is used with `Option` when you want to chain multiple computations, where each step may return an `Option`. If any step returns `None`, the entire chain stops immediately. Otherwise, the inner option value is passed to the next step in the chain.

The semantics of and_then are similar to those of map. More specifically, it applies a closure to the value inside Some, and the closure itself returns an Option. If the original Option is None, the result remains None, and the closure is never executed. The code in Listing 5-5 illustrates a scenario where and_then can be useful.

Listing 5-5. Code Example Explaining the Motivation for and_then

```
fn add_six_if_even(n: u32) -> Option<u32> {
    if n % 2 == 0 { Some(n + 6) } else { None }
}
fn divide_by_two_if_even(n: u32) -> Option<u32> {
    if n % 2 == 0 { Some(n / 2) } else { None }
}
```

The add_six_if_even function adds six to an input number only if the number is even. Similarly, the divide_by_two_if_even function divides the input number by two when the input value is even. The code in Listing 5-6 presents an example of the function introduced in Listing 5-5.

Listing 5-6. Using the Code in Listing 5-5 in main

```
fn main() {
    let input = Some(4);
    let result = match input {
        Some(value1) => match add_six_if_even(value1) {
            Some(value2) => match divide_by_two_if_even(value2) {
                Some(final_value) => Some(final_value),
                None => None,
            },
            None => None,
        },
        None => None,
    };
}
```

The code in Listing 5-6 begins by defining an input value wrapped in an Option. It then applies a sequence of transformations to this value using explicit pattern matching. First, the code checks whether the input is the Some variant. If it is, the contained value is passed to the add_six_if_even function, which conditionally transforms the value by adding five.

If this first transformation succeeds and returns Some, the resulting value is then passed to the divide_by_two_if_even function, which performs a second conditional transformation by dividing the value by two. At each stage, the code must explicitly handle both the Some and None cases. If any transformation fails and produces None, the computation stops immediately and the final result is None.

This nested pattern-matching structure highlights how quickly such code becomes verbose and difficult to read. There is where and_then come into play. The code in Listing 5-7 depicts how you can rewrite the same code in Listing 5-6 using and_then.

Listing 5-7. Refined Version of the Code in Listing 5-6 Using and_then

```
fn main() {
    let result = input
        .and_then(|x| add_six_if_even(x))
        .and_then(|x| divide_by_two_if_even(x));
}
```

This code chains two conditional transformations on input using the and_then combinator—by adding six to the value if it is even and then dividing the result by two, automatically short-circuiting and returning None if any step fails. Note that the input to the closure inside and_then is the inner Option value and the and_then must be an Option. Listing 5-7, compared to Listing 5-6, saves a lot of code and is more readable and precise.

As a side note, since the functions are not doing much in this case, you could also inline them, as depicted in Listing 5-8.

Listing 5-8. Updated Version of the Code in Listing 5-7 by Inlining the Functions Inside Closures

```
fn main() {
    let result = input
        .and_then(|x| if x % 2 == 0 { Some(x + 6) } else { None })
        .and_then(|x| if x % 2 == 0 { Some(x / 2) } else { None });
}
```

It must be noted that earlier in map, after the transformation, the value changes to an `Option` automatically (with writing any code). However, in case of `and_then`, you need to return an `Option` explicitly after transformation.

Finally, the code in Listing 5-7 can be even more compact, as shown in Listing 5-9.

Listing 5-9. An Even More Refined Version of Code in Listing 5-7

```
fn main() {
    let result = input
        .and_then(add_six_if_even)
        .and_then(divide_by_two_if_even)
}
```

This code works because function names in Rust can be used as closures, as long as the function signature matches the expected closure type.

In summary, this chaining ability is one of the key strengths of combinators. They make the code much easier to read and less error-prone, while still handling all the optional logic. The next section explains another commonly used combinator, called `or`.

The *or* Combinator

The `or` combinator, when used on `Option`, expresses a simple fallback strategy. If the `Option` already contains a value (i.e., it has the `Some` variant), the value is preserved with no change. If, however, the `Option` is `None`, it is replaced with an alternative `Option` value. This behavior is particularly useful when a primary source of data is preferred, but a secondary or fallback source should be used when the primary source is unavailable. For example, when working with multiple optional values, `or` allows you to select the first available value without resorting to explicit conditional checks or pattern matching. See Listing 5-10.

Listing 5-10. Basic Workings of the `or` Combinator

```
fn main() {
    let primary = Some(1);
    let alternative_value = Some(10);
    let result = primary.or(alternative_value);
}
```

In this code, calling the or on primary will return the value of primary, which is Some(1). If primary had a None variant, the result would have stored the fallback value to alternative_value. If both the primary value and the alternative_value were None, a situation that is typically unexpected but may occur due to an error, the primary.or(alternative_value); statement will result in None.

Let's now look at a more practical scenario and use case for or. Consider the code in Listing 5-11, which attempts to obtain a configuration value in a system from different sources in sequences.

Listing 5-11. A Practical Example of the or Combinator for Obtaining a Configuration Value from Multiple Sources

```
fn main() {
    let env_value = std::env::var("CONFIG_PATH").ok();
    let file_value = Some(String::from("Configuration values from a
    file"));
    let default_value = Some(String::from("default configuration"));

    let config_value = env_value.or(file_value).or(default_value);
}
```

This code defines three possible configuration sources. On the last line, we attempt to obtain a configuration value from multiple sources in a prioritized order. We first try to read the value from the environment variable using env_value. If this fails, we fall back to a value from a file given by file_value. If this also does not work, we use default_value. Overall, the last statement in Listing 5-11 means that we are selecting the first Some value encountered through successive uses of the or combinator.

The next section explores the or_else combinator, which is very similar to the or combinator.

The *or_else* Combinator

The or_else combinator differs from or in that it does not take an Option directly. Instead, it accepts a closure that lazily produces an Option only when required. This makes or_else particularly useful when the fallback value is expensive to compute or involves side effects, as the closure is evaluated only if the original Option is None. If the Option on which or_else is invoked contains a value, that value is returned unchanged. Otherwise, the closure is executed to compute and return an alternative Option.

The code in Listing 5-12 explains the basic workings of the or_else combinator.

Listing 5-12. An Example of the or_else Combinator

```
fn main() {
    let cached_result = Some(1);
    let resolved_result = cached_result.or_else(|| {
        println!("Computing expensive alternative value...");
        std::thread::sleep(std::time::Duration::from_secs(2));
        Some(42)
    });
}
```

The first line in this code defines a variable called cached_result, which is initialized from some value. We then call or_else on it, which accepts a closure returning an Option. Inside the closure, we include code representing a computationally expensive task. In this example, std::thread::sleep simulates a time-consuming operation, and the closure ultimately returns Some(42).

The cached_result already contains some value, so in Listing 5-12, the value will be returned immediately, and the closure will never be executed. This demonstrates *lazy evaluation,* where the potentially expensive fallback computation is performed only when necessary. Such on-demand evaluation avoids unnecessary work, conserving CPU resources and making the code more efficient. This is particularly useful in comparison to the or combinator. For instance, if or has an input parameter that's computed based on a returned value from some function, it will unnecessarily execute the function even if its value is not required.

The *unwrap_or* and *unwrap_or_else* Combinators

The unwrap_or and unwrap_or_else combinators are used to extract the value from an Option when it is a Some variant, and to supply a default value when it is None. This distinction mirrors that of or and or_else, where unwrap_or evaluates the default value eagerly, while unwrap_or_else computes it lazily by invoking a closure only when the Option is None.

Consider an example of unwrap_or_else. A similar explanation and behavior apply to unwrap_or, with the main difference being eager versus lazy evaluation of the default value. Consider a system that delivers greetings to users by first attempting to use a personalized greeting. If no user-specific greeting is available, the system falls back to providing a time-based greeting instead. The code in Listing 5-13 shows the implementation of the greetings in the code.

Listing 5-13. Code for Delivering Greetings to Users

```
use chrono::*;
fn main() {
    let greeting_for_user: Option<&str> = None;
    let greetings = greeting_for_user.unwrap_or_else(|| {
        let hour = Local::now().hour();
        if hour < 12 {
            "Good morning"
        } else if hour < 18 {
            "Good afternoon"
        } else {
            "Good evening"
        }
    });
}
```

In this code, `greeting_for_user` is defined as an `Option<&str>` that may or may not contain a user-specific greeting.[1] The `unwrap_or_else` method is then used to determine the final greeting. If a personalized greeting is present, it is unwrapped and used directly. Otherwise, the closure is executed to compute a fallback greeting. The fallback greeting is computed by obtaining the current hour using `Local::now().hour()`, which is next used for selecting an appropriate greeting.

It is important to note that the closure passed to `unwrap_or_else` is evaluated lazily. This means the time-based greeting logic is executed only when `greeting_for_user` is `None`, avoiding unnecessary computation when a user-specific greeting is already available.

[1] Listing <InternalRef RefID=”PC15”>5-13 uses the `chrono` crate, which provides robust date and time utilities.

The *filter* Combinator

The `filter` combinator on an `Option` allows you to conditionally keep the value only if it satisfies a given predicate given in the form of a closure. If the `Option` is `Some` and the closure returns true and the original `Some` value is retained otherwise, a `None` is returned. This is quite handy for lightweight validations.

Listing 5-14 provides an example of the filter combinator.

Listing 5-14. An Example of the Filter Combinator

```
fn main() {
    let child_age = Some(10);
    let is_adult = child_age.filter(|&a| a >= 18);
}
```

Here, `child_age` is an `Option<i32>` that may or may not contain an age value. The `filter` method is used to conditionally retain this value based on a predicate. The closure passed to `filter` receives a reference to the inner value of the `Option` and evaluates whether it satisfies the given condition. If the closure returns true, `filter` preserves the original `Some` variant and returns it unchanged. If the closure returns false, the value is discarded and `None` is returned. As a result, `is_adult` will be `None` for ages below 18 and `Some(age)` only when the condition is met.

Table 5-1 summarizes the key characteristics of the combinators covered in the section.

Table 5-1. Summary of the Combinators on Option

Combinator	Behavior for Some(value)	Behavior for None	Fallback Evaluation
map	Applies a closure/function and wraps the result in Some	Returns None	Eager
and_then	Applies a closure and returns an Option	Returns None	Eager
or	Retains the existing Some(value)	Returns the provided alternate Option	Eager
or_else	Retains the existing Some(value)	Invokes a closure to compute an alternate Option	Lazy
unwrap_or	Unwraps and returns the inner value	Returns the provided fallback default value	Eager
unwrap_or_else	Unwraps and returns the inner value	Invokes a closure to compute the default value	Lazy
filter	Retains Some(value) if the predicate is true	Returns None if the predicate is false	Eager

The same combinators discussed for Option can also be applied to the Result enum. Table 5-2 summarizes their key behaviors and characteristics in the context of Result.

Table 5-2. Combinator Behavior on Result

Combinator	Behavior for Ok(value)	Behavior for Err(Error)	Fallback Evaluation
map	Applies a closure/function to the Ok value	Returns the original Error	Eager
and_then	Applies a closure that returns another Result	Returns the original Error	Eager
or	Retains the existing Ok(value)	Returns the provided alternate Result	Eager
or_else	Retains the existing Ok(value)	Invokes a closure to compute an alternate Result	Lazy
unwrap_or	Retains Ok(value) if the predicate is true	Returns the provided default value	Eager
unwrap_or_else	Unwraps and returns the Ok value	Returns the provided default value	Lazy

This section explored some of the most basic and commonly used combinators. We have not covered all of them, but understanding these key combinators provides a solid foundation to grasp the remaining ones. For a complete reference, you can consult the official documentation, but the knowledge gained here will make learning the rest much easier.

Combinator Chains

Rust's strength with `Option<T>` lies not only in its individual combinators like `map`, `and_then`, and `or_else`, but also in how elegantly they can be composed. Idiomatic Rust encourages chaining these combinators to create concise, readable, and safe workflows for transforming, validating, and handling optional values. There are many ways to chain combinators in Rust. This section focuses on some common patterns. These are especially useful for routine programming tasks and handling optional values idiomatically.

Transform Validate Fetch

The first pattern uses combinators in the order of `map` → `filter` → `and_then`. This pattern applies when you want to transform a value, validate it, and then perform a fallible operation. It works well for processing raw user data, checking if it meets certain criteria, and then proceeding to a fallible operation, such as fetching information from a server or configuration.

Let's look at an example. We first define a `fetch_user` function shown in Listing 5-15.

Listing 5-15. Definition of the `fetch_user` Function

```
fn fetch_user(name: &str) -> Option<String> {
    println!("Looking for user in database: {name}");
    Some(format!("User({})", name))
}
```

This function takes a name, simulates a lookup for the name in some database, and returns it by wrapping in an `Option` as a formatted `String`. To simulate the pattern transform-validate-fetch, we consider a username, which we first transform by eliminating any leading or trailing spaces, following by validating that it is not empty, and finally fetching it from some database. The code in Listing 5-16 simulates this using the code in Listing 5-15.

Listing 5-16. Example of the Transform-Validate-Fetch Combinator Chain Pattern

```
fn main() {
    let user = Some("  alice  ")
        .map(str::trim) // Transform: remove whitespace
        .filter(|s| !s.is_empty()) // Retain only if non-empty
        .and_then(|name| fetch_user(name)); // Fallible operation
}
```

This code defines the `user` variable containing a username with leading and trailing spaces. We first apply the `map` on it for trimming the whitespace. This will return `Some("alice")`, which is passed to the `filter` combinator, which validates if the `Option` passed in contains a non-empty string. If all goes well, we finally use the `add_then` combinator to fetch the username using the `fetch_user` function. Note that the call to the function inside the and_then is essentially used in place of the closure body. This pattern helps when you need to clean and validate values before proceeding to more fragile or optional steps.

Multiple Fallible Steps, Followed by Transformation

This pattern uses combinators in the order of and_then → and_then → ... → map. This pattern is ideal when you have multiple fallible operations that are all followed by a transformation.

Consider a string value that must first be parsed into an unsigned integer. If the operation succeeds, the integer is used to select an appropriate configuration. Finally, the resulting configuration message is transformed to uppercase. The code in Listing 5-17 depicts this process.

Listing 5-17. Example of Multiple Fallible Operations Followed by a Transformation

```
fn main() {
   let result = Some("42")
        .and_then(|s| s.parse::<u32>().ok())
        .and_then(|s| match s {
            42 => Some("answer_config".to_string()),
            8080 => Some("web_server_config".to_string()),
            _ => None,
        })
        .map(|config| config.to_uppercase());
}
```

The first and_then attempts to parse the String value into an unsigned u32. If parsing succeeds, the next and_then selects a configuration based on the parsed number, returning a corresponding configuration String, or None if no match is found. This style of number-based configuration selection is common in scenarios such as server setup, where specific values (for example, port numbers like 8080) determine particular configurations. Finally, map is used to transform the selected configuration into uppercase. Each step in the chain executes only if the previous one succeeds.

Overall, the example in Listing 5-17 clearly illustrates a chain of multiple fallible operations composed using and_then, where each step may fail and short-circuit the computation. The final map demonstrates how, once all the fallible steps succeed, a pure transformation can be applied to the resulting value without introducing additional error handling.

Multiple Fallbacks, Followed by Value Extraction

This pattern uses combinators in the order of or_else → or_else → ... → unwrap_or. It is well suited for scenarios where multiple fallback options are attempted lazily, followed by a final extraction of a concrete value.

Consider a situation where a configuration path may come from several optional sources. The application may first attempt to read the path from an environment-specific configuration. If that is not available, it may fall back to a user-specific configuration file, and then to a default configuration provided by the system. The code in Listing 5-18 demonstrates this pattern in practice.

Listing 5-18. Example of Multiple Fallbacks, Followed by Value Extraction

```
fn main() {
    let env_config: Option<String> = None;
    let user_config: Option<String> = Some("/home/user/config.conf".to_
    string());
    let default_config: Option<String> = Some("/default.conf".to_string());

    let path = env_config
        .or_else(|| user_config)
        .or_else(|| default_config)
        .unwrap_or("/etc/default.conf".to_string());
}
```

The chain in this code begins by attempting to obtain a configuration path from env_config. If it is None, the first or_else lazily evaluates the user configuration. If that also fails, the next or_else attempts to use the default configuration. Finally, unwrap_or extracts the value if any of the previous steps succeeded, or provides a hardcoded fallback path when all options evaluate to None. Note that we provided a default hardcoded value in the unwrap_or in case it was not properly being set up.

Overall, this example illustrates how multiple fallback sources can be composed cleanly using `or_else`, with `unwrap_or` serving as the final safeguard. The pattern enables resilient defaulting while keeping the control flow concise, readable, and free from explicit conditional logic.

Validate, Transform, and Fallback

This pattern uses combinators in the order of `filter` → `map` → `unwrap_or_else`. It is appropriate when a value must first be validated, then transformed, and finally replaced with a computed fallback if necessary.

Consider a scenario where a port number is provided as an optional `String`. The application must ensure that the value is valid before using it and fall back to a default port when validation or transformation fails. The code in Listing 5-19 demonstrates this pattern.

Listing 5-19. Example of Validate, Transform, and Fallback

```
fn main() {
    let port = Some("8080")
        .filter(|s| s.chars().all(char::is_numeric))
  .map(|s| s.parse::<u16>().unwrap_or(0))
  .unwrap_or_else(|| 3000);
}
```

The chain begins with `filter`, which validates the input by ensuring that all the characters in the `String` are numeric. This prevents invalid values from proceeding further in the chain. The `map` combinator then attempts to parse the validated `String` into a u16. If parsing fails, a default value of 0 is produced. Finally, `unwrap_or_else` extracts the value when present or computes a fallback port of 3000 when the `Option` is `None`. Overall, this pattern demonstrates how validation, transformation, and fallback logic can be composed into a single, readable chain. It avoids explicit conditionals while ensuring that only valid data is used and sensible defaults are applied when needed.

Each pattern in this section shows how combinators can be composed to express logic clearly and concisely. They eliminate the need for verbose `match` statements. The examples also demonstrate lazy evaluation with closures. Additionally, they highlight the power of chaining when working with optional or missing data. The next section looks at some common transformations on vectors of optional types in Rust.

Transformations on Vectors

A vector containing optional values is a very practical and expressive data structure in Rust and is expressed as `Vec<Option<T>>`. It is used when you intend to represent partial data, missing values, or placeholders in a collection. It enables storing elements of type `T`, while explicitly handling cases where some elements might be missing. This avoids invalid default values and makes absence type-safe and explicit. The remainder of this section looks at some common transformations of this type using combinators. However, before covering the transformations on optional vectors, it is necessary to cover the iterators in the context of collections.

Using Combinators on Collections

In order to apply combinators on collections such as vectors, you first need to convert the collection into an iterator. This is because combinators cannot be directly applied on collections. The conversion from collection to iterators is done using one of three methods: `iter`, `iter_mut`, or `into_iter`. The `iter` method creates an iterator that immutably borrows each element; `iter_mut` creates a mutable borrow allowing in-place modification; and `into_iter` takes ownership of the collection, moving its elements. Once you have an iterator, you can chain combinators like `map`, `filter`, and `fold` to transform, filter, or aggregate elements efficiently.

Listing 5-20 shows an example of converting a vector into an iterator and then applying the combinators on the resulting iterator.

Listing 5-20. Converting a Vector Into an Iterator

```
fn main() {
    let numbers = vec![1, 2, 3, 4, 5];

    let processed = numbers
        .into_iter() // Convert vector into iterator
        .filter(|&n| n % 2 == 0)
        .map(|n| n * n)
        .collect::<Vec<i32>>();
}
```

In this example, `into_iter` converts the vector into an iterator. The `filter` combinator selects only even numbers and `map` transforms each number by squaring it. The `collect` method gathers the results into a new vector. It consumes the iterator and gathers all its elements into the specified collection type. The type of collection must be either inferred by the compiler or explicitly specified using *turbofish* syntax, such as `::<Vec<_>>`,. The `collect` method is commonly used at the end of iterator chains to finalize transformations into usable data structures.

Now that you understand how to convert a collection into an iterator to apply combinators, the following sections return to common transformations on vectors containing optional values.

Mandatory Value Transformation

This pattern focuses on unwrapping all `Some` values in a collection while applying a transformation to each element. It is useful when all the values are mandatory, and the presence of a `None` would indicate a serious problem, such as invalid input or incomplete data. By combining unwrapping with a transformation, you can safely process every element while performing additional computations in a concise manner.

Listing 5-21 contains an example of this pattern.

Listing 5-21. Example of a Mandatory Value Transformation

```
fn main() {
    let data = vec![Some(1), Some(2), Some(3)];
    let unwrapped = data
        .into_iter()
        .map(|x| x.unwrap() * 2)
        .collect::<Vec<i32>>();
}
```

In this listing, we call `into_iter` to consume the original data. Each element is mapped to its unwrapped value after multiplying it by two. The results are then collected in a new vector.

Inside the map, we can perform additional processing. For example, arithmetic operations, formatting, and other computations can be applied as part of the transformation. The call to unwrap inside the map ensures that if any value happens to None, the transformation will not apply and the program will immediately panic. This pattern provides a concise and idiomatic way to process mandatory values while safely performing additional computations.

Cleaning Option Values

This transformation involves unwrapping Some values while filtering out all None values. This happens when datasets contain optional values, which is common in applications dealing with incomplete user input, sensor data, or other sources where some values may be missing. In such cases, the goal is to process only the valid data while discarding the missing entries.

The code in Listing 5-22 puts this pattern into practice.

Listing 5-22. Example of Cleaning Option Values

```
fn main() {
    let data = vec![Some(1), None, Some(3), None, Some(5)];

    let filtered = data
        .into_iter()
        .filter(|x| x.is_some())
        .map(|x| x.unwrap())
        .collect::<Vec<i32>> ();
}
```

Here, we first call into_iter to consume the original data. The filter combinator keeps only the elements that are Some and discards all None values. In particular, the is_some method returns a true for elements that are Some and false for those that are None. Next, map unwraps the filtered values. Finally, collect gathers them into a vector of i32. The resulting vector will only contain the Some variants, removing all the None entries. This pattern provides a safe and concise way to clean datasets while retaining meaningful values.

The chain in Listing 5-22 can be further simplified by using the `flatten` combinator, as shown here:

```
let filtered = data.into_iter().flatten.collect::<Vec<i32>>();
```

The `flatten` combinator automatically removes all `None` values and unwraps the `Some` values. It returns only the inner values in a flat iterator, eliminating the need for separate `filter` and `map` steps. This makes the code more concise and expressive, while achieving the same result of extracting all valid values from a collection of options.

Filtering Out None While Preserving Some

This transformation involves removal of all the `None` variants while keeping the `Some` variants unchanged. This pattern differs from the earlier cleaning option values pattern in that it retains the `Some` values wrapped instead of unwrapping them, allowing the optional nature of the values to be preserved for further use or processing. This pattern is useful in scenarios like profile editors or form processors, where optional fields must be preserved for later use, re-insertion, or compatibility with systems that expect `Option` types.

Consider a data vector containing some `None` values, as shown in Listing 5-23.

Listing 5-23. Example of Filtering None and Preserving Some

```
fn main() {
    let mut data = vec![Some(1), None, Some(2), None, Some(3)];
    let data = data
        .into_iter()
        .filter(|x| x.is_some())
        .collect::<Vec<Option<i32>>>();
}
```

Here, we first call `into_iter` to consume the original vector. Next, the `filter` combinator removes all the `None` values while leaving the `Some` values wrapped. Finally, `collect` gathers the results into a vector of `Option<i32>`. This approach is concise and preserves the optional nature of the remaining elements, making it ideal for workflows that require `Option` types to be maintained. Table 5-3 summarizes the patterns considered in this section.

Table 5-3. *Summary of the Patterns on Vector of Option Type*

Transformation	Working	When Used
Mandatory value transformation	Unwrap all Some	When all values are mandatory
Cleaning optional values	Unwrap Some and filter out None	When there is incomplete data
Filtering out None while preserving Some	Remove None and keep Some	When preserving the Some wrappers

Combinators for Processing Vectors

This section covers additional combinators that are primarily designed for iterators and collections. These combinators help control iteration and aggregate values or add positional context. Unlike the combinators covered earlier, which transform or filter individual elements, the ones in this section operate on the collection as a whole or provide meta-level operations. This section demonstrates these combinators using vectors, although the same techniques can be applied to other collection types as well.

The *skip* Combinator

We begin with the `skip` combinator, which allows you to ignore the first few elements of a collection. This is particularly useful for bypassing headers or metadata. Consider the example in Listing 5-24.

Listing 5-24. A Vector Containing Data in CSV Style

```
fn main() {
    let csv_data = vec!["name,age", "Alice,30", "Bob,25"];
    let data_without_headers = csv_data.into_iter().skip(1).
    collect::<Vec<&str>>();
}
```

The `csv_data` vector contains CSV-style entries, with the first row representing the headers. The goal is to skip the headers and retain only the actual rows of data. We start by calling `into_iter` to convert the vector into an iterator. Next, we apply the `skip` combinator with an argument of `1` to ignore the first row only. Finally, we use `collect` to gather the remaining elements into a new vector. The `skip` in this case allows us to efficiently bypass irrelevant elements and focus more on meaningful data.

The *take* Combinator

This section explores the `take` combinator, which allows you to preview only the first few elements of a collection. This is particularly useful when working with large datasets and you want to inspect a small portion before processing the entire collection. Listing 5-25 demonstrates its use.

Listing 5-25. Using `take` to Preview a Portion of the Data

```
fn main() {
    let data = vec![
        String::from("row1"),
        String::from("row2"),
        String::from("row3"),
        String::from("row4"),
    ];

    let preview = data.iter().take(2).collect::<Vec<&String>>();
    println!("{:?}", preview); // ["row1", "row2"]
}
```

Here, we start with a vector and call `iter()` to create an iterator using the original data by reference. Then, `take(2)` selects only the first two elements by reference. Finally, `collect` gathers the results into a new vector.

Note that `take` operates on iterators, not on the original data directly, and it preserves the order of the elements. This makes it an efficient way to inspect or sample the beginning of a collection without modifying the original dataset.

The *enumerate* Combinator

We next examine the `enumerate` combinator, which allows you to attach an index to each element while iterating over a collection. This is particularly useful for tracking positions in tasks like logging, debugging, or building code formatting tools.

Consider the example in Listing 5-26.

Listing 5-26. Using `enumerate` to Add Line Numbers to the Code Lines

```
fn main() {
       let code = vec!["fn main() {", " println!(\"Hello\")", "}"];
    let code_with_line_numbers = code.into_iter().enumerate().
    collect::<Vec<(usize, &str)>>();
}
```

The variable code contains elements that correspond to code lines in a Rust program. By calling `enumerate` on the iterator, we pair each line with its index. Finally, `collect` gathers these pairs into a new vector.

In the resulting vector, each entry consists of a line number and its corresponding content. This approach is especially useful for debugging, displaying annotated data, or generating reports where the position of each element matters.

The *fold* Combinator

The `fold` combinator is a powerful tool for reducing a collection into a single accumulated value while processing each element. It gives you complete control over the accumulation logic. Let's go through an example of this combinator, as shown in Listing 5-27.

Listing 5-27. Using `fold` to Compute the Sum of Squares of a Vector

```
fn main() {
    let nums = vec![1, 2, 3, 4];
    let sum_of_squares = nums.iter().fold(0, |acc, &x| acc + x * x);
}
```

In this code, we start with a vector of numbers. To calculate the sum of squares, we use `fold`. The first argument initializes the accumulator at zero, and the second argument is a closure with two inputs. The first input is the accumulator that stores the accumulated values and the second argument represents the individual values of the iterators. In this case, each value of the vector will be multiplied by itself and then added to the already accumulated result.

fold is versatile combinator and can be used to compute sums, products, concatenations, or other aggregation operations. It provides a concise and powerful way to reduce a collection into a single value while retaining full control over the computation.

The *reduce* Combinator

Finally, we explore the reduce combinator. Reduce is similar to fold, but it does not require an initial accumulator. Instead, it uses the first element of the collection as the starting point and combines the remaining elements pairwise. Listing 5-28 shows an example of how reduce can be used to find the maximum value in a vector of integers.

Listing 5-28. Using reduce to Find the Maximum Value in a Vector

```
fn main() {
    let nums = vec![1, 2, 3, 4];
    let result = nums.into_iter().reduce(|a, b| a.max(b));
}
```

In this code, reduce finds the maximum value by comparing each element to the current maximum. Internally, the computation proceeds as follows. During the first call, a is the first element and b is the second. The result of this comparison becomes the new a, and the next element becomes b. This process continues until all the elements have been processed. Note that reduce returns an Option<T> because the original collection could be empty, in which case there would be no value to return.

Table 5-4 summarizes the common combinators discussed in this section.

Table 5-4. *Common Combinators for Collection Processing*

Combinator	Working	Use
skip	Skip the first *N* items of a collection	Useful for ignoring headers
take	Take only the first *N* items	Good for previewing large datasets
enumerate	Attach an index to each item	Useful for logging or labeling
fold	Accumulate values with custom logic	Apply custom accumulation logic
reduce	Combine elements pairwise	Combine elements into a single result

Debugging Iterator Pipelines

This section explains how to debug iterator pipelines or chains in Rust. This is important because it helps you understand how data flows through each transformation step and identify where unexpected behavior or incorrect results occur. Since iterator chains can be concise but complex, debugging helps ensure that each combinator is working as intended and improves code reliability and correctness.

We discuss two approaches for debugging iterator chains. The first approach breaks the chain after each combinator and manually inspects the intermediate results. The second approach relies on the inspect combinator to observe values as they flow through the chain.

Debugging by Breaking Iterator Chains

To understand the basics of this approach, consider the code in Listing 5-29.

Listing 5-29. An Iterator Chain for Illustrating Debugging Through Incremental Inspection

```
fn main() {
    let inputs = vec![" 23 ", "NaN", "", "42", "abc", "35"];
    let avg = inputs
        .into_iter()
        .map(str::trim)
        .filter(|s| !s.is_empty() && s.chars().all(char::is_numeric))
        .map(|s| s.parse::<u32>().unwrap())
        .fold((0, 0), |(sum, count), x| (sum + x, count + 1));

    let average = avg.0 as f64 / avg.1 as f64;
}
```

This code processes a vector of string inputs to compute the average of the valid numeric values. It begins by converting the vector into an iterator and trimming leading and trailing whitespace from each element. Next, it filters out empty strings and any values that contain non-numeric characters, ensuring that only valid numeric inputs remain. These filtered strings are then parsed into u32 values.

The final stage uses fold to accumulate two pieces of information at once using a tuple. This includes the running sum of numbers and the count of valid entries. The accumulator is a tuple, where the first element tracks the sum and the second tracks how many values have been processed. After the fold completes, the average is computed by dividing the total sum by the count and printing it as a floating-point value.

This chain is concise but may be hard to comprehend and debug if the output isn't what you expect. To inspect what's happening at each step, we can break the chain into explicit stages. After each method call, we can collect the result and display the intermediate result to inspect the values and see the result of the transformation. This is depicted in Listing 5-30.

Listing 5-30. Revising the Code in Listing 5-29 to Break the Chain into Explicit Stages

```
fn main() {
    let inputs = vec![" 23 ", "NaN", "", "42", "abc", "35"];
    let stage1 = inputs.into_iter().collect::<Vec<_>>();
    println!("Stage 1 (raw): {:?}", stage1);

    let stage2 = stage1.into_iter().map(str::trim).collect::<Vec<_>>();
    println!("Stage 2 (trimmed): {:?}", stage2);

    let stage3 = stage2
        .into_iter()
        .filter(|s| !s.is_empty() && s.chars().all(char::is_numeric))
        .collect::<Vec<_>>();
    println!("Stage 3 (filtered valid): {:?}", stage3);

    let stage4 = stage3
        .into_iter()
        .map(|s| s.parse::<u32>().unwrap())
        .collect::<Vec<_>>();
    println!("Stage 4 (parsed ints): {:?}", stage4);

    let avg = stage4
```

```
        .iter()
        .fold((0, 0), |(sum, count), &x| (sum + x, count + 1));

    let average = avg.0 as f64 / avg.1 as f64;

}
```

In this code, we collect the values right after calling the `into_iter`. Next, we repeatedly apply the same and collect values after each combinator. This approach is helpful for observing intermediate transformations and understanding how the vector evolves at each step. However, it comes at the cost of additional boilerplate, as it requires extra variables and repeated collection solely to inspect intermediate results.

Debugging with the *inspect* Combinator

The `inspect` combinator allows you to observe values as they flow through an iterator chain without modifying them. This makes it a powerful debugging tool. Unlike when breaking the chain into stages, it does not require additional variables to store intermediate results. Using the same chain as in Listing 5-29, we can revise the code and insert `inspect` calls after each combinator to examine the intermediate values as they are produced. This modified code is shown in Listing 5-31.

Listing 5-31. Revising the Code in Listing 5-29 to Observe Intermediate Values Using `inspect`

```
fn main() {
    let inputs = vec![" 23 ", "NaN", "", "42", "abc", "35"];
    let avg = inputs
        .into_iter()
        .inspect(|s| println!("[raw] {:?}", s))

        .map(str::trim)
        .inspect(|s| println!("[trimmed] {:?}", s))

        .filter(|s| !s.is_empty() && s.chars().all(char::is_numeric))
        .inspect(|s| println!("[valid]  {:?}", s))
```

```
        .map(|s| s.parse::<u32>().unwrap())
        .inspect(|x| println!("[parsed] {}", x))
        .fold((0, 0), |(sum, count), x| (sum + x, count + 1));

    let average = avg.0 as f64 / avg.1 as f64;

}
```

In this code, inspection occurs on a per-element basis. Each element flows through the entire chain of transformations and `inspect` calls before the next element is processed. As a result, the inspections reflect the step-by-step progression of each individual value through the iterator pipeline. This behavior contrasts with the earlier approach, where the entire vector was processed in discrete stages, and each stage operated on the full collection before moving to the next transformation.

Summary

This chapter introduced combinators as a central abstraction for expressing data transformations in a concise manner. It began by establishing the role of combinators such as `map`, `filter`, `and_then`, `or_else`, and `unwrap_or`, and it showed how they enable fluent chaining over optional and iterable data without resorting to verbose `match` statements. The discussion then extended to applying combinators on collections by first converting them into iterators using `iter`, `iter_mut`, and `into_iter`, followed by common transformation patterns on vectors containing `Option` values, including unwrapping mandatory data, filtering out missing values, and preserving optional structure when required. The chapter further explored iterator-focused combinators such as `skip`, `take`, `enumerate`, `fold`, and `reduce`, highlighting their role in controlling iteration, aggregating results, and adding contextual information. Finally, it addressed practical debugging techniques for iterator chains, covering debugging by breaking chains and debugging without breaking the chain using the `inspect` combinator. Overall, the chapter demonstrated how combinators promote clarity and reduce excessive code.

The next chapter explores lifetime relationships and delves into some of Rust's less commonly discussed topics, including variance, covariance, and contravariance.

CHAPTER 6

Relationships in Lifetimes

As references flow through functions, structs, and traits, the relationships between their lifetimes become increasingly significant. Understanding lifetime relationships in Rust allows developers to precisely express how long data must remain valid, enabling the compiler to enforce memory safety across complex borrowing scenarios without relying on runtime checks.

This chapter explores the intricate relationship between lifetimes and type bounds in Rust, focusing on how they govern reference safety and flexibility. It begins with a background on lifetimes and then moves to lifetime bounds, explaining how they define relationships between lifetimes and ensure that data remains valid for safe access.

The discussion then moves to implied bounds, where the compiler automatically infers certain lifetime or type relationships, reducing redundancy while maintaining safety. It then examines subtyping and variance, key concepts that describe how types with different lifetimes can interact or substitute for one another.

The chapter further explains covariance, contravariance, and invariance, showing how each affects function signatures, generic types, and trait implementations. Through clear examples and careful reasoning, you will gain a solid understanding of how these principles work together to give Rust its unique blend of flexibility, expressiveness, and memory safety.

Background of Lifetime Topics

This section provides the conceptual background needed to understand advanced lifetime topics. It introduces concrete lifetimes, generic lifetimes, and the `'static` lifetime. These concepts form the foundation for later discussions on lifetime bounds, implied bounds, subtyping, and variance. This section does not intend to provide complete and detailed information on lifetimes, but rather serves as a quick refresher. It begins with a brief introduction to concrete lifetimes.

N. Azam, *Advanced Rust*, https://doi.org/10.1007/979-8-8688-2992-5_6

Concrete Lifetimes

A *concrete lifetime* refers to the actual duration during which a value exists in memory. A value's lifetime begins when it is created and ends when it is dropped, either because its scope ends or because ownership is transferred. The code in Listing 6-1 provides examples of concrete lifetimes.

Listing 6-1. Demonstrating Concrete Lifetimes Using Scope Boundaries and Ownership Transfer

```
fn main() {
    let x = 5;
    let y = x;

    {
        let z = 10;
    }

    let a = String::from("abc");
    let b = a;

    println!("{x}");
    println!("{a}"); // Error
}
```

In this listing, x and y are stack-allocated values. Since both of them are defined in the main scope, their lifetimes begin at their declarations and end when main finishes execution. The variable z is declared inside an inner scope and therefore its lifetime begins at its declaration and ends when the inner block terminates.

The variables a and b demonstrate ownership transfer for heap-allocated data. When a is moved into b, the lifetime of a ends immediately. Any attempt to use a afterward results in a compilation error, even though the surrounding scope is still active.

When references are involved, Rust enforces an additional rule. According to the rule, a reference must never outlive the value it borrows. Consider Listing 6-2.

Listing 6-2. Example of a Dangling Reference

```
fn main() {
    let r;
```

```
    {
        let x = 5;
        r = &x; // Error
    }
    println!("{r}");
}
```

In this example, the reference `r` exists beyond the inner scope since it is defined in the `main` scope; however, the value it is referring to is limited to the inner scope. Accessing `r` in the outside scope will therefore lead to an invalid reference, which is also called a *dangling reference.*

Unlike owned values, whose lifetimes are strictly tied to lexical scopes, the lifetimes of references are determined by their actual usage within a scope. This behavior is known as *non-lexical lifetimes*. Rust's borrowing rules allow either multiple immutable references or a single mutable reference at any given time. Rust enforces this using the non-lexical lifetimes. For instance, consider Listing 6-3.

Listing 6-3. Non-Lexical Lifetimes and References

```
fn main() {
    let mut x = vec![1, 2, 3];

    let y = &x;
    println!("{y}");

    let z = &mut x;
    z.push(4);
    println!("{z}");
}
```

Although both references appear in the same `main` function scope, the immutable reference `y` is no longer used after the first `println!`. The compiler therefore ends its lifetime early on the print line, allowing the mutable reference `z` to be created safely. As a result, the immutable and mutable references do not overlap.

Generic Lifetimes

Concrete lifetimes describe when values exist. *Generic lifetimes* describe how the lifetimes of references relate to one another, which becomes essential when functions return references. The code in Listing 6-4 demonstrates this.

Listing 6-4. Missing Lifetime Specifier Due to an Ambiguous Return Reference

```
fn pick(x: &i32, y: &i32) -> &i32 { // Error
    if rand::random() {
        x
    }
    else {
        y
    }
}
```

The value returned by this function is a reference to an integer. However, the lifetime of that reference is unclear. The returned reference may point to either x or y, and each of these references may have a different lifetime. Because this relationship is not explicitly stated in the function signature, the borrow checker cannot determine how long the returned reference is guaranteed to be valid. As a result, the compiler reports an error of "missing lifetime specifier: this function's return type contains a borrowed value, but the signature does not specify whether it is borrowed from x or y."

Generic lifetime specifiers (which start with a tick (')), can resolve issues like those shown in Listing 6-4. Listing 6-5 demonstrates how to fix Listing 6-4 using these specifiers.

Listing 6-5. Using a Generic Lifetimes to Fix the Code in Listing 6-4

```
fn pick<'a>(x: &'a i32, y: &'a i32) -> &'a i32 {
    if rand::random() { x } else { y }
}
```

Adding a generic lifetime specifier to this code establishes a relationship between the lifetimes of the parameters i and j and the returned value. The returned reference will have the lifetime of the shorter of the two parameters. For instance, if i has a shorter lifetime than j, the returned reference lifetime is tied to i. However, if j is shorter, it is tied to `j`. This ensures that the reference never outlives the data it points to, thereby preventing dangling references. Note that not all parameters must share the same lifetime. If a function always returns a reference to a specific parameter, only that parameter needs a lifetime annotation.

The *'static* Lifetime

The `'static` lifetime in Rust denotes that a reference can live for the entire duration of the program. It is commonly used for string literals or data stored in global. The following code lines demonstrate how to declare a variable with a static lifetime.

```
let s: &'static str = "Hello, Rust!";
```

The string literal `"Hello, Rust!"` has a `'static` lifetime, meaning that it is valid for the entire runtime of the program, irrespective of which scope it is defined in.

It is important to note that references to slices have static lifetimes. This is demonstrated in Listing 6-6.

Listing 6-6. References to Slices Have Static Lifetimes

```
fn main() {
    let mut str_slice_1: &str;
    {
        let str_slice_2 = "";
        str_slice_1 = str_slice_2;
    }
    println!("{str_slice_1}");
    println!("{str_slice_2}"); // Error
}
```

The `str_slice_1` in this code is declared in the outer scope or `main` scope. Inside the inner scope, another string slice `str_slice_2` is defined, and `str_slice_2` is assigned to `str_slice_1`. After the inner scope ends, we access `str_slice_1` and `str_slice_2` in print statements in the outer scope. Although `str_slice _2` is not accessible after the inner scope and the compiler gives an error, `str_slice_1`, which holds its references, is still available. This is because string slices have static lifetimes.

In summary, generally speaking when a scope ends, the value created inside the scope is cleaned up and the variable is dropped. In case of string slices, only the variable is dropped; the value remains. This behavior of slices is different from the owned types.

Listing 6-7 will also compile for the same reason.

Listing 6-7. Assigning a String Slice in an Inner Scope

```
fn main() {
    let mut str_slice_1: &str;
    {
        str_slice_1 = "";
    }
    println!("{str_slice_1}");
}
```

The `str_slice_1` refers to a string defined in the inner scope. However, because string slices have a `'static` lifetime, the code compiles successfully, and `str_slice_1` can be accessed outside the inner scope without any errors.

A final note in this regard is that `String` or array slices created from owned types have non-static lifetimes. The code in Listing 6-8 demonstrates this.

Listing 6-8. String Slice Created from an Owned String Type

```
fn main() {
    let str_slice_from_string: &str;
    {
        let string = String::from("");
        str_slice_from_string = &*string; // Error
    }

    println!("{str_slice_from_string}");
}
```

Listing 6-8 declares a string slice in the outer scope. Inside the inner scope, a `String` is created, and a string slice is obtained by dereferencing the `String` and taking a reference. The dereference converts the `String` into a `str`, and the reference produces a string slice or `&str` type. Accessing the slice after the inner scope causes an error.

This is surprising, because in the previous example in Listings 6-6 and 6-7, the reference to string slice was accessible outside the scope. However, in this case it is not.

The reason is that `String` is an owned type. Owned values exist only within the scope where they are defined unless explicitly returned. Any reference to them outside that scope becomes dangling, leading to lifetime issues.

Lifetime Elision Rules

Lifetime elision in Rust enables the compiler to automatically infer the lifetimes of references in function and method signatures, making code more concise and easier to read. The compiler applies three lifetime elision rules. If the lifetimes remain unclear after applying these rules, an error is raised, and explicit lifetime annotations are required. The rules are as follows:

- Each reference parameter receives its own lifetime parameter.
- If there is exactly one input lifetime, it is assigned to all output lifetimes.
- If there are multiple input lifetimes, but one is a reference to `self` or a mutable reference to `self`, the lifetime of `self` is assigned to all output lifetimes.

Consider the following function without any lifetime annotations:

```
fn return_str(s_1: &str) -> &str { s_1 }
```

This function returns a reference, yet the compiler accepts it without any errors. In Listing 6-4, we saw that functions returning references usually require explicit lifetime annotations. Here, however, the function compiles, due to lifetime elision rule.

In the `return_str` function, we have one input parameter. Therefore, according to the first rule, it will get its own lifetime parameter. The function after adding the lifetime parameter will look like this:

```
fn return_str<'a>(s_1: &'a str) -> &str {
      s_1
}
```

According to the second rule, if there is exactly one input lifetime parameter, that lifetime is assigned to an output lifetime. After applying this rule, it will result in the following:

```
fn return_str<'a>(s_1: &'a str) -> &'a str {
        s_1
}
```

By applying the first two rules, Rust can automatically determine the lifetimes of references in the function signature. In a similar manner, the third rule can be used to reason about function signatures and apply lifetime elision.

With this necessary background, we can now jump into the deeper lifetime topics. The next section starts with lifetime bounds.

Lifetime Bounds and Subtyping

Lifetime bounds define constraints on the lifetimes of references. They indicate that one lifetime must be at least as long as another, establishing a clear relationship between multiple lifetimes. By specifying these bounds, Rust can determine how references relate to each other throughout the program. The next section covers the basics of lifetimes.

Basic Lifetime Bounds

Consider the code in Listing 6-9, which defines a function that takes in a couple of references.

Listing 6-9. Definition of the Largest Function That Takes in a Couple of References

```
fn largest(x: &u8, y: &u8) -> &u8 // Error
{
    if x > y { x } else { y }
}
```

The function takes in a couple of references to u8 values and returns the largest one. The compiler is unable to resolve the lifetime of the output, based on the lifetime elision rules, and therefore gives an error. We can now add lifetimes annotations based on elision rules.

According to first rule, each parameter that is a reference gets its own lifetime parameter. Applying this rule will lead to Listing 6-10.

Listing 6-10. Function After Applying the First Elision Rule

```
fn largest<'a, 'b>(x: &'a u8, y: &'b u8) -> &u8
{
    if x > y { x } else { y }
}
```

The second rule is that, if there is exactly one input lifetime parameter, that lifetime is assigned to all output lifetime parameters. In this case, we have two and not one input lifetime parameter. So this rule does not apply. The third rule applies to methods and therefore is also not applicable in this case.

This means that the lifetime for the output of the function cannot be resolved by the compiler and we have to manually do it. Let's add the lifetime of 'a to the return value. This is shown in Listing 6-11.

Listing 6-11. Function After Applying the First Elision Rule

```
fn largest<'a, 'b>(x: &'a u8, y: &'b u8) -> &'a u8
{
    if x > y { x } else { y } // Error
}
```

The code still does not compile. The return value may be either x or y, depending on the call to the function. For x, this is fine since it also has the same lifetime, but for y, it will be invalid. If we inspect the error message, it gives a very useful hint "consider adding the following bound: 'b: 'a".

Lifetime bounds in Rust are used to specify that one lifetime must outlive another. It is written as in the following syntax 'a: 'b. This essentially means that lifetime 'a must be at least as long as 'b. More concretely, 'a: 'b -> 'a outlives 'b or 'a lasts at least as long as 'b.

Sometimes, the syntax 'a: 'b is also referred to as subtyping, where 'a is considered a subtype of 'b. Let's add a lifetime bound to the function, as shown in Listing 6-12.

Listing 6-12. Updated Function Definition with a Lifetime Bound

```
fn largest<'a, 'b>(x: &'a u8, y: &'b u8) -> &'a u8
where
    'b: 'a,
{
    if x > y { x } else { y }
}
```

The code now compiles. Lifetime bound in this case means that lifetime 'b outlives lifetime 'a. In other words, 'b is some lifetime which is longer than lifetime 'a. The compiler is happy now because for the returned reference, it expects any lifetime that is at least as long as 'a. If x is returned, we are returning exactly 'a; however if y is returned, we are providing a lifetime 'b which is longer than 'a. The compiler will only report an error if we provide any lifetime that is shorter than 'a.

What happens if we swap the lifetime bound condition in Listing 6-12, as shown in Listing 6-13?

Listing 6-13. Updated Function Definition with Lifetime Bounds Swapped

```
fn largest<'a, 'b>(x: &'a u8, y: &'b u8) -> &'a u8
where
    'a: 'b,
{
    if x > y { x } else { y } // Error
}
```

The code does not compile since it was expecting any lifetime that is at least as long as 'a; however, 'b is shorter then 'a.

Implied Bounds

Lifetime bounds are sometimes implied, meaning they do not need to be stated explicitly and are instead inferred by the compiler. Consider a struct with a field containing a reference to a generic, as shown here:

```
struct GenericWithLifetime<'a, T> {
      b: &'a T,
}
```

For the type to be valid, the generic T must outlive the lifetime 'a. Otherwise, it will not be accessible. This is required because the field b holds a reference with lifetime 'a to a value of type T. For the reference with lifetime 'a to be valid, the value of type T (which may happen to be a reference itself) must live for at least as long as 'a. If T were allowed to contain references with a shorter lifetime, those references could expire while b is still in use.

This requirement can be expressed using the notion of subtype, as covered in the previous section. According to subtyping, 'a: 'b means that 'a outlives 'b and now T: 'a will be inferred ,which means that T outlives 'a. This is required for the type to be well formed.

Being well formed in this context means that the lifetimes of references and the type it refers to are correctly specified and valid according to Rust's borrowing rules. This will ensure memory safety and prevent dangling references. If Rust can infer that a type parameter must outlive a certain lifetime for the type to be well-formed, it enforces this relationship using subtyping, to maintain safety guarantees. In summary, the bound is inferred from the type in the struct GenericWithLifetime.

The following examples show cases in which the lifetime bounds are inferred. Consider a function that takes in the GenericWithLifetime struct as input.

```
fn lifetime_bound_implied_fn<'a, T>(x: GenericWithLifetime<T>) {}
```

The input struct, as seen earlier, requires the lifetime bound of T to be a subtype of 'a and therefore it will be inferred whenever we use the struct. In particular, the bound T: 'a is implied in the function signature.

Consider another function that takes a reference to a generic type U as its parameter:

```
fn lifetime_bound_implied_fn_1<'b, U>(x: &'b U) {}
```

In this case, the lifetime bound is also implied. Since the parameter x is a reference with lifetime 'b to a value of type U, the value of type U must live for at least the duration of 'b. Otherwise, the reference would not be valid. For this reason, the compiler infers the bound U: 'b, which is required for the type to be well formed.

Sometimes, lifetime bounds are not implied, even in closely resembling scenarios. Consider the following function:

```
fn lifetime_bound_not_implied<'a, T>() {}
```

This function has no input parameters. Since neither the lifetime 'a nor the type T is used in any reference within the function signature, the compiler has no basis to infer a relationship between them. As a result, no lifetime bound is implied in this case.

Let's also consider an example involving traits. Consider the following definition of a trait:

```
trait Trait<'a, T: 'a> {}
```

This trait is generic over the lifetime 'a and the T, with T being a subtype of 'a. The compiler will generate an error if we try to implement it for the unit type, as shown here:

```
impl<'a, T> Trait<'a, T> for () {} // Error
```

This gives an error of "the parameter type T may not live long enough, so that the type T will meet its required lifetime". The parameter type T must be valid for the lifetime 'a as defined in the trait definition. The problem in this case is that from the type of unit, the bound is not inferred. There is no type from which T being a subtype of 'a or T: 'a is implied. The error will go away if we implement it from a reference to T, as shown here:

```
impl<'a, T> Trait<'a, T> for &'a T {}
```

In this case, for the implementing type (i.e., &'a to T), the bound is implied and there are no issues.

Lastly, as a side note, it is important to note that only lifetime bounds are implied and inferred. Trait bounds are not implied and have to be mentioned explicitly. For instance, consider the following struct definition:

```
struct A<T: Clone>(T);
```

If we define a function using generics, as shown here:

```
fn doesnt_specify_T_Clone<T>(x: A<T>)  // Error
```

The compiler will give an error of "the trait bound `T: Clone` is not satisfied". Earlier in case of references, the compiler could infer the bound. However in this case, the compiler cannot infer it. This means we have to explicitly bind T by `Clone`, as shown here:

```
fn doesnt_specify_T_Clone<T: Clone>(x: A<T>) {}
```

Variance

Now that you understand subtypes, it's important to understand variance. Variance in Rust explains how subtyping relationships between the components of a type affect the subtyping of the type itself. It determines whether a type can be substituted with another type that has a shorter or longer lifetime. Understanding variance is essential for reasoning about how lifetimes propagate through references, structs, and generic types.

Covariance

There are three types of variance—covariance, contravariance, and invariance. This section starts with the details of covariance.

Variance Basics

It's best to understand the basics with the help of an example, as shown in Listing 6-14.

Listing 6-14. Definition of the Function `accepts_str` and Its Usage in `main`

```
fn accepts_str(s: &str) {}

fn main() {
    let s_1 = String::from("");
    let s_2 = "";      // 'static
    let s_3 = &*s_1;  // 'a

    accepts_str(s_2); // 'static
    accepts_str(s_3); // 'a
}
```

In this code, we define the `accepts_str` function, which takes a reference to a string slice. In `main`, we have several variables: `s_1` is an owned String, while `s_2` is a string slice. The `s_3` variable is also a string slice, created by dereferencing `s_1` (which produces a `str`) and then taking a reference to it to obtain a string slice.

As covered earlier, references to slices have static lifetimes, therefore `s_2` will have a static lifetime (indicated in Listing 6-14). However, references to slice created from owned types do not have static lifetimes.

The compiler will therefore not assign a static lifetime to `s_3` but some other concrete lifetime, let say `'a` (indicated in Listing 6-14). Note that `'a` in this case represents a concrete lifetime, which should not be confused with a generic lifetime parameter. A generic lifetime parameter can be substituted with another lifetime, whereas a concrete lifetime corresponds to a specific duration in the code where the reference is valid.

Also note that in the function `accepts_str` signature, the lifetime of the string slice is not mentioned. When lifetimes are not mentioned, the Rust compiler tries to infer them based on lifetime elision rules. According to the first lifetime elision rule, each parameter that is a reference gets its own lifetime parameter annotation. Following this rule, the function `accepts_str` signature is equivalent to the following:

```
// fn accepts_str(s: &'a str)
```

where `'a` is some lifetime that is not equal to the 'static lifetime, or simply put, it is a non-static lifetime. Also we are considering `'a` to be a non-generic lifetime, which we explain shortly.

The last two lines in Listing 6-14 call the `accepts_str` function with the two variables of `s_2` and `s_3`. The `s_2` variable has a `'static` lifetime, while `s_3` has a non-static lifetime. Although the function `accepts_str` signature expects a non-static lifetime, it works with both `'static` and other non-static lifetimes without producing a type mismatch error. This flexibility is a result of variance.

Variance in rust describes how subtyping relationships between components of a type relate to types themselves. For instance, given 'x is a subtype of `'y` or `'x: 'y`, what is the relationship between a type T over `'x`, with the type T over `'y` or `T<'x>` relationship with `T<'y>`? More concretely, `'x: 'y` => variance answers how `T<'x>` relates to `T<'y>`.

Understanding Covariance

Covariance is when we have some lifetime `'x: 'y` then, for any type `T`, we have `T<'x>: T<'y>`. This means that anywhere `T<'y>` is expected, we can provide `T<'x>` and the compiler will have no issues, due to covariance.

Returning to the code in Listing 6-14, we know that `'static: 'a`. This is because `'static` outlives any other lifetime `'a`, as it is valid for the entire duration of the program. Now according to covariance, for any type T, `T<'static>: T<'a>` (i.e., a type over `'static`) will be a subtype of the same type over `‘a`. Now if `T` happens to be a `&str` type (i.e., `T = &str`), the subtyping relationship can be summarized as follows:

`‘static: ‘a => T<’static>: T<‘a> => &’static str: &’a str`

This suggests that any where we expect the type `&’a str`, we can provide `&’static str` and the code will compile with no issues, due to covariance.

The `accepts_str` function in Listing 6-14 expects a value of type `&'a str`. Due to covariance, it can accept not only this exact type but also `&'static str`. As a result, the following calls in `main` both compile successfully:

```
accepts_str(s_2); // 'static
accepts_str(s_3); // 'a
```

This works because the function can accept `&'static str` and `&'a str`, with `'static` outliving `'a`.

Earlier, we noted that in this function signature obtained after applying lifetime elision:

```
// fn accepts_str(s: &'a str)
```

The lifetime `'a` should not be confused with a generic lifetime parameter. This is because if we explicitly annotate the generic lifetimes, as shown here:

```
fn accepts_str<‘a>(s: 'a str) {}
```

The calls to the function in `main` in Listing 6-14 will perform the static dispatch, where `‘a` will be substituted by the specific values for the lifetimes and therefore two separate versions of the same function will be created. An important point to note is that variance does not apply in this scenario.

Note When a function that uses generics is called with concrete types, the compiler generates a separate version of the function for each concrete type. This process is known as *static dispatch*, because the exact function implementation is determined at compile time.

The covariance can also be seen during variable assignment. For instance, consider the code in Listing 6-15.

Listing 6-15. Covariance During Variable Assignment

```
fn main() {

    let s_1 = String::from("");
    let mut x = &*s_1;              // 'a
    let y: &'static str = "";       // 'static

    x = y;
}
```

The lifetime of variable x in this code is a non-static concrete lifetime, `let` say `'a`. The lifetime of y is `‘static`. Since `‘static: 'a` as covered earlier, the type `&'static str: &'a str`. This means that x can be assigned a type `&'a str` and can also be assigned something with type `&'static str`. In summary, the assignment on the last line in Listing 6-15 is valid because of covariance.

Contravariance

Covariance represents one type of relationship between the types over `‘x` and `'y` given that `'x` is a subtype of `'y`. The covariance relationship can be summarized as shown here:

```
If 'x: 'y then T<'x>: T<'y>
```

This section examines another kind of relationship, known as *contravariance.* If `'x` is a subtype of `'y`, then a type `T<'y>` is considered a subtype of `T<'x>`. This is summarized as follows:

```
if 'x: 'y  then T<'y>: T<'x>
```

This behavior is the opposite of covariance and arises in specific situations, most notably when function pointers (discussed in Chapter 4) are used as arguments to other functions.

Contravariance in Function Pointers

Let’s go over an example to learn the concept. Consider the following function signature:

```
fn str_fn(f: fn(&str)) {}
```

This function can be called with any function that accepts a string slice with some arbitrary lifetime such as `'a`. The type `fn(&str)` denotes a function pointer.

We next define a function that accepts a string slice and then uses it as an argument to call the `str_fn` in `main`, as shown in Listing 6-15.

Listing 6-16. Definition of `accepts_str_1` and Using it to Call `str_fn`

```
fn accepts_str_1(s: &'static str) {}
fn main() {
    str_fn(accepts_str_1); // Error
}
```

The `accepts_str_1` function accepts a string slice with a lifetime that is strictly `‘static`. The code does not compile, due to contravariance. To understand it, we focus on the definition again. According to the definition, we have the following:

```
if 'x: 'y  then T<'y>: T<'x>
```

We know that `'static` lifetime is a subtype of some lifetime, `'a` or `'static: 'a`. So according to the definition contravariance, any type over `'a` should be a subtype of any type over `‘static` or `T<'a>: T<'static>`. If we assume the type `T` to be a function pointer, we will have `fn(&'a str): fn(&'static str)`. This means that anywhere we expect the type `fn(&'static str)` involving a static lifetime, we can provide the type `fn(&'a str)` with the shorter lifetime, `‘a`. In summary, a function expecting a functinal pointer with a shorter lifetime should not be provided with a functional pointer having a longer lifetime. We will look into the reason for this shortly.

In the function signature `fn str_fn(f: fn(&str)) {}`, the compiler expected a function pointer with some non-static lifetime, say `'a`. However, we provided a function pointer with a `'static` lifetime. With functional pointers following contravariance, only shorter lifetimes are expected, so the compiler gives an error.

The code in Listing 6-15 will compile if we provide another function pointer with a non-static lifetime, as shown in Listing 6-16.

Listing 6-17. Definition of `accepts_str_2` and Using it to Call `str_fn`

```
fn str_fn(f: fn(&str)) {}

fn accepts_str_2(s: &str) {}
fn main() {
    str_fn(accepts_str_2);
}
```

The code in this listing now compiles. This is because the function `accepts_str` signature, according to the first elision rule, will be converted internally to something like this:

```
// fn accepts_str_2(s: &'a str) {}
```

This function signature is based on some non-static lifetime, `'a`. Since this satisfies the requirement of the function `str_fn` as explained, the code compiles.

Additional Insights on Contravariance

This section explores why function pointers must be given shorter, rather than longer, lifetimes. The `fn str_fn(f: fn(&str)) {}` function can only handle a string slice that has some arbitrary but non-static lifetime. If you provide it with something that is more useful, such as a type with a `'static` lifetime, it cannot handle that because it is not being defined that way. We can change the signature of the function to accept a static lifetime, as shown in Listing 6-17.

Listing 6-18. Updated Definition of `str_fn` Using a Static Lifetime

```
fn str_fn(f: fn(&'static str)) {}

fn accepts_str_1(s: &'static str) {}
```

```
fn accepts_str_2(s: &str) {}

fn main() {
    str_fn(accepts_str_1);
    str_fn(accepts_str_2);
}
```

The updated function `str_fn` now accepts a string slice having a `'static` lifetime. It can now handle static and shorter lifetimes now.

An analogy of a child learning in school can help build an intuitive mental model of contravariance in function pointers. Consider a child in Grade 2. Books designed for Grades 4 and 5 contain more advanced material and may be valuable, but the child cannot effectively use them due to a lack of the required skills. In contrast, books from lower grades are easily manageable, as they fall within the child's current level of understanding.

Contravariance also happens during variable assignment. Consider the code in Listing 6-18.

Listing 6-19. Contravariance with Variables

```
fn str_fn(f: fn(&'static str)) {}

fn accepts_str_1(s: &'static str) {}
fn accepts_str_2(s: &str) {}
fn main() {

   let mut x: fn(&str) = accepts_str_2;         // fn(&'a str)
   let mut y: fn(&'static str) = accepts_str_1;  // fn(&'static str)

    x = y; // Error
    y = x;
}
```

The variables `x` and `y` are functional pointers. They contain a pointer to `accept_str_2` with a `'static` lifetime and `accept_str_1` with some non-static lifetime of say `'a`.

Assigning `x` to `y` is not valid because `x` is a functional pointer with a shorter lifetime. Therefore `y` cannot be assigned to it because it is a functional pointer with a longer lifetime. The assignment of `y` to `x` is however valid. This is because `y` has a longer lifetime and can be assigned to something having a shorter lifetime.

Invariance

The third type of variance is called *invariance*. If some lifetime 'x is a subtype of 'y, then there are cases where we do not have any subtype relationship between the type T over 'x and the type T over 'y. This is expressed in summarized form as follows:

```
if 'x: 'y then T<'x> has no relationship with T<'y>
```

This typically occurs when the lifetimes are inside some mutable context.

Invariance Example

Consider the code in Listing 6-19.

Listing 6-20. Example of Invariance

```
fn accept_vec(str_vec: &mut Vec<&str>, s: &str) {
    str_vec.push(s)
}
fn main() {
    let mut vec: Vec<&'static str> = vec!["", ""];
    let non_static_str = &*String::from("");
    accept_vec(vec, non_static_str);  // Error
}
```

In Listing 6-20, we first declare a vector vec containing string slices having 'static lifetimes. We also create a string slice called non_static_str from a String, which has a non-static lifetime. Next, we define the accept_vec function, which takes a mutable reference to a vector of string slices and a string slice and attempts to push the slice into the vector. In main, we call accept_vec to add non_static_str to vec.

This code does not compile and produces a lifetime-related error. Let's examine the code, starting from the signature of the function. The function signature, based on the first lifetime elision rule, will be converted internally to something similar to this:

```
// fn(&mut Vec<&'a str>, &'a str)
```

Again note that `'a` is not a generic lifetime parameter, and we used it to indicate some arbitrary lifetime, which is some non-static lifetime. In Listing 6-19, in `main`, the call to the function from a lifetime perspective has the following form:

```
fn(&mut Vec<&'static str>, &'a str)
```

Summarizing this, we can say that:

```
function expects this: fn(&mut Vec<&'a str>,       &'a str)
We provided this:      fn(&mut Vec<&'static str>, &'a str)
```

There is nothing wrong with the second argument for what the function expects and what we provided. The function was expecting a string slice, with some arbitrary lifetime, and we provided one. However, for the first argument, the function is expecting a vector of string slices, with some arbitrary non-static lifetimes, and we provided a more useful static lifetime.

Now this should be fine based on covariance. The arguments to functions are covariant except functional arguments, which are contravariant. This section explains this a bit further.

According to covariance, we can provide a type over a longer lifetime to a function that is expecting a type over a shorter lifetime. This makes sense because if we can access some value everywhere in the longer scope, then we must be able to access it everywhere in the shorter scope. Therefore, the compiler can automatically convert longer references into shorter references. This, however, is not true if the lifetimes are associated with mutable references.

All the references in the vector in Listing 6-19 are static, which means that they will live for the entire duration of the program. The vector itself is also defined in `main`, so it will last until the end of the `main`. Inside the function we are updating the vector by pushing a string slice. The string slice that is pushed in the vector has a shorter lifetime (something that is non-static), which may allow a possible use after it's free. This is because the vector has a longer life and will remain there for a longer period, but the values we are pushing into it have a shorter lifetime, which may not live as long as the vector itself. This of course leads to a problem, which is solved by the concept of invariance.

Invariance means that you must provide exactly what is being asked for. You cannot provide something that is longer or shorter. You must stick exactly to what is being asked for. Specifically in the context of mutable references, you must provide a type over a lifetime that has exactly the same lifetime, not shorter, not longer. This in summary means that mutable references are invariant in their types, meaning that lifetime or subtyping relationships do not apply to the types they refer to.

In the literature, the phrasing for representing invariance with mutable references is that "mutable references are invariant in their type." We explain this along with some additional characteristics of mutable references in the next section.

Mutable References Invariant in Types and Covariance in Lifetimes

The summary from the previous section is that mutable references are invariant in their types. This means that when mutable references are involved, the type they refer to must match exactly and subtyping or lifetime relationships do not apply. An additional property of mutable references is that they are covariant in their lifetimes. This is hard to grasp and digest. Listing 6-21 shows an example.

Listing 6-21. Understanding Mutable References Being Covariant in Their Lifetimes

```
fn update_reference<'longer, 'shorter>(mut u_1: &'longer mut u8, mut u_2:
&'shorter mut u8)
where
    'longer: 'shorter,
{
    u_2 = u_1;
}
fn main() {
    let mut x1: u8 = 8;
    let mut x2: u8 = 10;
    let mut y = &mut x1;
    {
        let mut z = &mut x2;
        update_reference(y, z);
    }
}
```

This code first defines two `u8` variables in `main` and creates mutable references to them. The reference `y` has a longer lifetime, while `z` has a shorter lifetime because it is scoped inside an inner block. Next, the code defines the `update_reference` function, which takes two mutable references with generic lifetimes `'longer` and `'shorter`. We add a lifetime constraint `'longer: 'shorter`, meaning `'longer` outlives `'shorter`. Inside the function, we assign `u_2 = u_1`.

In `main`, we call `update_reference` with mutable references `y` and `z`. Note again that the mutable reference `y` has a longer lifetime compared to `z`, which is limited to the scope in which it is defined. The important point to note in the context of the previous example is that we are talking about lifetimes of the mutable references and not about the lifetimes associated with the type the mutable references are pointing to. These are two distinct lifetimes and we need to be clear about it. This distinction is clearer when examining a type like `&'a mut &'b str`. There are two lifetimes: `'a` is associated with the outer mutable reference, and `'b` is associated with the inner string slice. In this context, we are primarily concerned with the lifetime `'a` of the mutable reference.

Coming back to the code in Listing 6-20, the function works because the mutable reference `y` passed in has a longer lifetime then mutable reference `z`. When the compiler looks at the assignment statement, it sees that `u_2` has a shorter lifetime and therefore expects something with a shorter lifetime to be assigned to it. However, we are providing it a mutable reference with a longer lifetime. This works due to covariance. The mutable references are covariant in their lifetimes; however, they are invariant in the types they refer to.

In Listing 6-20, `longer` is a subtype of `shorter` (i.e., `longer: shorter`), which means anywhere `shorter` is expected, we can provide the `longer` lifetime. This is what is meant by the statement that mutable references are covariant in their lifetimes.

The covariance of mutable references makes sense because if we have a mutable reference with a certain lifetime, we can be sure that there will be no immutable access to the data during that time. Additionally, any shorter lifetime will also ensure that there is no immutable access to the data.

Summary

This chapter examined how lifetime relationships shape Rust's borrowing and type system, enabling precise and safe reasoning about references. It began with core concepts such as concrete and generic lifetimes, non-lexical lifetimes, and the `'static` lifetime, followed by an explanation of lifetime elision rules and when explicit annotations are required. The discussion then moved to lifetime bounds and subtyping, showing how outlives relationships express validity guarantees between references. Implied bounds were introduced to explain how the compiler infers necessary lifetime constraints to ensure well-formed types. The chapter concluded with an in-depth treatment of variance, clarifying covariance, contravariance, and invariance, and explaining their practical impact on references, function pointers, and mutable borrowing. Together, these ideas illustrate how Rust combines expressiveness with strict compile-time safety guarantees.

The next chapter covers advance topics in traits, such as traits limitations, object safety, and the orphan rule.

CHAPTER 7

Trait Limitations, Object Safety, and the Orphan Rule

While traits provide powerful abstraction and polymorphism, their use is governed by deliberate constraints. Rust's trait limitations, object safety rules, and orphan rule define clear boundaries on where and how traits can be implemented, ensuring coherence, predictability, and soundness across large and evolving codebases.

This chapter examines some of the most important boundaries and design rules that shape traits and trait objects in Rust. It begins by exploring the limitations of trait objects, explaining why not all traits can be turned into trait objects and how Rust enforces these constraints for safety and clarity. The discussion then moves to multiple traits and associated types, explaining how they interact and how they affect the way traits can be implemented or combined.

This chapter also studies methods with generic parameters and functions without a `self` parameter, two cases that often influence whether a trait is object-safe or not. The chapter further investigates how type size impacts trait objects and why dynamically sized types add complexity to trait-based designs. It then explores partial object safety, identifying scenarios where only part of a trait can be used dynamically.

Finally, it covers the orphan rule, a fundamental restriction that governs how and where traits can be implemented, thereby preventing conflicts and maintaining coherence across crates. By the end of this chapter, you will have a solid grasp of Rust's trait system boundaries, the reasoning behind them, and how to design traits that are both flexible and safe for real-world applications

N. Azam, *Advanced Rust*, https://doi.org/10.1007/979-8-8688-2992-5_7

Trait Object Limitations

In Rust, trait object safety defines the conditions under which a trait can be used for dynamic dispatch, such as through `&dyn Trait` or `Box<dyn Trait>`. A trait is object-safe when its methods can be called without knowing the concrete implementing type at compile time, ensuring safe and consistent runtime behavior. However, not all traits meet these criteria. This section explores the main limitations that prevent traits from being object-safe, focusing on how multiple traits, associated types, methods with generics, and functions without a `self` parameter each introduce constraints that restrict trait objects and influence Rust's balance between flexibility, type safety, and performance.

Multiple Traits

To demonstrate the fundamental concepts, we present the code examples in the next few listings. Consider the `Drawable` and `Movable` traits, each containing a single method for drawing and moving, as shown in Listing 7-1.

Listing 7-1. Definition of the `Drawable` and `Movable` Traits

```
trait Drawable {
    fn draw(&self);
}

trait Movable {
    fn move_to(&mut self, x: f64, y: f64);
}
```

Next, we define a couple of structs called `Circle` and `Square`. Their definitions are given in Listing 7-2.

Listing 7-2. Definition of the `Circle` and `Square` Structs

```
struct Circle {
    x: f64,
    y: f64,
    radius: f64,
}
```

```
struct Square {
    x: f64,
    y: f64,
    side: f64,
}
```

The Circle is defined by its center point, specified by the x and y coordinates and the radius. A square, on the other hand, is defined by its starting point given by the x and y coordinates along with the side length. Since all sides of a square are equal, specifying a single side value is sufficient to represent its dimensions.

Next, we have the implementation of the Circle and Square structs, depicted in Listing 7-3.

Listing 7-3. Implementation of Drawable and Movable for Circle and Square

```
impl Drawable for Circle {
    fn draw(&self) {
        println!(
            "Drawing a circle at ({}, {}), radius {}",
            self.x, self.y, self.radius
        );
    }
}

impl Movable for Circle {
    fn move_to(&mut self, x: f64, y: f64) {
        self.x = x;
        self.y = y;
        println!("Moved circle to ({}, {})", self.x, self.y);
    }
}

impl Drawable for Square {
    fn draw(&self) {
        println!(
            "Drawing a square at ({}, {}), side {}",
```

```
            self.x, self.y, self.side
        );
    }
}

impl Movable for Square {
    fn move_to(&mut self, x: f64, y: f64) {
        self.x = x;
        self.y = y;
        println!("Moved square to ({}, {})", self.x, self.y);
    }
}
```

The Drawable implementation for Circle prints the circle at the specified position with a prescribed radius. The Movable implementation for Circle updates the circle's x and y coordinates to move it to a new position. In the same way, the implementations of Drawable and Movable for Square print and move the position of the square.

Now assume we want to implement a function called move_and_draw, which will move an object and then draw it. The definition of this function is depicted in Listing 7-4.

Listing 7-4. Definition of the move_and_draw Function

```
fn move_and_draw(obj: ____, x: f64, y: f64) {
    obj.move_to(x, y);
    obj.draw();
}
```

The input to this function is an object that we intend to move and draw, along with its location using x and y coordinates of the points. Notice that the type of the object is intentionally empty; we will come back to it soon. Inside the function, we make a call to move and then draw.

The move_and_draw function may be called for different types, such as Circle and Square, which are both Movable and Drawable. Ideally we will use a trait object here. However, trait objects are defined based on a single trait and not multiple ones. In this case, we have two traits. What we need is some type of trait object that is both drawable and movable, as shown in Listing 7-5.

Listing 7-5. Definition of the `move_and_draw` Function with an Added Type Annotation for the Argument

```
fn move_and_draw(obj: &mut (dyn Drawable + Movable), x: f64, y: f64) {
// Error
    obj.move_to(x, y);
    obj.draw();
}
```

This however does not compile and gives an error. The reason lies in how Rust manages trait objects through vtables.

Rust crates *vtables* in the background to manage trait objects and dynamic dispatch. A vtable is essentially a data structure that contains pointers to method implementations for a given type, allowing for method calls on trait objects to be resolved at runtime. They are created at compile time and a separate *vtable* is created for each concrete type for a given trait. For the implementations in Listing 7-3, the Rust compiler will construct the following four vtables.

- vtable 1: `Drawable` for `Circle`
- vtable 2: `Drawable` for `Square`
- vtable 3: `Movable` for `Circle`
- vtable 4: `Movable` for `Square`

In order for the `obj: &mut (dyn Drawable + Movable)` syntax to work, we need to know both where the `draw` method is and where the `move_to` method is. However, they are contained in different vtables corresponding to different traits. We have vtables for `drawable` for the concrete types (vtable 1 and vtable 2), and we also have vtables for movable for the concrete types (vtable 3 and vtable 4). Rust only allows multiple vtables to exist for a single type, with one vtable generated for each trait implementation. A combined vtable derived from multiple traits for a single type is not supported in Rust.

Another way to look at the problem is that when the functions are called using some concrete type, say `Circle`, the compiler doesn't know whether to look in vtable 1 or vtable 3 to dynamically resolve the function call.

The compiler gives this error message for the code in Listing 7-5: "only auto traits can be used as additional traits in a trait object". It further elaborates: "consider creating a new trait with all of these as supertraits and using that trait here instead". It also gives nice syntax for how to do it: "trait `NewTrait: Drawable + Movable {}`". Let's use the suggestion and create a new trait called `DrawableMovable`, which will require the types to be `Drawable` and `Movable`.

```
trait DrawableMovable: Drawable + Movable {}
```

The traits of `Drawable` and `Movable` are now *supertraits* of `DrawableMovable` (see the following note). The requirement due to supertraits of `Drawable` and `Movable` is that any type that implements the base trait of `DrawableMovable` must also implement `Drawable` and `Movable`. Next, we add the implementation of `DrawableMovable` for `Circle` and `Square`.

```
impl DrawableMovable for Circle {}
impl DrawableMovable for Square {}
```

Note The syntax of `Trait: Trait1 + Trait2 { ... }` is called a *supertrait* declaration in Rust. Here, `Trait1` and `Trait2` are supertraits of `Trait`. This means that any type implementing `Trait` must also implement `Trait1` and `Trait2`.

We can now update the `trait` object in the function definition in Listing 7-5 based on the trait of `DrawableMovable`, as shown in Listing 7-6.

Listing 7-6. Updated Function Definition Based on the Trait of `DrawableMovable`

```
fn move_and_draw(obj: &mut dyn DrawableMovable, x: f64, y: f64) {
    obj.move_to(x, y);
    obj.draw();
}
```

The code now compiles. This is because now a single vtable per trait is generated for a type. More specifically, the following two vtables are generated:

- vtable 5: `DrawableMovable` for `Circle`
- vtable 6: `DrawableMovable` for `Square`

The vtables now contain all the methods in the two traits for each type. For instance, for `Circle`, the vtable 1 contains pointers to all the methods in the two traits of `Movable` and `Drawable` for Circle. This also means that vtable 5 and vtable 6 will be larger compared to vtable 1 to vtable 4, as they now contain more pointers to methods.

A final point to note in the same context is that auto traits can be used as additional traits in a trait object. For instance, consider the code in Listing 7-7.

Listing 7-7. Using of Auto Traits as Additional Traits in a Trait Object

```
fn move_and_draw(obj: &mut (dyn Drawable + Send), x: f64, y: f64) {
    obj.draw();
}
```

Listing 7-7 uses the same syntax as in Listing 7-5, which previously failed to compile. The reason this version compiles is that auto traits such as Send and Sync do not define any associated methods. As a result, they have empty vtables, which do not cause conflicts or issues during compilation, since no dynamic method dispatch is required.

Note Auto traits in Rust are special traits that the compiler automatically implements for types based on their composition. Examples include `Send` and `Sync`, which indicate whether a type can be safely transferred or shared across threads. Unlike user-defined traits, auto traits do not contain methods or associated items, and their implementations are inferred automatically rather than written explicitly by the programmer.

Associated Types

Using associated types with trait objects is not allowed directly in Rust. Associated types must be known at compile time. Trait objects, however, use dynamic dispatch, which is resolved at runtime. This creates a mismatch because the compiler cannot determine the concrete type of the associated type during execution. To preserve type safety, Rust disallows this combination. Let's look at an example to see how this limitation appears in practice.

Consider the `Drawable` trait introduced in Listing 7-1. We add an associated type to the trait definition, as shown in Listing 7-8.

Listing 7-8. Updated Trait Definition of `Drawable` with an Associated Type of `SomeType`

```
trait Drawable {
    type SomeType;
    fn draw(&self);
}
```

Let's revise the implementation of `Drawable` for the `Circle` and `Square`, as shown in Listing 7-9.

Listing 7-9. Implementation of `Drawable` for `Circle` and `Square` with an Associated Type

```
impl Drawable for Circle {
    type SomeType = f64;
    fn draw(&self) {
        println!(
            "Drawing a circle at ({}, {}), radius {}",
            self.x, self.y, self.radius
        );
    }
}
impl Drawable for Square {
    type SomeType = f64;
    fn draw(&self) {
        println!(
            "Drawing a square at ({}, {}), side {}",
            self.x, self.y, self.side
        );
    }
}
```

The implementations are the same as in Listing 7-3, but with the associated type set to `f64` for both `Circle` and `Square`. Next, we consider a `draw` function that takes in a mutable reference to a trait object, as shown in Listing 7-10.

Listing 7-10. Definition of the `draw` Function

```
fn draw(obj: &dyn Drawable) { // Error
    obj.draw();
}
```

This function gives this error: "the value of the associated type `SomeType` in `Drawable` must be specified". You can't just mention that the function can take any `Drawable` thing, regardless of what its associated type is. The reason behind this is that the information regarding the associated type can't be captured in the vtable, since it is a type and a type does not have an address in the binary to which an entry of the vtable may point to (recall that a vtable contains pointers). To resolve this issue, we can use syntax that conveys that `obj` is `Drawable` but has a `Sometype` of `f64`. The function definition in Listing 7-11 will work in this case.

Listing 7-11. Updated Definition of the `draw` Function with an Associated Type Mentioned Explicitly

```
fn draw(obj: &dyn Drawable<SomeType = f64>) {
    obj.draw();
}
```

This code now compiles. We now have a vtable specifically for anything that implements `Drawable` where the associated type is `f64`. This means that the associated type is now being glued to the trait object in its type information.

It is pertinent to note that using associated types with trait objects is not ideal. For instance, associated types are not necessarily the same in each implementation. If they remain the same, there is no point to define them. For instance, in the `Drawable` for `Square`, `SomeType` could be `f32`, as shown in Listing 7-12.

Listing 7-12. Updated Implementation of `Drawable` for `Square` with `SomeType = f32`

```
impl Drawable for Square {
    type SomeType = f32;
    ...
}
```

The function in Listing 7-11 will now only work for `Circle`. For instance, consider the code in `main`, as shown in Listing 7-13.

Listing 7-13. Using the `draw` Function in `main`

```
fn main() {
    let circle = Circle {
        x: 5.0,
        y: 6.0,
        radius: 6.0,
    };

    let square = Square {
        x: 2.0,
        y: 3.0,
        side: 6.0,
    };

    draw(&circle);
    draw(&square); // Error
}
```

This code gives this error: "type mismatch resolving `<Square as Drawable>::SomeType == f64`". This is because the `draw` function is only defined to accept anything that implements the `Drawable` with an associated type of `f64`. Since the associated type does not match the provided type in case of the function call `draw(&square)`, we get an error.

To fix the code in Listing 7-10, we have to make another version of the function where `SomeType = f32`, as shown in Listing 7-14.

Listing 7-14. Another Version of the `draw` Function with `SomeType = f32`

```
fn draw_1(obj: &dyn Drawable<SomeType = f32>) {
    obj.draw();
}
```

The code in Listing 7-13 will now compile.

Resolving associated types in this way for trait objects works, but it introduces a couple of issues. First, the function names must differ, which breaks consistency and makes the interface harder to use. Second, a separate function is required for each possible value of the associated type, effectively reverting to a form of static dispatch and undermining the very purpose of using trait objects for dynamic dispatch.

Methods with Generics

The next limitation of trait objects is that traits containing generic methods cannot be turned into trait objects. This section explains the details with the help of the same traits and structs introduced in the earlier sections.

An Illustrative Example

Consider a modified definition of the `Drawable` trait containing a generic function, as shown in Listing 7-15.

Listing 7-15. Modified Definition of the `Drawable` Trait with a Generic Function

```
trait DrawableWithGenericFn {
    fn draw_with_generic<T: std::fmt::Debug>(&self, color: T);
}
```

The function contains a generic color parameter `T`, with a `Debug` bound. We next implement the trait for `Circle` (`Circle` was defined in Listing 7-2). The implementation is given in Listing 7-16.

Listing 7-16. Implementation of `DrawbaleWithGenericFn` for `Circle`

```
impl DrawableWithGenericFn for Circle {
    fn draw_with_generic<T: std::fmt::Debug>(&self, color: T) {
        println!(
            "Drawing a circle at ({}, {}), having radius {}, with
            color {:?}",
            self.x, self.y, self.radius, color
        );
    }
}
```

The draw_with_generic method takes a generic with color that can be any type that implements the Debug trait and prints information about the circle's position, radius, and the provided color value. Next, we add a draw function that will take a trait object of DrawableWithGenericFn and a generic color parameter. The function definition is given in Listing 7-17.

Listing 7-17. Definition of the draw Function

```
fn draw<T: std::fmt::Debug>(obj: &dyn DrawableWithGenericFn, color: T) {
    obj.draw_with_generic(color); // Error
}
```

This code gives this error: "the trait DrawableWithGenericFn cannot be made into an object. Consider moving draw_with_generic to another trait". It further explains: "for a trait to be object-safe, it needs to allow building a vtable to allow the call to be resolvable dynamically".

Generic Methods and Vtables

A trait is considered to be object-safe if it can be turned into a trait object or, alternatively, if we can construct a vtable for it, given the constraints of the vtable data structure. Recall from the discussion in the previous section that a vtable is constructed for each implementing type of a trait and contains a single entry for each specific method corresponding to a concrete type. The entry for a method in a table contains a pointer to the method definition of the implementing type.

In case of generics, we have a static dispatch, which results in multiple implementations for the same method. To better understand this, consider the code in main depicted in Listing 7-18.

Listing 7-18. Calling the draw Method from main with an Instance of Circle

```
fn main() {
    let circle_1 = Circle {
        x: 0.0,
        y: 0.0,
        radius: 5.0,
    };
```

```
    let circle_2 = Circle {
        x: 10.0,
        y: 10.0,
        radius: 2.0,
    };
    draw(&circle_1, "red");
    draw(&circle_2, (255, 0, 0));
}
```

In Listing 7-18, we created a couple of `Circle` instances and called the `draw` function with the created instances. The first call in this code specifies the generic `color` parameter using a string slice, while in the second call mentions the generic `color` parameter in the form of a triple of (red, blue, green). The function calls in `main` and creates two instances of the `draw` function due to static dispatch. The created functions will look something like Listing 7-19.

Listing 7-19. Functions Created Due to Static Dispatch Resulting from the Calls in `main`

```
// fn draw_str<T: std::fmt::Debug>(obj: &dyn DrawableWithGenericFn<T>,
color: &str) {
//     obj.draw(String);
// }

// fn draw_Tuple<T: std::fmt::Debug>(obj: &dyn DrawableWithGenericFn<T>,
color: (i32,i32,i32)) {
//     obj.draw((i32,i32,i32));
// }
```

The created functions will lead internally to two implementations for the `draw` method of the `DrawableWithGenericFn` trait due to static dispatch. This is because they call the `draw` method, which itself is a generic method. The two created methods look something like Listing 7-20.

Listing 7-20. The Specialized Version of the `Draw` Function Created Due to Static Dispatch

```
impl DrawableWithGenericFn for Circle {

    // fn draw_with_generic_str(&self, color: &str) {
    //     println!(
    //         "Drawing a circle at ({}, {}), having radius {}, with
               color {:?}",
    //         self.x, self.y, self.radius, color
    //     );
    // }
    // fn draw_with_generic_tuple(&self, color: (i32,i32,i32)) {
    //     println!(
    //         "Drawing a circle at ({}, {}), having radius {}, with
               color {:?}",
    //         self.x, self.y, self.radius, color
    //     );
    // }
}
```

The first implementation in this listing is for the concrete type of string slice and the second for the tuple. This means that the generic T is realized in the first version as a `&str` type and realized in the second version as `(i32,i32,i32)`.[1]

This leads to an issue from the vtable perspective. Recall that Rust creates a separate vtable for each concrete type, trait pair. This means that a single vtable is constructed per concrete type for each trait it implements. Recall also that a vtable contains pointers to the implementations of a trait's methods for a specific concrete type. Now when Rust tries to construct a vtable (i.e., vtable of `DrawableWithGenericFn` for `Circle`), it won't know which implementation of the `draw` method in Listing 7-20 it should refer to. The design of the vtable only allows a single pointer for each method. In general, if there are more concrete types for the generic of T, there can be potentially more concrete methods

[1] Note that when generics are substituted, you do not need them to define them explicitly using angled brackets. Moreover, the syntax used in Listing <InternalRef RefID=”PC22”>7-20 is for illustrative purposes and may not exactly represent the internal realization of the specific version of the functions.

(due to static dispatch) and therefore the compiler will have no way of determining which one to put in the vtable. This is why traits containing generic methods cannot be turned into trait objects.

Another way of understanding why traits containing generic methods cannot be turned into trait objects is that you are essentially mixing static and dynamic dispatch. In the implementation block in Listing 7-20, we are doing static dispatch and when we try to make a trait object in Listing 7-17 (in the function parameter list), we are mixing it with dynamic dispatch. Static and dynamic are two different approaches and should not be mixed. A clear decision has to be made before implementation regarding which one to choose, by considering the advantages and disadvantages of each. This does not mean that we do not have other ways of mixing the two, but we should not be doing that unless and until there are compelling reasons for doing so.

Generic Traits and Trait Objects

The previous section noted that traits containing generic methods cannot be turned into trait objects. However, generic traits themselves can be converted into trait objects.

Consider a generic version of the trait considered in the previous section, along with its implementation for the `Circle` struct. The code is shown in Listing 7-21.

Listing 7-21. A Specialized Version of the `Draw` Function Created Due to Static Dispatch

```
trait GenericDrawable<T: std::fmt::Debug> {
    fn draw(&self, color: T);
}
impl<T: std::fmt::Debug> GenericDrawable<T> for Circle {
    fn draw(&self, color: T) {
        println!(
            "Drawing a circle at ({}, {}), having radius {} with
            color {:?}",
            self.x, self.y, self.radius, color
        );
    }
}
```

This listing defines a generic trait containing a draw method. Unlike in Listing 7-16, the generic is now associated with the trait and not with the method inside the trait. The code implements trait for the Circle depicted in Listing 7-22.

Listing 7-22. Updated Definition of the draw Function

```
fn draw<T: std::fmt::Debug>(obj: &dyn GenericDrawable<T>, color: T) {
    obj.draw(color);
}
```

The draw function now calls the draw method of the implementation in Listing 7-22. Next, consider the same code in main given in Listing 7-18, which is also given in Listing 7-23.

Listing 7-23. Using the draw Method in Implementation in Listing 7-22

```
fn main() {
    let circle_1 = Circle {
        x: 0.0,
        y: 0.0,
        radius: 5.0,
    };

    let circle_2 = Circle {
        x: 10.0,
        y: 10.0,
        radius: 2.0,
    };
    draw(&circle_1, "red");
    draw(&circle_2, (255, 0, 0));
}
```

The calls in main will lead to an internal creation of two versions of the draw function due to static dispatch. The created versions of the functions will look something similar to Listing 7-24.

Listing 7-24. Implementation of the `draw` Function Due to Static Dispatch

```
// fn draw_str(obj: &dyn GenericDrawable<&str>, color: &str) {
//     obj.draw(color);
// }

// fn draw_tuple(obj: &dyn GenericDrawable<(i32,i32,i32)>, color:
(i32,i32,i32)) {
//     obj.draw(color);
// }
```

The syntax in this listing for the trait objects `&dyn GenericDrawable<&str>` is similar to the syntax for trait objects already seen in the case of associated types. In particular, the created functions in Listing 7-24 will lead to the creation of two implementations for the `GenericDrawable` trait due to the use of specific concrete types for the generics. The two internally created implementations will look something like Listing 7-25.

Listing 7-25. Internal Implementations of GenericDrawable for Circle for Concrete Types

```
// impl GenericDrawable<&str> for Circle {
//     fn draw(&self, color: &str) {
//         println!(
//             "Drawing a circle at ({}, {}), having radius {} with
               color {:?}",
//             self.x, self.y, self.radius, color
//         );
//     }
// }

// impl GenericDrawable<(i32, i32, i32)> for Circle {
//     fn draw(&self, color: (i32,i32,i32)) {
//         println!(
//             "Drawing a circle at ({}, {}), having radius {} with
               color {:?}",
//             self.x, self.y, self.radius, color
//         );
//     }
// }
```

The first implementation is for the string slice and the second implementation is for a tuple. This depicts a situation that is very similar to the case of associated types. This works because you have two different vtables for the circle.

- vtable 1: `GenericDrawable<&str>` for `Circle`
- vtable 2: `GenericDrawable<(i32,i32,i32)>` for `Circle`

Each vtable will point to its respective method and there are no issues. Recall that one vtable is created for each type that implements a given trait. However, in this case, multiple vtables are generated for the same generic type `T`. This happens because, internally, each concrete instantiation of `T` results in a distinct implementation of the trait. For every specific realization of `T`, the Rust compiler produces a separate vtable corresponding to that implementation. In the previous example, two concrete realizations lead to two distinct vtables for the same type. The same principle applies when traits use associated types. Each unique associated type results in a separate implementation and, consequently, a separate vtable generated by the compiler.

Functions without *self* Parameters

Functions that do not take `self` as a parameter cannot be turned into trait objects. Trait objects depend on the presence of `self` to identify which concrete instance the method should operate on during dynamic dispatch. Without `self`, the compiler has no way to associate the method call with a specific instance, making trait object creation invalid. This section explores this limitation and discusses why such functions are not considered object-safe.

Basic Illustration with an Example

Consider the code in Listing 7-26.

Listing 7-26. Definition of `SomeTrait` and Types A and B

```
trait SomeTrait {
    fn no_self() {}
}

struct A;
struct B;
```

```
impl SomeTrait for A {}
impl SomeTrait for B {}

fn main() {
    let a = A;
    let obj: &dyn SomeTrait = &a; // Error
}
```

Listing 7-26 defines a trait called SomeTrait containing a function called no_self. The trait also provides a default implementation for the function, which means that the specific implementations of the trait are not required to provide an explicit implementation for the trait. Next, we define a couple of types and implement the trait for them. In main, we create an instance of A and then try to convert it into a trait object of type dyn SomeTrait. However, the compiler does not allow this and throws this error: "the trait SomeTrait cannot be made into an object". It further explains: "for a trait to be object-safe, it needs to allow building a vtable to allow the call to be resolvable dynamically". The error additionally provides a hint for a possible solution, stating that "consider turning no_self into a method by giving it a &self argument: &self". This error originates from the fact that functions that do not take self as a parameter cannot be turned into trait objects. Let's explore this limitation in detail to understand why such functions are not compatible with trait objects.

Imagine trying to call the no_self function inside main using the trait object. We cannot use the syntax obj.no_self() for this, because no_self does not take self as a parameter and is therefore not tied to any specific type, such as A or B in this example. In other words, it behaves like a static function rather than a method. Moreover, such functions cannot be placed in a vtable, since vtables are constructed for specific type-based implementations of trait and contain pointers to methods that operate on concrete instances of a type. Because no_self lacks the type association, it has no corresponding entry in the vtable and cannot be called through the dot syntax.

Multiple Implementations of Functions with No *self*

In the case of Listing 7-26, since the trait provides a default implementation, it may seem like there is no major issue or concern. After all, there is only one default implementation. However, problems arise when multiple types provide their own implementations of the same method. These implementations may differ from the default one defined in the trait. This is perfectly valid in Rust because default methods can be overridden. To illustrate this, Listing 7-27 adds separate `no_self` implementations for types `A` and `B`.

Listing 7-27. Implementation of `no_self` from Listing 7-26 for `A` and `B`

```
impl SomeTrait for A {
    fn no_self() {
        print!("no_self() for A");
    }
}
impl SomeTrait for B {
    fn no_self() {
        print!("no_self() for B");
    }
}
```

In this code, `A` and `B` both provide their own implementations of the `no_self` function from the `SomeTrait`, overriding any default behavior and defining type-specific versions of the method. In `main`, you might think that you could use some sort of syntax like `(dyn SomeTrait)::no_self();` to access the method using a trait object. Of course, this syntax is not allowed, but let's say for instance that you could use something along the same lines.

The problem now is how the compiler would know whether to call the one for type `A` or Type `B` or the default one. The trait objects are type erased. There is no concrete type corresponding to `dyn SomeTrait`. In summary, this situation is not something the compiler can meaningfully resolve. For regular methods, the presence of `self` allows the compiler to determine the concrete type of the object at runtime. However, for functions without `self`, there is no instance to associate with the call. Only the trait object remains, and without a concrete type to dispatch to, the compiler cannot determine which implementation to invoke.

From the trait object safety perspective, this means that the `SomeTrait` trait is not object-safe because we cannot handle the `no_self` function inside the vtable. In other words, the construction of the vtable to accommodate `no_self` function is not possible.

Keeping No *self* Functions While Ensuring Object Safety

What if you still want to keep the `no_self` function in the trait, even though it cannot be called through a trait object? In this case, your goal is to make the trait object-safe while accepting that `no_self` will remain usable only through the concrete types, and not via a trait object.

This can be accomplished by explicitly marking `Self` to be `Sized`, as shown in Listing 7-28.

Listing 7-28. Keeping `no_self` accessible Through Concrete Types While Ensuring Object Safety

```
trait SomeTrait {
    fn no_self() where Self: Sized {}
}
```

Adding the `Self:Sized` constraint will enable the code in Listing 7-26 to compile, removing the error on this line:

```
let obj: &dyn SomeTrait = &a;
```

The constraint of `where Self: Sized` tells the compiler that the `no_self` function can only be called on types whose size is known at compile time. Since trait objects are unsized by nature, this effectively excludes `no_self` from being part of a trait object's vtable. In other words, this constraint informs the compiler that `no_self` should only be available for concrete types, not for trait objects. See Listing 7-29.

Listing 7-29. Updated Definition of `SomeTrait`

```
trait SomeTrait {
    fn no_self() where Self: Sized {}
    fn fn1(&self){};
}
```

For the types implementing `SomeTrait`, only the `fn1` method will be part of the vtables. The `no_self` method will not be part of the vtables.

Note In Rust, types are categorized as sized or unsized. A *sized type* is one whose memory size is known at compile time. For example, primitives (`i32`, `bool`), arrays with fixed lengths, and most structs and enums. An *unsized type* has an unknown or variable size at compile time, which includes slices (`[T]`), trait objects (`dyn Trait`), and string slices (`str`).

Since the compiler cannot determine the memory size of an unsized type, such types cannot be used directly as standalone values. Instead, they must be placed behind some kind of pointer or reference that provides the necessary size information at runtime. For instance, you cannot write `let s: str = "hello";` or `let t: dyn Drawable = Circle;` directly. This will not compile. Instead, you must use references such as `let s: &str = "hello";` and `let t: &dyn Drawable = Circle;`. These references store the extra metadata (such as length or vtable pointer) needed for the compiler to handle unsized types safely.

The type-specific version of `no_self` can now be called from `main` using the fully qualified paths, as shown in Listing 7-30.

Listing 7-30. Updated Code in `main` After Adding the Size Constraint to `no_self`

```
fn main() {
    let a = A;
    let obj: &dyn SomeTrait = &a;

    A::no_self();
    B::no_self();
}
```

Note, however, that the default implementation cannot be called directly using the syntax such as `SomeTrait::no_self();`. This gives this error: "cannot call associated function on trait without specifying the corresponding impl type. Cannot call associated function of trait".

A last point to note is that the previous section highlighted that functions using generics are not trait object-safe. You can however mark them as `Sized`—just like `no_self` function in this example—if you want to keep them while ensuring object safety. For instance, the code in Listing 7-31 will compile.

Listing 7-31. Updated Definition of SomeTrait with a Generic Function Having a Size Constraint

```
trait SomeTrait {
    fn no_self() where Self: Sized, { }
    fn generic_fn<T>(&self, generic: T)  where Self: Sized{}
    fn draw(&self);
}
```

The addition of generic_fn with the size constraint will allow the creation of the trait object for SomeTrait. The code in main given in Listing 7-30 will therefore still compile with no errors.

The next section goes a bit deeper and discusses the implications of making a function sized for a trait.

Size and Trait Objects

In the previous section, you learned that traits that contain a function without a self parameter cannot be turned into trait objects. That section explained some preliminary reasons with respect to vtables. This section goes a bit deeper and discusses some additional reasons.

Implications of Size Constraints on Traits and Methods

All traits are optionally sized by default. The following trait declaration will give an error:

```
trait SomeTrait: ?Sized {} // Error
```

The error states that "traits are ?Sized by default". So, what are the implications on a trait being optionally sized by default (i.e., traits can sized or unsized)? Let's focus on its implications.

Note In Rust, every trait is implicitly declared as trait TraitName: ?Sized by default. The ?Sized bound means that the trait can be implemented for sized and unsized types.

We first add a method to the trait that takes `self`, as shown in Listing 7-32.

Listing 7-32. Definition of `SomeTrait` Containing a Single Method

```
trait SomeTrait {
    fn method(self);
}
```

As mentioned, traits are optionally sized by default, meaning that they can be implemented for both sized and unsized types. Since unsized types cannot be passed by value, they must be passed by reference instead. Therefore, we might expect this code to produce an error, as it takes `self` by value. However, somewhat surprisingly, it compiles successfully. If we, however, add a default implementation for the method, as shown in Listing 7-33, the error is caught.

Listing 7-33. Updated `SomeTrait` with a Default Implementation for Method

```
trait SomeTrait {
    fn method(self) {} // Error
}
```

The error is "function arguments must have a statically known size, the size for values of type `Self` cannot be known at compilation time". To make sure that only sized types can use the implementation, you can add the sized constraint to the trait, as shown in Listing 7-34.

Listing 7-34. Updated `SomeTrait` with `Sized` Constraint

```
trait SomeTrait: Sized {
    fn method(self) {}
}
```

This fixes the error. However, this also limits the types for which it can be implemented. For instance, you can implement it for `i32` but not for an array slice of `u8`, as shown here:

```
impl SomeTrait for i32 {}
impl SomeTrait for [u8] {} // Error
```

The error message is exactly pointing this. It states that "the size for values of type [u8] cannot be known at compilation time, required by a bound in `SomeTrait`".

To make the trait more flexible, there is a more granular and precise way to mark individual methods as `Sized`, instead of the making the trait `Sized`. This technique is shown in Listing 7-35.

Listing 7-35. Updated `SomeTrait` with Sized Constraint Added to the Method Instead of to the Trait Itself

```
trait SomeTrait {
    fn method(self) {} where Self:Sized, {}
}
```

The implementations for `i32` and `[u8]` are now fine and do not generate an error.

You can also use the method of `SomeTrait` in `main` with some types, as shown in Listing 7-36.

Listing 7-36. Using the Method in `main` Using Sized and Unsized Types

```
fn main() {
    let x = 5;
    let y: &[u8] = &[4, 5, 6];
    x.method();
    y.method(); // Error
}
```

Variable x in this code is a sized type, while variable y is unsized. We can call the method on the sized i32 type (variable x), but cannot call it for unsized array slice (variable y). This makes sense because an array slice is unsized, and it should not be allowed to call the method, which is sized. But why does Rust allow the implementation of the trait for unsized types?

The answer is that the trait may contain some additional methods, which may be used by the unsized types. For instance, let's add one more method to the `SomeTrait` definition with a default implementation, as shown in Listing 7-37.

Listing 7-37. Updated SomeTrait with an Additional Method Having No Size Constraint

```
trait SomeTrait {
    fn method(self) {} where Self:Sized, {}
    fn method_1(&self) {}
}
```

The added method of method_1 in this definition has no size constraint, so it can be called by sized and unsized types. The code in Listing 7-38 shows how we can use method_1 for both sized and unsized types.

Listing 7-38. Using the Method in main with Sized and Unsized Types

```
fn main() {
    let x = 5;
    let y: &[u8] = &[4, 5, 6];
    x.method_1();
    y.method_1();
}
```

In summary, an unsized type implementing a trait can only access unsized methods.

Implications of Sized Methods for Trait Objects

This section looks at the consequences and implications of marking methods inside a trait for trait objects. It starts by implementing SomeTrait for its corresponding trait object using this line:

```
impl Some_Trait for dyn Some_Trait {} // Error
```

This line gives this error: "the object type (dyn Some_Trait + 'static) automatically implements the trait SomeTrait". This means that we do not need to do it manually because the compiler takes care of it for us. The dyn SomeTrait is unsized just like the array slice of [u8]. This means that with the implementing type of dyn SomeTrait (which represents a trait object), we can only access unsized methods. To see this more clearly, consider the code in main, as shown in Listing 7-39.

Listing 7-39. Creating a Trait Object from the `x` Variable

```
fn main() {
    let x = 5;
    let x: &dyn SomeTrait = &x;
    x.method(); // Error
    x.method_1();
}
```

This code creates a trait object from the variable `x`. This is allowed as we earlier implemented `SomeTrait` for i32. With the trait object `x`, we cannot access the sized `method`; however, we can access the `method_1`.

In conclusion, by marking a method or function as `Sized`, you exclude it from the set of methods available to trait objects. As a result, such methods are not included in the vtable.

A Use Case of Sized Methods (Partial Object Safety)

Sized functions inside a trait can be useful in certain contexts, even though they cannot be called through trait objects. These functions allow traits to define behavior that applies only to sized types, while still keeping the rest of the trait object-safe. This approach provides flexibility. Specifically, developers can include both object-safe methods for dynamic dispatch and `Sized` methods for compile-time use within the same trait. This is referred to as *partial object safety.*

Consider the following updated `Drawable` trait definition in Listing 7-40.

Listing 7-40. Definition of the `Drawable` trait with a Sized `scale` Method

```
trait Drawable {
    fn draw(&self);
    fn scale<T>(&mut self, factor: T)
    where Self: Sized, T: Into<f64>;
}
```

The trait contains a `draw` and a `scale` method. The added `scale` method may be required for scaling the size of an object before drawing, for better visualization. The method takes a mutable reference to self and a generic `T` and will resize the object based on the factor `T`. The added bound of `Into<f64>` will enable converting the generic `T` to `f64` type during computation.

A couple of things to note with regard to the `scale` method. Firstly, it uses a generic to allow a flexible API for the method usage. Secondly, as discussed in the previous section, because it uses a generic, it cannot be used via trait objects.

We next implement the `Drawable` trait for `Circle` and `Square` (defined in Listing 7-2 earlier). The implementation is shown in Listing 7-41.

Listing 7-41. Implementation of `Drawable` (Containing a Sized Scale Method) for `Circle` and `Square`

```
impl Drawable for Circle {
    fn draw(&self) {
        ...
    }
    fn scale<T>(&mut self, factor: T)
    where
        Self: Sized,
        T: Into<f64>,
    {
        let factor = factor.into();
        self.radius *= factor;
        println!("Scaled circle to radius {}", self.radius);
    }
}
impl Drawable for Square {
    fn draw(&self) {
        ...
    }
    fn scale<T>(&mut self, factor: T)
    where
        Self: Sized,
        T: Into<f64>,
```

```
    {
        let factor = factor.into();
        self.side *= factor;
        println!("Scaled square to side {}", self.side);
    }
}
```

The draw function has the same definition as in Listing 7-3, so we skip its detail here. The implementations of scale for Circle first covert the factor to f64, and then resize the radius based on the factor. Finally, the circle is displayed with an updated radius. The Square has a similar implementation.

The two implementations are used in main using the code in Listing 7-42.

Listing 7-42. Using the Implementation in Listing 7-41 in main

```
fn main() {
    let mut circle = Circle {
        x: 0.0,
        y: 0.0,
        radius: 5.0,
    };

    let mut square = Square {
        x: 10.0,
        y: 10.0,
        side: 2.0,
    };

    let mut shapes: Vec<&mut dyn Drawable> = vec![&mut circle, &mut square];

    shapes[0].draw();
    shapes[1].draw();

    shapes[0].scale(2); // Error
    shapes[1].scale(3); // Error

    circle.scale(2);
    square.scale(1.5);
}
```

In this code, we first define instances of `Circle` and `Square` and then define an array containing trait objects. The `draw` function is available via trait objects. Therefore, the `shapes[0].draw();` and `shapes[1].draw();` calls are valid. This is because these are object-safe methods. The `scale` methods are not available via trait objects since they use a generic and therefore are not object-safe. They can however be called with the concrete types using the dot syntax since they use `self` as a parameter. The last two calls in Listing 7-42—given by `circle.scale(2);` and `square.scale(1.5)`—are therefore valid.

In summary, traits in Rust can be partially object-safe. The object-safe methods can be accessed through trait objects, while the remaining methods must be called directly on concrete instances if they take `self`, or through fully qualified syntax if they do not. This completes our discussion of traits objects and their size-related issues. The next section covers more advanced issues related to traits.

The Orphan Rule

The orphan rule in Rust defines where trait implementations can be written. It requires that either the trait or the type being implemented must be defined within the current crate. This rule helps maintain coherence across crates and prevents conflicts that could occur if multiple implementations for the same combination were allowed in different crates.

This section helps illustrate this rule using an example. Consider the following code in Listing 7-43, which is included in the library crate.

Listing 7-43. Definition of a `Point` Struct and `Printable` Trait in `lib.rs`

```
pub struct Point {
    pub x: i32,
    pub y: i32,
}

pub trait Printable {
    fn print(&self);
}
```

This code defines a `Point` struct with two public fields, `x` and `y`, and a `Printable` trait that declares a `print` method to be implemented by types that want to define their own printing behavior.

Next in the binary crate, we implement the `Printable` trait for a point given in Listing 7-44.

Listing 7-44. Implementing the `Printable trait` for `Point` in the Binary Crate of `main.rs`

```
use rust_book::{Point, Printable};

impl Printable for Point{} // Error
fn main() {}
```

The trait and the struct are first brought into scope and then we try to implement the trait for the type. The Rust compiler does not allow the implementation and gives this error: "Only traits defined in the current crate can be implemented for types defined outside of the crate. Point is not defined in the current crate". The error occurs because the code in the binary crate violates the orphan rule.

The orphan rule states that to implement a trait for a given type, either the trait or the type must be defined within the current crate. Without this restriction, multiple crates could define different implementations of the same trait for the same type, leading to ambiguity about which implementation Rust should use. In this case, the `Printable` trait and the `Point` type are both defined outside the current crate, which is why the implementation is not allowed.

To fix the error in Listing 7-44, we can define a wrapper struct to wrap the `Point` struct, as shown in Listing 7-45.

Listing 7-45. Definition of a `PointWrapper` Struct and Its Implementation for `Printable`

```
struct PointWrapper(Point);
impl Printable for PointWrapper {
    fn print(&self) {
        println!("x-axis: {}, y-axis: {}", self.0.x, self.0.y);
    }
}
```

The `PointWrapper` in this case is a tuple struct (see the following note). Since the `PointWrapper` is defined within the current crate or the binary crate, the Rust compiler allowed the implementation of the `Printable` trait on it. In the definition of `print`, the `self.0` case means the `Point` struct instance, which is next used to access the individual fields. The orphan rule is now satisfied, which requires that one of the implementing type or trait must be defined within the current crate implementing the trait.

Note In Rust, a *tuple struct* is a type of struct that behaves like a tuple and a struct. It has named structure but unnamed fields, which are accessed by position rather than by name. Tuple structs are useful when you want to create a distinct type with tuple-like behavior but still give it a meaningful name. For example:

```
struct Color(i32, i32, i32);
struct Point(f64, f64);
```

Here, `Color` and `Point` are distinct types even though they both contain numeric fields. The fields can be accessed using dot notation with an index, such as `color.0` or `point.1`.

The orphan rule becomes a bit more complex when generics are involved. Consider extending the existing library in Listing 7-43, which already defines the `Point` struct and the `Printable` trait, by adding another generic trait, as shown in Listing 7-45.

Listing 7-46. Updated Library in Listing 7-43 with an Added Trait of `Addition`

```
...
pub trait Addition<T, U> {
    fn add(self, rhs: T) -> U;
}
```

The generic trait called `Addition` has two type parameters, `T` and `U`, representing a generic addition operation that takes a right side value of type `T` and returns a result of type `U`. If you try to define the `Addition` trait in your binary crate, as shown in Listing 7-46, you will get an error.

Listing 7-47. Implementation of `Addition` for `Point` in the Binary Crate of `main.rs`

```
impl Addition<Point, Point> for Point { // Error
    fn add(self, rhs: Point) -> Point {
```

```
        Point {
            x: self.x + rhs.x,
            y: self.y + rhs.y,
        }
    }
}
```

This implementation defines how two `Point` values can be added using the `Addition` trait, returning a new `Point` whose `x` and `y` coordinates are the sums of the corresponding coordinates from the two input points. The code in Listing 7-46 does not compile for obvious reasons. Neither the `Point` type nor the `Addition` trait is defined in the current crate (i.e., `main.rs`), which means it violates the orphan rule.

Consider adding a `Line` struct to the binary crate. The definition is shown in Listing 7-48.

Listing 7-48. Definition of the `Line` struct in the Binary Crate

```
struct Line {
    start: Point,
    end: Point,
}
```

A `Line` consists of two `Point` values of `start` and `end`, representing the endpoints of a line segment. In some contexts, it may make sense to add one point to another to produce a line. To represent this behavior, we add an implementation of the `Addition` trait for the `Line` type in the binary crate, as shown in Listing 7-49.

Listing 7-49. Implemenation of `Addition` for `Point` in the Binary Crate with One Generic Defined Locally

```
impl Addition<Point, Line> for Point {
    fn add(self, rhs: Point) -> Line {
        Line {
            start: self,
            end: rhs,
        }
    }
}
```

This implementation defines that adding one Point to another using the Addition trait creates a Line connecting the two points as its start and end. The implementations in Listing 7-47 and Listing 7-49 are both implementing the Addition for Point in the binary crate. The code in Listing 7-47 does not compile but the code in Listing 7-49 does. This is because in cases of traits involving generics, at least one generic should represent a type that is locally defined. In case of Listing 7-48, one of the generics is replaced by the Line type, which is defined locally in the same crate.

Lastly, if we try to implement the Addition trait for types that are in the standard library ,such as i32 as shown here:

```
impl Addition<i32, i32> for i32 {} // Error
```

This will generate an error. The type i32 is not local. It is defined in the standard library and not in the current crate. The requirement that at least one type should be local has been violated.

Sealed Traits

In Rust, sealed traits provide a way to restrict trait implementations to a specific module or crate, preventing external types from implementing them. Unlike regular traits, which can be implemented anywhere they are visible, sealed traits use a private subtrait to enforce encapsulation. This design pattern is useful when you want to expose a trait's functionality but maintain strict control over its implementations.

You can see the details of how this sealed pattern can be implemented in code. Consider the code in the in the library crate, shown in Listing 7-50.

Listing 7-50. Example Demonstrating the Sealed Trait Pattern with Some Code in the Library

```
pub mod my_module {
    mod private_mod {
        pub trait Sealed {}
    }
}
```

The code in Listing 7-50 contains a pub module of my_module containing a private submodule called private_mod. The private module contains a public Sealed trait.

Next, we intend to add a trait to this code that exposes functionality but maintains strict control over its implementation. This means that the trait provides certain functionalities that types can use, but it restricts which types can implement it. The code in Listing 7-51 shows how to add such a trait to the code in Listing 7-50.

Listing 7-51. Updated Code in Listing 7-50 with an Added SomeTrait Having a Supertrait of Sealed

```
pub mod my_module {
    use private_mod::Sealed;

    pub trait SomeTrait: Sealed {
        fn some_fn(&self);
    }

    mod private_mod {
        pub trait Sealed {}
    }
}
```

We first bring the Sealed trait into scope and then define SomeTrait. The SomeTrait trait has a single some_fn method. It also has a supertrait called Sealed, which ensures the achievement of the intended sealing behavior. It allows the exposure of functionality but maintains control over the implementations. This section explains this in some detail.

From basic Rust modules, we know that public items of a private child module are visible only to the parent module. In Listing 7-51, this means that the Sealed trait is only available within the parent my_module module. Moreover, the supertrait of Sealed ensures that any type that implements SomeTrait must also implement the Sealed trait. Since the Sealed trait is only visible within the parent my_module, the type implementing SomeTrait must also be within my_module. This suggests that any type that is not in the parent module cannot access the Sealed trait and therefore cannot implement it.

Let's add code to implement SomeTrait within the parent module for some type. This code is shown in Listing 7-52.

Listing 7-52. Updated Code in Listing 7-51 with My Type and Its Implementation for the Traits

```
pub mod my_module {
    ...
    pub struct MyType1;
      impl SomeTrait for MyType1 {
          fn some_fn(&self) {
              println!("You can access me");
          }
      }

      impl Sealed for MyType1 {}
}
```

This code defines the `MyType1` type and implements the `SomeTrait` and `Sealed` traits for it.

We can now use `Mytype1` and the implemented functionalities in `main`. This is shown in Listing 7-53.

Listing 7-53. Using `MyType1` and Its Implementation in `main`

```
use rust_book::my_module::{MyType1, SomeTrait};
fn main() {
    let item1 = MyType1;
    item1.some_fn();
}
```

This code first brings `MyType1` and `SomeTrait` into scope. It then defines an instance of `MyType1` and accesses the functionality provided the `SomeTrait`.

Note that although we can access the functionality provided by `SomeTrait` outside the module in which it is defined, we have restrictions over its implementation. In particular, the implementation for types is restricted to the module in which they are defined. For instance, the code in Listing 7-54 in the binary crate will not compile.

Listing 7-54. Defining `MyType2` and Using it to Implement `SomeTrait` in the Binary Crate of `main.rs`

```
use rust_book::my_module::SomeTrait;

struct MyType2;
impl SomeTrait for MyType2 { // Error
    fn some_fn(&self) {
        println!("External Code");
    }
}
```

We define `MyType2` and then try to implement it for `SomeTrait`. This code does not compile. The error message in this case is very informative: "the trait bound `private_mod::Sealed` is not satisfied, the trait `Sealed` is implemented for `MyType1` only". Lastly, it gives the exact root cause of the problem: "`SomeTrait` is a sealed trait". It also explains very nicely the reason for sealed traits by mentioning "this is usually done to force you to use one of the provided types that already implement it".

Lastly, it is important to note that the sealing pattern does not prevent you from defining other traits within the same parent module that do not use the sealing behavior. Such traits can be intentionally left unsealed, allowing external types to implement them freely. This can be done by defining additional public traits that do not include the `Sealed` trait as a supertrait. As a result, types outside the current crate are permitted to implement these traits.

Summary

This chapter examined the key limitations and safety rules that govern traits in Rust. It began with a discussion of trait object limitations, explaining that only object-safe traits can be used for dynamic dispatch through vtables. Using examples like `Drawable` and `Movable`, it illustrated how vtables link trait objects to concrete types and why combining multiple traits into a single trait object is not allowed. The chapter then explored associated types and generic methods, emphasizing that they cannot be represented in vtables and therefore make a trait object unsafe. The chapter also covered functions without a `self` parameter, clarifying that such methods cannot participate in dynamic dispatch since they are not tied to an instance. The discussion of sized and unsized types explained how `Sized` and `?Sized` bounds influenced trait implementation and object safety. The concept of partial object safety was introduced, showing that some traits can include both object-safe and non-object-safe methods.

The chapter then covered the orphan rule, which enforces that either the trait or the type have to be defined in the same crate to prevent conflicting implementations. Lastly, sealed traits were covered. They restrict the implementations to a controlled scope for design consistency.

The next chapter turns the focus to downcasting, exploring how trait objects can be converted back into their concrete types to enable safe runtime type inspection in Rust.

CHAPTER 8

Downcasting

In complex systems, values are often handled through abstract interfaces rather than concrete types, trading specificity for flexibility. There are moments, however, when recovering the original concrete type becomes necessary to make informed decisions at runtime. Rust's approach to downcasting allows such transitions to occur in a controlled and explicit manner, preserving safety while enabling selective access to underlying implementations.

The focus of this chapter is the concept of *downcasting* in Rust, a powerful yet subtle feature that lets developers recover concrete types from trait objects at runtime. The chapter begins by clarifying what downcasting means within Rust's static type system and why it becomes useful when dealing with traits. Through practical examples, you'll see how to safely downcast a trait object using standard library tools. The discussion then covers conversions between trait objects, explaining when they are valid and how they relate to Rust's strict type safety.

The chapter also examines methods for checking a value's type without downcasting, offering alternatives for dynamic behavior while keeping code clear and efficient. Finally, the chapter highlights common pitfalls, type mismatches, and the role of the `Any` trait in runtime type inspection. By the end of this chapter, you will know how to use downcasting wisely, design trait-based systems that minimize its need, and write robust, idiomatic Rust code.

Downcasting Basics

Downcasting in Rust refers to converting a trait object back into a concrete type. Since trait objects erase the original type information at runtime, downcasting allows recovering the concrete type. Recovering a concrete type can be useful when working with trait objects, enabling type-specific behavior that wouldn't be possible with dynamic dispatch alone. The next section looks at the basics of downcasting.

N. Azam, *Advanced Rust*, https://doi.org/10.1007/979-8-8688-2992-5_8

The *Any* Trait

The core idea of downcasting is that, given a trait object in either immutable (&dyn Trait) or mutable (&mut dyn Trait) form, you want to recover its original concrete type. In other words, downcasting allows you to convert a trait object back into the specific type that implements it. Downcasting is made possible using a special trait in the standard library called Any. It is implemented for all types that have a static lifetime by default. This includes most types in Rust, except for those that contain non-static references. The following example make things clear.

Consider Listing 8-1.

Listing 8-1. Definition of the Animal Trait with Any as a Supertrait

```
use std::any::Any;

trait Animal: Any {
    fn make_sound(&self);
}
```

The Animal trait in this code contains a method called make_sound. To make sure that any type that implements the Animal trait also implements the Any trait, it's mentioned as a supertrait. The Any trait will allow you to convert a trait object of &dyn Animal type to its concrete type.

Next we define a couple of structs and implement the Animal trait for them, as shown in Listing 8-2.

Listing 8-2. Definition of Dog and Cat and Their Implementation for Animal

```
struct Dog;
struct Cat;

impl Animal for Dog {
    fn make_sound(&self) {
        println!("Woof!");
    }
}
```

```
impl Animal for Cat {
    fn make_sound(&self) {
        println!("Meow!");
    }
}
```

The code defines the Dog and Cat structs and implements the Animal trait for both types. Notice that Any is declared as a supertrait of Animal. As discussed in the previous chapter, when a trait is defined in a base-supertrait relationship, any type that implements the base trait must also implement the supertrait. In this case, this means that any type implementing Animal must also implement Any. Interestingly, the Dog and Cat types do not explicitly implement Any, yet the code compiles successfully. This is because the Any trait is automatically implemented for all types with a 'static lifetime, so it does not need to be implemented manually. This implies that since types already have this trait by default, it is not necessary to declare Any as a supertrait in Listing 8-1. It was included there only to illustrate the concept more clearly.

Immutable Conversion to *&dyn Any*

A common pattern in Rust for using the Any trait is introducing a method of as_any. Listing 8-3 updates the definition of Animal to include the as_any method.

Listing 8-3. Updated Definition of the Animal Trait with an Added as_any Method

```
use std::any::Any;

trait Animal: Any {
    fn make_sound(&self);
    fn as_any(&self) -> &dyn Any;
}
```

Given any type implementing the Animal trait, the as_any method will convert a reference to an instance of the implementing type, to a trait object of type &dyn Any. Let's implement it for the Dog and Cat types. This implementation is shown in Listing 8-4.

Listing 8-4. Updated Implementations of Dog and Cat in Listing 8-2 with the as_any Method

```
impl Animal for Dog {
    ...
    fn as_any(&self) -> &dyn Any {
        self
    }
}

impl Animal for Cat {
    ...
    fn as_any(&self) -> &dyn Any {
        self
    }
}
```

In both implementations, the as_any method returns self, which refers to the current instance of the implementing type (Dog or Cat). However, the return type from the methods is &dyn Any, meaning that self is automatically converted into a trait object of type &dyn Any. This works because, as discussed earlier, the Any trait is implemented for nearly all types, which makes this conversion valid and allows instances of these types to be treated as Any trait objects.

Next, we use the implementations in Listing 8-4 inside a function called identify_and_make_sound. The definition of the function is shown in Listing 8-5.

Listing 8-5. Definition of identify_and_make_sound

```
fn identify_and_make_sound(animal: &dyn Animal) {
    if let Some(dog) = animal.as_any().downcast_ref::<Dog>() {
        println!("It's a Dog");
        dog.make_sound();
    } else if let Some(cat) = animal.as_any().downcast_ref::<Cat>() {
        println!("It's a Cat");
        cat.make_sound();
```

```
    } else {
        println!("Unknown animal");
    }
}
```

The function takes in a reference to dyn Animal. It first checks if the type passed in is a Dog using the if let syntax. The as_any will convert the instance into a trait object of type dyn Any (i.e., &dyn Animal -> &dyn Any). The downcast_ref method of the Any trait attempts to downcast a reference to a trait object of type &dyn Any into an Option wrapping a reference of a specific concrete type, such as &Dog or &Cat. The overall meaning of the right side of the first if let in Listing 8-5 means that if the cast to Dog is successful, it returns Some(&Dog); otherwise, it returns None. The inner value of the Option is extracted in the variable dog using the if let. If the extraction is successful, it prints that it's a dog and calls the appropriate make_sound implementation for the type. Similarly, the second if let in Listing 8-5 checks if the type passed in is a Cat and does the appropriate action. If neither case holds, it prints that it is an unknown animal.

The code in Listing 8-6 shows how the function can be used in main.

Listing 8-6. Using identify_and_make_sound in main

```
fn main() {
    let dog = Dog;
    let cat = Cat;
    let animals: Vec<&dyn Animal> = vec![&dog, &cat];

    for animal in animals {
        identify_and_make_sound(animal);
    }
}
```

We created an instance of Dog and Cat. The created variables are borrowed and stored in a vector of trait objects of type &dyn Animal. The code iterates over the vector, passing one element to the identify_and_make_sound function in each iteration. At the point of the function call inside the loop (before the function is executed), the concrete type of each element is not known statically. The call to the identify_and_make_sound function performs runtime type identification through downcasting and executes the behavior specific to the detected type. When the first element is processed, the function identifies it as a Dog and prints the corresponding message and sound. When the second element is processed, it is identified as a Cat, and the appropriate output is produced. This example illustrates how trait objects enable heterogeneous collections while still allowing type-specific behavior when combined with controlled runtime downcasting.

Mutable Conversion to *&mut dyn Any*

The downcast_ref method returns an immutable reference over a type. The Any trait has another method called downcast_mut, which gives a mutable reference over the type. To access this method, we add it to the Animal trait and implement it for the two types. The updated Animal trait and the implementations of Dog and Cat are shown in Listing 8-7.

Listing 8-7. Updated Animal Trait and Implementations of Dog and Cat

```
trait Animal {
    ...
    fn as_mut_any(&mut self) -> &mut dyn Any;
}

impl Animal for Dog {
    ...
    fn as_mut_any(&mut self) -> &mut dyn Any {
        self
    }
}

impl Animal for Cat {
    ...
    fn as_mut_any(&mut self) -> &mut dyn Any {
        self
    }
}
```

The as_mut_any method provides a mutable conversion from a trait object of type &mut dyn Animal to a mutable trait object of type &mut dyn Any. The implementation of the method for Dog and Cat converts the respective types to &mut dyn Any. This conversion works since the Any trait is automatically implemented for these types.

We can also update the definition of identify_and_make_sound given in Listing 8-5. The updated code is shown in Listing 8-8.

Listing 8-8. Updated Definition of `identify_and_make_sound` Based on `as_mut_any`

```
fn identify_and_make_sound(animal: &mut dyn Animal) {
    if let Some(dog) = animal.as_mut_any().downcast_mut::<Dog>() {
        println!("It's a Dog");
        dog.make_sound();
    } else if let Some(cat) = animal.as_mut_any().downcast_mut::<Cat>() {
        println!("It's a Cat");
        cat.make_sound();
    } else {
        println!("Unknown animal");
    }
}
```

This definition is similar to the definition in Listing 8-5. However, we are now using `as_mut_ref` instead of `as_ref` and `downcast_mut` instead of `downcast_ref`. The `as_mut_ref` performs the conversion from `&mut dyn Animal` to `&mut dyn Any` while `downcast_mut` performs the conversion from `&mut dyn Any` to `&mut Dog` or `&mut Cat`.

The code in Listing 8-9 shows how the new definition in Listing 8-8 can be used in `main`.

Listing 8-9. Using the Function in Listing 8-8 in `main`

```
fn main() {
    let mut dog = Dog;
    let mut cat = Cat;
    let animals: Vec<&mut dyn Animal> = vec![&mut dog, &mut cat];

    for animal in animals {
        identify_and_make_sound(animal);
    }
}
```

We now create mutable variables of the `Dog` and `Cat` types. The vector is defined as a mutable vector of type `&mut dyn Animal` and contains mutable references to the two types.

Removing the *as_any* and *as_mut_any* Methods

This section further explains how you can refine the implementations of Dog and Cat in Listing 8-7. As pointed out a few times, almost all types implement the Any trait. Therefore, all the types can be casted to trait objects of type dyn Any. For instance, Listing 8-10 shows how you can cast the references to Dog and Cat into a reference to dyn Any.

Listing 8-10. Casting References to Concrete Types to References to dyn Any

```
fn main() {
    let mut dog = Dog;
    let mut cat = Cat;
    let dog = &mut dog as &mut dyn Any;
    let cat = &mut cat as &mut dyn Any;
}
```

This code creates mutable Dog and Cat instances and then explicitly castes the mutable references into mutable trait object references of type &mut dyn Any. Earlier we noted that the function in Listings 8-5 and 8-8 was doing two types of conversion:

- &dyn animal to &dyn Any using as_any or &mut dyn to &mut dyn Any using as_mut_any
- &dyn Any to &(Dog, Cat) using downcast::ref or &mut dyn Any to &mut (Dog, Cat)

The casting in main shown in Listing 8-10 performs the first type of conversion. That means that in the function definitions in Listings 8-5 and 8-8 we do not need as_any or as_mut_any. We can now revise the definition of the identify_and_make_sound function in Listing 8-8 without using the as_mut_any. This is shown in Listing 8-11.

Listing 8-11. Updated Definition of the Code in Listing 8-8 Without as_mut_any

```
fn identify_and_make_sound(animal: &mut dyn Any) {
    if let Some(dog) = animal.downcast_mut::<Dog>() {
        println!("It's a Dog");
        dog.make_sound();
    } else if let Some(cat) = animal.downcast_mut::<Cat>() {
```

```
        println!("It's a Cat");
        cat.make_sound();
    } else {
        println!("Unknown animal");
    }
}
```

Since the function now accepts a trait object of type &dyn Any, it no longer requires manual conversion to this type. In the same way, we can revise the definition of the function in Listing 8-5 based on immutable references.

Since as_any and as_mut_any are no longer required, we can update the Animal trait definition and its implementations for Dog and Cat in Listing 8-7. This is shown in Listing 8-12.

Listing 8-12. Updated Definition of the Animal trait and Its Implementation for Dog and Cat

```
trait Animal {
    fn make_sound(&self);
}

impl Animal for Dog {
    fn make_sound(&self) {
        println!("Woof!");
    }
}

impl Animal for Cat {
    fn make_sound(&self) {
        println!("Meow!");
    }
}
```

The implementations are now reduced and do not require methods for conversion to the dyn Any type, as shown in Listing 8-13.

Listing 8-13. Demonstrating How to Use `identify_and_make_sound` in `main`

```
fn main() {
    let mut dog = Dog;
    let mut cat = Cat;
    let dog = &mut dog as &mut dyn Any;
    let cat = &mut cat as &mut dyn Any;
    let animals: Vec<&mut dyn Any> = vec![dog, cat];

    for animal in animals {
        identify_and_make_sound(animal);
    }
}
```

Since the values in the vector are already casted to the required `&mut dyn Any` type, we can mention them directly as vector elements. Lastly, the `for` loop is used to call the function for each element.

Downcasting Use Case

The example presented in the previous section was primarily illustrative and not intended to reflect a realistic scenario. This section shifts the focus to a more practical use case, where downcasting provides a tangible value, particularly in situations that require type-specific handling at runtime. To ground the discussion, we introduce an event detection example, which demonstrates how downcasting can be used to identify and process different kinds of events.

Consider a scenario where different kinds of events—such as mouse clicks and keyboard input—must be handled dynamically based on their specific characteristics. A mouse event, for example, carries information such as cursor coordinates, while a keyboard event contains data about the key that was pressed. Although these events share a common set of behaviors through a shared trait, each type also defines its own data and processing logic. As a result, even though all events belong to the same conceptual family and can be treated uniformly at an abstract level, the event-handling logic must be able to distinguish between their concrete types at runtime in order to process them correctly. To handle this distinction, we need a way to figure out the exact type of the event at runtime. We can simulate this scenario and see how downcasting can help in determining the concrete type of an event.

The code in Listing 8-14 depicts this scenario.

Listing 8-14. Code Setup for the Event Handling Scenario

```
use std::any::Any;
trait Event {}

struct MouseEvent {
    x: i32,
    y: i32,
}

struct KeyBoardEvent {
    key: char,
}

impl Event for MouseEvent {}
impl Event for KeyBoardEvent {}
```

The code defines an `Event` trait that represents shared behavior among the events and allows different kinds of events to be handled uniformly. Next, it defines a couple of concrete event types, namely `MouseEvent` and `KeyBoardEvent`. The `MouseEvent` struct contains `x` and `y` fields that represent the position of the mouse cursor, while the `KeyBoardEvent` struct stores the character corresponding to the key that was pressed. Finally, we implement the `Event` trait for both structs.

To properly handle events, we add an `event_handling` function. The definition of the function is given in Listing 8-15.

Listing 8-15. Definition of the `event_handling` Function

```
fn event_handling(event: &dyn Any) {
    if let Some(mouse) = event.downcast_ref::<MouseEvent>() {
        println!("Mouse event at ({}, {})", mouse.x, mouse.y);
    } else if let Some(keyboard) = event.downcast_ref::<KeyBoardEvent>() {
        println!("Keyboard event, with key pressed: {}", keyboard.key);
    } else {
        println!("Unknown event");
    }
}
```

The code is very similar to the code in Listing 8-11. The `event_handling` function accepts a reference to a trait object of type `&dyn Any`. Inside the function, `downcast_ref` is used to attempt a safe downcast to a specific concrete event type. If the value is successfully identified as a `MouseEvent`, the function accesses its `x` and `y` coordinates and prints the corresponding message. If the first downcast fails, the function then attempts to downcast the value to a `KeyBoardEvent` and, if successful, prints the key that was pressed. When neither downcast succeeds, the function falls back to handling the event as an unknown type. This example illustrates how downcasting enables a single, generic event handler to distinguish between different event variants at runtime while still operating through a common abstraction.

The code in Listing 8-16 can be used to use the function in Listing 8-15 in main.

Listing 8-16. Using the `event_handling` Function in `main`

```
fn main() {
    let mouse_event = MouseEvent { x: 100, y: 200 };
    let keyboard_event = KeyBoardEvent { key: 'A' };

    event_handling (&mouse_event);
    event_handling (&keyboard_event);
}
```

We create instances of `MouseEvent` and `KeyBoardEvent` and call the function for the two events.

Downcasting for Converting Between Trait Objects

Downcasting can also be used to determine whether a value stored behind a trait object can be safely converted into another trait object. This capability is particularly useful when working with values that may implement multiple traits, but are accessed through a single, abstract interface. By attempting such conversions at runtime, a program can adapt its behavior based on the additional traits an object implements, without requiring compile-time knowledge of its concrete type.

Let's examine the conversion between trait objects through a concrete example to better understand how this works in practice. Consider the example code in Listing 8-17.

Listing 8-17. Code Setup for Understanding Trait Conversion Using Downcasting

```
use std::any::Any;
trait Shape {
    fn area(&self) -> f32;
}

trait Drawable {
    fn draw(&self);
}

struct Rectangle {
    width: f32,
    height: f32,
}

impl Shape for Rectangle {
    fn area(&self) -> f32 {
        self.width * self.height
    }
}

impl Drawable for Rectangle {
    fn draw(&self) {
        println!(
            "Drawing a rectangle with width: {} and height: {}",
            self.width, self.height
        );
    }
}
```

This code defines two independent traits of `Shape` and `Drawable`, representing different capabilities of computing area and rendering an object, respectively. The `Rectangle` struct implements both traits, allowing it to be treated as a `Shape` when area computation is required and as a `Drawable` when drawing behavior is needed.

Using the previous setup, we now demonstrate how a single concrete type can support multiple trait interfaces and how trait-based abstractions can be used interchangeably. To accomplish this, we define the `check_if_convertable` function, as shown in Listing 8-18.

Listing 8-18. Definition of the `check_if_convertable` Function

```
fn check_if_convertable(shape: &dyn Any) {
    if let Some(drawable) = shape.downcast_ref::<&dyn Drawable>() {
        println!("This shape is drawable");
        drawable.draw();
    } else {
        println!("This shape is not drawable");
    }
}
```

The `check_if_convertable` function accepts a trait object of type `&dyn Any`, allowing it to perform runtime checks on the underlying value. Inside the function, `downcast_ref::<&dyn Drawable>()` is used to determine whether the value behind the trait object can also be viewed as a `Drawable` trait object. If the downcast yields `Some(&dyn Drawable)`, the function prints an appropriate message and invokes `draw` on the instance. Otherwise, it reports that the given shape cannot be treated as `Drawable`. The function illustrates how downcasting can be used to test trait-to-trait compatibility at runtime.

Listing 8-19 demonstrates how the function in Listing 8-18 can be used in `main`.

Listing 8-19. Using the Function in Listing 8-18 in `main`

```
fn main() {
    let rect = Rectangle {
        width: 5.0,
        height: 10.0,
    };
    let some_shape: &dyn Shape = &rect;

    check_if_convertable(&some_shape);
}
```

This code creates an instance of Rectangle, which is converted to a Shape trait object. Finally, it is passed to the check_if_convertable function to see if it can be converted to Drawable.

In summary, the ability to check if a type has a certain trait and converting between trait objects is useful in scenarios where a type exhibits multiple behaviors, but you only have access to one of its traits at a given moment. This enables dynamic behavior selection at runtime, allowing you to extend functionality without modifying existing code. In real-world applications, this can be beneficial in frameworks where objects conform to a base interface but may also implement additional capabilities that need to be discovered dynamically, such as a type that has a Shape can also be Drawable in a graphics engine.

Checking Type Without Downcasting

Downcasting makes it possible to recover concrete types from trait objects. However, there are situations when a full downcast is unnecessary. In many runtime-driven contexts such as input/output processing, it is often sufficient to determine the actual type of a value without converting it. In such cases, direct type inspection becomes more appropriate and efficient. This is enabled through the type_id method of the Any trait.

The type_id method returns a unique TypeId associated with a type at runtime. Since Any is implemented for all types with a 'static lifetime, type_id enables dynamic type comparison without performing a downcast. In other words, it allows types to be compared directly, based solely on their identity, without requiring explicit conversion to a concrete type.

Consider a scenario where values are received by a program from various sources such as database reads, input from users, and values received from a network. We would like to determine their exact type at runtime and take appropriate actions on them. The function in Listing 8-20 simulates this scenario.

Listing 8-20. Definition of the check_type Function

```
use std::any::{Any, TypeId};

fn check_type<T: Any>(value: &T) {
    if value.type_id() == TypeId::of::<i32>() {
        println!("The type is i32.");
```

```
    } else if value.type_id() == TypeId::of::<String>() {
        println!("The type is String.");
    } else {
        println!("Unknown type.");
    }
}
```

The check_type function accepts a generic parameter T with the trait-bound Any, which allows runtime type inspection. Inside the function, the type_id method provided by the Any trait is used to retrieve the runtime TypeId of the value being examined. This identifier is then compared against TypeId::of::<i32>(), an associated function that returns the unique TypeId corresponding to the i32 type defined by the standard library.

If the two identifiers match, the function concludes that the value is of type i32 and executes the corresponding branch. The same comparison is then performed for String using TypeId::of::<String>(). If none of the comparisons succeed, the function falls back to the default case and reports the type as unknown. Listing 8-21 shows how the function in Listing 8-20 can be used in main.

Listing 8-21. Using the Function in Listing 8-20 in main

```
fn main() {
    let num = 42;
    let text = String::from("Hello");
    check_type(&num);
    check_type(&text);
}
```

The first call will produce the output of The type is i32 and the second call will produce the output of The type is String.

The function in Listing 8-20 demonstrates how type_id enables type checking at runtime without requiring downcasting. The approach can be quite useful for dynamic type checking in applications like logging systems, type registries, and event handling frameworks.

Summary

This chapter presented a comprehensive exploration of downcasting in Rust, focusing on how concrete types can be safely recovered from trait objects at runtime. It began by introducing the motivation for downcasting and the role of the `Any` trait in enabling runtime type inspection within Rust's otherwise static type system. Through progressively refined examples, the chapter demonstrated immutable and mutable downcasting using `downcast_ref` and `downcast_mut`, along with common design patterns such as `as_any` and `as_mut_any`. It also showed how these helper methods can be eliminated by performing explicit conversions to `&dyn Any`, leading to simpler and more idiomatic designs. Practical use cases were discussed in detail, including event handling systems and scenarios involving trait-to-trait conversion, where a value implementing multiple traits must be dynamically queried for additional capabilities. The chapter further explored how to check types without downcasting by using `type_id`, highlighting cases where full conversion is unnecessary.

The next chapter examines the drop check process, focusing on how Rust ensures memory safety during destruction and how lifetimes and ownership interact at drop time.

CHAPTER 9

Drop Check

Resource management does not end with ownership alone; it extends into the precise moment when values are destroyed. As programs grow in complexity, ensuring that references remain valid during destruction becomes a subtle but critical concern. Rust's drop check mechanism enforces strict guarantees around value lifetimes at destruction time, preventing use-after-free scenarios and maintaining soundness even in the presence of custom destructors.

This chapter focuses on one of Rust's most distinctive features related to memory management (i.e., the drop check mechanism). The chapter begins by exploring the `Drop` trait, which defines how and when values are automatically cleaned up when they go out of scope. From there, the chapter moves into the drop check process, a compile-time analysis that ensures resources are not used after being moved or dropped, thus preventing subtle memory safety issues.

The chapter then explains how partial moves interact with drop semantics and what rules Rust enforces to maintain consistent ownership behavior. It also examines the order of dropping, explaining how Rust determines which values are destroyed first and why this order matters in real-world programs. In addition, we'll look deeper into the nuances of the drop system, including advanced scenarios involving structs, references, and nested resources.

The chapter discusses techniques for avoiding automatic drops when necessary, providing fine-grained control over resource lifetimes. Finally, it concludes with an essential discussion on panic safety, exploring how Rust ensures memory integrity and prevents double drops even in the presence of runtime panics. By the end of this chapter, you will have a thorough understanding of how Rust's drop system enforces deterministic cleanup, memory safety, and robustness without the need for a garbage collector.

N. Azam, *Advanced Rust*, https://doi.org/10.1007/979-8-8688-2992-5_9

Drop Check Basics

This section goes over the basics of drop check in Rust. Building on the basics, it will move to advanced details, including drop order, self-referencing, and panic safety.

Effects of Manually Implementing Drop

Consider the code in Listing 9-1.

Listing 9-1. Definition of a Struct A and Its Implementation for the `Drop` Trait

```
struct A<'a> {
    a: &'a mut i32,
}

impl<'a> Drop for A<'a> {
    fn drop(&mut self) {
        println!("Dropping");
    }
}
```

The code defines a struct `A` and then implements the `Drop` trait for it. The struct field contains a reference and therefore the mandatory lifetime annotations are added. The `Drop` trait in Rust lets you define cleanup code through the `drop` method. This method runs automatically when the value goes out of scope.

Now consider the code in `main`, shown in Listing 9-2.

Listing 9-2. Code with a Variable and a Mutable Reference to It

```
fn main() {
    let mut x = 45;
    let y = &mut x;
    println!("{x}");
}
```

The code in Listing 9-2 creates a mutable variable `x` and then takes a mutable reference to it using `y`. This code compiles as it passes the borrowing rules.

Now look at similar code to Listing 9-2, but with type `A` defined in Listing 9-3.

Listing 9-3. Code Similar to Listing 9-2 But with Type A

```
fn main() {
    let mut x = 45;
    let b = A { a: &mut x };
    println!("{}", x); // Error
}
```

As in Listing 9-2, we first created a mutable variable and then created a mutable reference to it stored in the field to A. Finally, we print the variable x. The code in Listings 9-2 and 9-3 is almost identical. The only difference is that, in Listing 9-2, we use a primitive variable to hold a mutable reference, whereas in Listing 9-3, we use a field of the struct. However, the compiler is not happy with Listing 9-3 and gives an error, even though the borrow rules are not being violated. This is kind of confusing. If you inspect the error message it says, "cannot borrow x as immutable because it is also borrowed as mutable". The error message further explains "mutable borrow might be used when b is dropped and runs the Drop code for type A".

From the error message, it appears that the drop implementation may be causing an issue. We can comment it out, as shown in Listing 9-4.

Listing 9-4. Updated Code in Listing 9-3 Without the Drop Implementation

```
struct A<'a> {
    a: &'a mut i32,
}

/* impl<'a> Drop for A<'a> {
    fn drop(&mut self) {
        println!("Dropping");
    }
} */
fn main() {
    let mut x = 45;
    let b = A { a: &mut x };
    println!("{}", x);
}
```

The code surprisingly compiles. This indicates that the `Drop` implementation is causing the issue. But what exactly is the problem?

You can now execute the code in Listing 9-3 to see some useful hints. It first indicates a mutable borrow on the line `let b = A { a: &mut x };` with no issues. Next, it indicates an immutable borrow on the line `println!("{}", x);` with an error. This means that the printing line is causing the issue. The precise error is that "mutable borrow might be used here (on printing line), when `b` is dropped and runs the `Drop` code for type `A`". This seems interesting. The `drop` is called when the values goes out of scope or when an explicit call to it is being made. In this case, there is no explicit call to `drop`. This means that it will be called at the end of main where the value is dropped. If we look at the error message again it says, "mutable borrow might be used, when `b` is dropped". This means that somehow the compiler thinks that the mutable reference, which is created above the print line in Listing 9-4, is used by the drop implementation, which is used at the end of the `main`. If this is the case, it is clearly a violation of the borrowing rules, which do not allow coexistence of immutable and immutable references.

We can update the code in `main` by calling the drop before the print line statement, as shown in Listing 9-5.

Listing 9-5. Updated Code of `main` in Listing 9-4 with an Explicit Call to `drop`

```
fn main() {
    let mut x = 45;
    let b = A { a: &mut x };
    drop(b);
    println!("{}", x);
}
```

This code makes an explicit call to `drop` before printing. This means that the mutable reference to `x` will be dropped before printing. The code compiles now. This suggests that the compiler is assuming that the call to `drop` is using the mutable reference.

If you, however, look at the `Drop` implementation shown in Listing 9-1, you can see that it does not use a mutable reference. This may seem strange because, even though the `drop` method does not explicitly use a mutable reference, the compiler must assume that it could. In reality, nothing prevents you from writing a line inside `drop` that uses a mutable reference to modify the internal value. While no practical `Drop` implementation would normally do this, the language itself does not forbid it. If such a modification occurs, it would clearly be unsafe and therefore unacceptable.

In general, the compiler assumes that dropping a type may access the values contained within it. This is referred to as *drop check*. In particular, if you have a type such as TypeA<T>, then while dropping TypeA, the compiler assumes that T may be accessed, regardless of whether it is actually used. With this check, the compiler is trying to guard you from some sort of a Drop implementation that might use the value, because any intervening use of the value may lead to a violation of the borrowing rules. In the absence of a manual Drop implementation, the compiler is satisfied because the inner value cannot be touched by anyone.

Addressing Drop Check Constraints

In the presence of the drop check constraints enforced during manual Drop implementation, you might wonder if you always have to explicitly call drop before using the value later in the code? This will put a lot of burden on the programmer and at times will get very complex. The other solution is to never include a Drop implementation. This would not work either, as there are scenarios in unsafe Rust where you have to explicitly clear memory resources.

So, what is the way out? How do you communicate to the compiler that the inner value is not being accessed? Unfortunately, this is not possible in the stable compiler version. Therefore, you need to switch to the nightly version and use the *drop check eyepatch* feature. To switch to the nightly version of Rust, use the following command:

```
rustup default nightly
```

The code in Listing 9-6 shows the updated implementation of Drop with the unstable eye patch feature.

Listing 9-6. Updated Drop Implementation with the dropck_eyepatch Feature

```
#![feature(dropck_eyepatch)]
struct A<'a> {
    a: &'a mut i32,
}

unsafe impl<#[may_dangle] 'a> Drop for A<'a> {
    fn drop(&mut self) {
        *self.a *= 2;
        println!("Dropping");
```

```
    }
}
fn main() {
    let mut x = 45;
    let b = A { a: &mut x };
    println!("{}", x);
}
```

Listing 9-6 uses the `#![feature(dropck_eyepatch)]` feature, which is a permanently unstable feature. It allows you to opt out of the drop check rules. This feature may remain permanently unstable because it is not considered a permanent solution to the problem. Listing 9-6 uses an unsafe implementation with the `#[may_dangle]` attribute. This serves as a guarantee that the code inside `drop` will not access the inner value.

The compiler now knows that the call to the drop at the end of the `main` in Listing 9-6 will not be accessing the inner mutable reference. The use of mutable references to `x` is therefore limited only to the line on which we created the variable `b` and has no overlap with other accesses to it.

Drop and Partial Move

Having explored the drop check rules and manual `Drop` implementations in detail, this section now turns to *partial moves* and their interactions with drop semantics in Rust.

A partial move in Rust occurs when one or more fields of a composite type, such as a struct, are moved while the remaining fields stay accessible. In Rust, this is allowed when the struct as a whole is not used later in the program, and only the portions that have not been moved are accessed afterward. This section quickly recaps the concept of a partial move. Consider the code in Listing 9-7.

Listing 9-7. Partial Move of a Struct Field

```
struct Student {
    name: String,
    age: u32,
}

fn main() {
    let student = Student {
```

```
        name: String::from("Ali"),
        age: 20,
    };

    let name = student.name;      // Partial move
    println!("{}", student.age); // Allowed: unmoved field
    println!("{}", student);     // Error: Not allowed:
}
```

In this example, `student.name` is moved into `name`, but `student.age` can still be accessed because it was not moved. However, using `student` as a whole after moving the `name` field is not allowed. Now you'll see how the partial move interacts with the `drop` semantics.

Consider a struct and its `drop` implementation, as shown in Listing 9-8.

Listing 9-8. Definition of a Struct and its `drop` Implementation

```
struct A<'a> {
    a: &'a mut i32,
    s: String, // add later on
}

impl<'a> Drop for A<'a> {
    fn drop(&mut self) {
        println!("Dropping");
    }
}
```

The struct in this listing is similar to the struct defined in Listing 9-1 but with an additional string field. Next, we create an instance of the struct and try to partially move the string field out of it. This is depicted in Listing 9-9.

Listing 9-9. Definition of a Struct and its `drop` Implementation

```
fn main() {
    let mut x = 45;
    let b = A {
        a: &mut x,
```

```
        s: String::from("some str"),
    };
    let c = b.s; // Error
}
```

The field s is of type string, which is heap allocated. Assigning it to some variable will lead to a change of ownership. This means the line `let c = b.s` will move the ownership of field s from variable b to variable c. This is an example of a partial move explained earlier in Listing 9-7.

The compiler does not allow the partial move in this case. The error in this case reads as "cannot move out of type A, which implements the Drop trait". The code will compile if we remove the Drop implementation.

Earlier in Listing 9-7 we noted that Rust allows partial moves as long as the whole struct is not used later and only the unmoved parts are accessed. With the manual drop implementation, it is not allowed. More precisely, we are not allowed to move out the fields from a type. This is logical because the drop takes a mutable reference to `self`, where `self` means the whole instance and not parts of it. Another perspective of this is that the drop needs to perform clean up. Trying to clear up something that is already moved out will cause errors and unexpected behavior.

Drop Order

After understanding how drop check governs whether values can be safely accessed during destruction, it is equally important to understand *drop order,* which determines the sequence in which those values are actually destroyed.

Rust automatically drops values when they go out of scope. Generally speaking, values are dropped in the reverse order of their creation. For instance, consider a couple of structs and their drop implementations in Listing 9-10.

Listing 9-10. Definition of a Couple of Structs Along with their Respective Drop Implementations

```
struct A;
struct B;

impl Drop for A {
    fn drop(&mut self) {
```

```
        println!("Dropping value of type A");
    }
}

impl Drop for B {
    fn drop(&mut self) {
        println!("Dropping value of type B");
    }
}
```

As discussed, the `drop` method of the `Drop` trait is automatically invoked when a value goes out of scope and is dropped. Now we'll use the code in Listing 9-10 in `main`, as shown in Listing 9-11.

Listing 9-11. Using the Code in Listing 9-10 in `main`

```
fn main() {
    let a = A;
    let b = B;
}
```

This code creates an instance of the two structs in `main`. Executing this code will result in the following output:

```
Dropping value of type B
Dropping value of type A
```

Since `b` is created last, its destructor was called first. This is the general pattern of dropping variables in Rust (i.e., they are dropped in reverse order of their creation).

The same pattern can be observed in arguments to a function. For instance, consider Listing 9-12.

Listing 9-12. Dropping of Variables Passed to a Function

```
fn some_fn(a: A, b: B) {}
fn main() {
    let a = A;
    let b = B;
    some_fn(a, b);
}
```

The variable a is the passed first to the function and variable b is passed last. According to the reverse order, variable b will be dropped first, followed by variable a. An important reason for dropping simple variables in reverse order is that later variables may contain references to earlier values, whereas the reverse is generally not the case.

Exceptions to Reverse Drop Order

Rust does not follow reverse drop order in every case. An exception to this are types that are based on multiple values, such as arrays, vectors, tuples, and structs. Values in such types are dropped in the source-code order. For instance, consider the code in Listing 9-13.

Listing 9-13. Definition of Containers Based on Structs A and B Defined in Listing 9-10

```
struct Container {
    a: A,
    b: B,
}
fn main() {
    let c = Container { a: A, b: B };
}
```

The Container type is based on structs A and B, as defined in Listing 9-10. Assuming the same drop implementations for A and B in Listing 9-10, this code will result in the following output.

```
Dropping value of type A
Dropping value of type B
```

The drop order in this case follows the source-code order and not the reverse order. Additionally, note that the order in which you initialize the fields does not matter. For instance, this line will result in the same drop order:

```
let c = Container { b: B, a: A };
```

This is because the order is based on the definition of the struct fields in the struct definition.

Dropping nested values in source-code order makes sense. If you construct an array containing two values, it will seem odd for the last element to be dropped first. This goes against the natural left-to-right order in which the values are written and understood in the source code. The same logic applies to tuples, where the most intuitive behavior is to drop the first element first, then the second, and so on.

Listing 9-14 shows a tuple containing instances of A and B.

Listing 9-14. A Tuple Containing Instances of A and B

```
struct A;
struct B;

impl Drop for A { ...}
impl Drop for B { ... }

fn main() {
    let x = (A {}, B {});
}
```

In main, we create a tuple x containing values of type A and B, which allows us to observe the drop order of tuple elements. If we execute the code in Listing 9-14, the drop order follows the source-code order.

The tuple will drop in regular reverse drop order if the values in the tuple are destructured. For instance, consider this code line:

```
let (a, b) = (A {}, B {});
```

In contrast to the code line in Listing 9-13 (i.e., `let x = (A {}, B {})`), variables a and b are now local variables in main and not elements of the tuple. Moreover, since b was created after a, it is dropped first. In general, when values are moved out of the compound types and stored as individual variables, they are dropped in reverse order and not in source-code order. This is because they are not part of the compound type any more.

The drop in source-code order is also not followed when such values are not contained within the type itself. Meaning that the type does not have the ownership but rather uses references to values that reside outside the type. For instance, consider the following code line:

```
let x = (&A {}, &B {});
```

In this case, the values are not contained within the tuple. The tuple only has reference to values that reside outside the tuple. In this case, the two values will be dropped in reverse order.

The same can also be observed with vectors. To store types A and B inside the same vector, you can use the trait objects shown in Listing 9-15.

Listing 9-15. Defining a Vector Containing References to A and B

```
struct A;
struct B;

impl Drop for A {...}

impl Drop for B {…}

trait T {}
impl T for A {}
impl T for B {}
fn main() {
    let v: Vec<&dyn T> = vec![&A {}, &B {}];
}
```

This code defines a common trait between A and B and implements it for the two types. In main, we created a vector of type dyn T to store references to A and B. Again, since the values are not contained within the vector, the values will be dropped in regular reverse order.

Let's go over one final example where the values are contained within the vector. Consider the code in Listing 9-16.

Listing 9-16. Defining Struct A, its Drop Implementation, and a Vector Containing Instances of A

```
struct A {
    value: String,
}

impl Drop for A {
    fn drop(&mut self) {
        println!("Dropping value of type A with value {}", self.value);
```

```
    }
}

fn main() {
    let vec = vec![
        A {
            value: String::from("First"),
        },
        A {
            value: String::from("Second"),
        },
        A {
            value: String::from("Third"),
        },
    ];
}
```

This code defines struct A, which unlike its previous definitions, now contains a String field. In Drop implementation, we are displaying the String field of the instance. This will help us exactly determine the instance of A, which is being dropped. In main, we define a vector containing instances of A. Note that all the instances of ` are contained within the vector and therefore they will be dropped in insertion or source-code order. Executing this code will therefore produce the following output:

```
Dropping value of type A with value First
Dropping value of type A with value Second
Dropping value of type A with value Third
```

Table 9-1 summarizes the drop order rules covered in the section.

Table 9-1. *Summary of the Drop Order Rules*

Data Type	Drop Order
Owned data in tuples/structs	Drop in declaration order
Owned data in vectors	Drop in insertion order
Local variables	Drop in reverse declaration order
References	Don't affect the drop order of the referenced data

As a developer, it is important to be aware of Rust's dropping rules. This ensures that you can rely on a consistent drop order, which is crucial when managing resources such as files, network connections, locks, and other values that require proper cleanup.

Drop Order and Self-Referential Structs

After understanding how Rust determines the order in which values are dropped, it is natural to explore scenarios where this destruction process becomes more delicate. One such case arises with *self-referential types,* where a value may internally hold references to its own data, making questions of validity, movement, and eventual dropping significantly more subtle.

A self-referential type is one in which one element references another element contained within the same type. Rust does not support true self-referential types because of its borrowing rules, as attempting to create them can lead to dangling references when an instance of the type is dropped. The following example illustrates why Rust does not allow true self-referential types.

For the sake of ease of understanding, we use the same code from earlier. See Listing 9-17.

Listing 9-17. Code Similar to the Code in Listings 9-10 and 9-13

```
struct A;
struct B;
impl Drop for A { … }
impl Drop for B { … }
struct Container {
    a: A,
    b: B,
}

fn main() {
    let a = A;
    let b = B;
    let c = Container { a: a, b: b };
    let tuple = (c, &c); // Error
}
```

The code is similar to the code in Listings 9-10 and 9-13. In the last line, we define a tuple that contains instance of `c` along with its reference. As mentioned, self-referencing occurs when a type contains elements that reference other elements within the same type. The tuple in the previous listing may be considered a self-referencing type. In this case, the second element of the tuple references other element within the same type (i.e., the first element of the tuple). The Rust compiler does not allow defining such types. The last line in Listing 9-17 does not compile and gives an error of "borrow or move value".

Although the tuple in Listing 9-17 appears to be a self-referential type, in the truest sense, it is not. This is because when we assign variable `c` to the first element of the tuple, it is essentially moved into the first element. This is because when struct instances are assigned, they are moved and not copied. The variable `c` is moved, so it does not exist in `main`. Therefore a reference to the same variable will lead to a dangling reference. Note that because Rust does not allow self-referencing to resolve the reference to `c` in the second element of a tuple, the compiler will look at the code and not consider the variables in the tuple itself. The gives an error since `c` is already being moved out. It is not a true self-referential type since the resolution of `&c` depends on the code tuple and not the tuple itself.

You may think that you can create the value inside the tuple itself and then reference it, as shown in this code line:

```
let mut tuple = (String::from(""), &tuple.0);
```

This is also not valid since, for the resolution of variable `tuple`, the compiler will investigate the code defined before the line on which the `tuple` is declared. If it fails to find such a variable, it will throw an error. Even if it found a variable with the name of the tuple, it will shadowed by the declaration line, making the earlier declaration and a reference to it invalid. In summary, there is no way to reference the first element within the same tuple. This leads to the fact that Rust does not allow true self-referential types.

Example of Self-Referential Structs

In the same way, self-referencing structs are also not allowed. For instance, consider the code in Listing 9-18.

Listing 9-18. Example of Self-Referential Structs

```
struct SelfRef<'a> {
    s: String,
    s_ptr: &'a String,
}
fn main() {
    let text = String::from("Hi");
    let linked_str = SelfRef {
        s: text,
        s_ptr: &text, // Error
    }
}
```

The code defines a struct called `SelfRef` that contains two fields: `s`, which owns a `string`, and `s_ptr`, which is intended to hold a reference to a `String` with lifetime `'a`. In `main`, an instance of this struct is being created where `s` stores the string `"Hi"`, while `s_ptr` is intended to reference the `s` field of the same struct instance, making it a self-referential type. This gives the same error as encountered in Listing 9-17. The variable `text` is moved in the field `s` and subsequent attempts to refer to it are not possible. Rust will throw an error, even if you try to create the value inside the instance itself, as shown in this code line:

```
let linked_str = SelfRef {
     s: String::from("Hi"),
     s_ptr: &linked_str.s, // Error
}
```

You cannot reference a value within the struct for reasons explained earlier in the context of tuples.

Self-Referential Stack Allocated Copy Types

The syntax depicting self-referential types such as `tuple = (c, &c)` is allowed for stack-allocated types such as primitives, which are copied and not moved. This section goes over some examples.

Consider the code in Listing 9-19.

Listing 9-19. Example of Self-Referential Stack-Allocated Types

```
fn main() {
let x = 5;
    let mut tuple = (x, &x);
}
```

The code defines a tuple containing an `i32` value and a reference to the same value. In this code, using the variable `x` as the first element of the tuple will make a copy of the original variable `x`. There is no transfer of ownership in this case. The original variable remains in `main`. The second element of the tuple, which is a reference to `x`, is therefore valid since it is pointing to the variable `x` defined before the declaration of the tuple. To see this clearly, we will update the value inside the tuple and display `x` and the tuple elements. See Listing 9-20.

Listing 9-20. Updated Listing 9-19 Code

```
fn main() {
    let x = 5;
    let mut tuple = (x, &x);
    tuple.0 = 20;
    println!("x is: {x}, tuple.0: {}, tuple.1: {}", tuple.0, tuple.1);
}
```

Executing this code will generate the following output:

```
x is: 5, tuple.0: 20, tuple.1: 5
```

The variable in `main` is not updated and the second element of the tuple points to the variable in `main` and not to the first element of the same tuple. The tuple in Listing 9-20 is genuinely not a self-referential type since the second element of the tuple is referencing a value that does not reside inside the tuple.

Avoiding Drop

There are scenarios in which you might intentionally want to avoid calling the `drop` method automatically. This typically arises when you need finer control over resource management, ownership transfer, or when a value must remain in memory beyond its usual scope-based lifetime. This section looks at a scenario in which this can happen.

Consider a struct called Data and its implementation block containing the new associated constructor function. The code is shown in Listing 9-21.

Listing 9-21. Definition of Data struct, its impl Block, and the Implementation for Drop

```
struct Data {
    vec: Vec<i32>,
}

impl Data {
    fn new() -> Self {
        Self {
            vec: Vec::with_capacity(0),
        }
    }
}
impl Drop for Data {
    fn drop(&mut self) {
        // expensive_operation();
        println!("Dropping Data");
    }
}
```

The Data struct contains a single field of an i32 vector. The constructor creates a new Data instance containing an empty vector. The Drop implementation is assumed to be using an expensive_operation() function, which is simulating code that contains some expensive operations before the drop. There may be situations where the Data instance is created but is never initialized from some useful values. In such cases, if the Drop implementation is called, it will unnecessarily execute the expensive_operation() function.

To avoid calling the drop, you can use the forget function provided by the standard memory module. The code in Listing 9-22 shows how to use the function.

Listing 9-22. Using forget to Avoid Calling drop

```
fn main() {
    let data = Data::new();
    let data_initialized = false;
```

```
    if !data_initialized {
        mem::forget(data);
    }
}
```

This code initialized an instance of Data. The data_initialized variable is used to determine if the variable is initialized. If data is not initialized, we will call the forget function, passing in the variable data. The forget function forces the Rust compiler to forget about the value (i.e., it no longer keeps track of the value).

When the value goes out of scope, its destructor is therefore not executed. If you were to execute the code, you might note that the drop implementation is not being invoked. In this case, it makes sense because the value has not been allocated any heap space since with_capacity(0) does not lead to any heap allocation.

An important aspect of the forget function is that it takes the ownership of the value. This means that the value that is forgotten cannot be used in subsequent code and is no longer available for use.

Use Case of *forget* in Benchmarking

A useful use case of the forget function is in benchmarking, when you are interested in the running time of your code and not in the time for deallocations. Consider the simple code for benchmarking depicted in Listing 9-23.

Listing 9-23. Using forget in Benchmarking

```
fn main() {
    let start = std::time::Instant::now();
    for _ in 0..1_000_000 {
        {
            let v = vec![0; 100];
            mem::forget(v);
        }
    }
    let duration = start.elapsed();
}
```

The code starts by recording the starting time. The `now()` function returns a value representing a specific moment in time. Although this value is not human-readable, it is ideal for measuring the duration between events in a program. Inside the loop, we have the code that we want to benchmark. Finally, we compute the time taken using the `elapsed()` function. The `elapsed()` method returns a `Duration` value representing the amount of time that has passed since the `Instant` variable was created.

Typically, in benchmarking, we are interested in measuring the performance of our code while excluding the time taken for deallocations. To avoid deallocation overhead, the `forget()` function is used in Listing 9-23. Note that if `forget` is not used, the destructor will be invoked many times inside the benchmarking loop, which can significantly affect the running cost of the measured code. In such cases, it becomes important to manage and free resources carefully.

Manually Dropping Data

In addition to forgetting the dropping of a value, Rust provides the ability to manually drop using its wrapper struct called `ManuallyDrop`. The code in Listing 9-24 shows its use.

Listing 9-24. Using `ManuallyDrop` to Control Cleanup of `data`

```
fn main() {
    let data = Data::new();

    let mut data = ManuallyDrop::new(Data::new());
    unsafe {
       ManuallyDrop::drop(&mut data);
    }
}
```

This code first creates an instance of `Data`, which is then wrapped by `ManuallyDrop`. The wrapping process suppresses Rust's automatic destructor call, giving the programmer explicit control over when the value is dropped. Inside the `unsafe` block, `ManuallyDrop::drop(&mut data)` is used to explicitly invoke the destructor for the wrapped `Data` instance. This operation is placed inside `unsafe` because Rust cannot guarantee at compile time that the value will not be accessed again after being manually dropped, and any such access would lead to undefined behavior. Therefore, the programmer must ensure that the manual drop is performed correctly and that the value is not used afterward.

The `ManuallyDrop` functionality can be useful in scenarios where ownership of a Rust-managed resource is being transferred to external code, such as C libraries. In such cases, the resource can be wrapped in `ManuallyDrop` to prevent Rust from automatically dropping it, thereby avoiding potential double-free errors. The data wrapped inside `ManuallyDrop` can later be explicitly destroyed by calling the special `drop` function associated with the `ManuallyDrop` type.

Note that both `ManuallyDrop::drop` and the regular `drop` method of the `Drop` trait destroy values, but they serve different purposes and operate under different safety constraints.

Panic Safety

The behavior of `drop` becomes particularly important when normal program execution is interrupted by a panic. In such situations, Rust relies on `drop` to release resources during stack unwinding, which makes the concept of *panic safety* closely tied to the correctness of `drop` implementations.

When a panic occurs, Rust unwinds the program stack, which is the region of memory used to store active function calls, local variables, and temporary values during program execution. Each function call adds a new stack frame to this stack, and as functions return, their frames are removed.

What Happens When Programs Panic

During a panic, Rust begins unwinding this stack. This means that everything that has been pushed onto the program stack is removed in the reverse order in which it was added. Besides other things, this includes the dropping of all owned values, ensuring that resources such as heap-allocated memory are properly cleaned up. At this stage, for any owned value that has a custom-defined `Drop` trait, its `drop` method is executed before its memory is freed. This section goes over some code so you can better understand this.

Consider the code in Listing 9-25.

Listing 9-25. Definition of BadResource and its Drop implementation

```
struct BadResource;

impl Drop for BadResource {
    fn drop(&mut self) {
        println!("Dropping BadResource");
    }
}
```

The code defines a struct called BadResource and implements the Drop for it. The code in Listing 9-26 uses BadResource in main and calls a panic.

Listing 9-26. Using the Code in Listing 9-25 in main

```
fn main() {
    let _br = BadResource;
    panic!("Main function panicked!");
    println!("This will execute"); // unreachable code
}
```

When the main panics on the second line, the program will stop executing any lines below it. The last line in the code therefore will not execute. The compiler indicates the same and issues a warning on the last line stating, "unreachable statement".

When the program encounters a panic, it tries to clear up everything in the stack. In Listing 9-26, we have a variable br in main when the panic is encountered. Rust will try to clear it or drop it due to the panic. This will invoke its drop method even though the end of main has not been reached. Executing the code in Listing 9-26 will generate the following output:

```
thread 'main' (21244) panicked at src\main.rs:24:5:
Main function panicked!
note: run with `RUST_BACKTRACE=1` environment variable to display a
backtrace
Dropping BadResource
```

This indicates that a panic occurred and then the drop method was called for the br variable.

Understanding Double Panics

In Rust, a *double panic* occurs when a panic happens while unwinding from another panic. This situation is critical because Rust's panic mechanism relies on unwinding the stack to properly clean up its resources. When a second panic occurs during this unwinding process, Rust aborts the program immediately, skipping all remaining cleanup logic.

The code in Listing 9-27 depicts a double panic.

Listing 9-27. A Double Panic Situation

```
struct BadResource;

impl Drop for BadResource {
    fn drop(&mut self) {
         println!("Dropping BadResource");
        panic!( "Panic in Drop");
    }
}
fn main() {
    let _br = BadResource;
    panic!("Main function panicked!");
 }
```

In this code, there are two panics—the main panic and the drop implementation panic. In this case, when the second panic occurs, the remaining unwinding process will immediately stop, which means some resources may not be cleaned up properly. If you execute the code, you might see very long output that will look something like this:

```
thread 'main' (21800) panicked at src\main.rs:24:5:
Main function panicked!
note: run with `RUST_BACKTRACE=1` environment variable to display a
backtrace
Dropping BadResource
thread 'main' (21800) panicked at src\main.rs:11:9:
panic in drop
stack backtrace:
   0:      0x7ff73134b372 - std::backtrace_rs::backtrace::win64::trace
```

```
at /rustc/25d319a0f656ee8faa7a534da299e76e96068a40/library\std\src\..\..\
backtrace\src\backtrace\win64.rs:85
   1:      0x7ff73134b372 - std::backtrace_rs::backtrace::trace_
unsynchronized
                                            at /rustc/25d319a0f656ee8faa7a534da299e7
6e96068a40/library\std\src\..\..\backtrace\src\backtrace\mod.rs:66
   ...
   ...
  59:      0x7ffcf572e8d7 - BaseThreadInitThunk
  60:      0x7ffcf6aac3fc - RtlUserThreadStart
error: process didn't exit successfully: `target\debug\rust_course.exe`
(exit code: 0xc0000409, STATUS_STACK_BUFFER_OVERRUN)
```

The detailed output is basically showing the stack backtrace, which is the sequence of function calls at the lower level, providing details about where the error originated. The situation of double panic can be quite dangerous, as not all the resources are cleared up cleanly. The `catch_unwind()` function can be used to remedy this. The next section explains this function and then we will come back to handling double panics using this function.

Handling Panics Using *catch_unwind()*

The `catch_unwind()` function is used to catch panics at runtime, allowing the program to continue execution even if a piece of code panics. It essentially provides an opportunity to handle the panic gracefully, which can be particularly useful in robust applications and libraries. By catching the panic, the program can decide how to respond, such as logging the error, cleaning up resources, or continuing with alternative logic. The code in Listing 9-28 explains the basic functionality of this function.

Listing 9-28. Basic Workings of `catch_unwind()`

```
use std::panic;
fn main() {
    let _br = BadResource;
    let result = panic::catch_unwind(|| {
        panic!("Main function panicked!");
        println!("This will not execute"); // Not reachable
```

```
    });
    println!("This will execute");
}
```

The catch_unwind() function takes in a closure and executes it. This function has some nice properties. It returns a Result, which in case of panic returns an Error variant and otherwise returns an Ok variant. The remainder of the code outside the closure executes normally, even if there is a panic. This means that the last print line in Listing 9-28 will always execute. This was not possible previously. The panic will only stop the execution of the code inside the closure. The last statement inside the closure is therefore not reachable.

The returning Result enum also allows you to properly handle the panic using a match statement. For instance, the code in Listing 9-29 can be used to determine whether a panic occurred.

Listing 9-29. Handling a Panic Using the catch_unwind()

```
use std::panic;

fn main() {
    let _br = BadResource;

    let result = panic::catch_unwind(|| {
        let x = _br;
        panic!("Main function panicked!");
        println!("This will not execute");
    });

    match result {
        Ok(_) => println!("Code ran fine"),
        Err(e) => println!("Caught a panic"),
    }
}
```

The closure passed into the catch_unwind function runs in a protected environment or, more specifically, inside the closure body. Its affects are therefore limited. For instance, in Listing 9-29, the instance of BadResource will not be dropped immediately due to the panic in main. It will be dropped at the end of main. Even though the effects are limited to the closure body, there still might be side effects from the closure itself. For example, if the closure writes to a file, sends a message, or modifies an atomic value, those effects are not contained within the closure.

Handling Double Panics with *catch_unwind()*

This section shows how you to use `catch_unwind()` to handle double panics. You can isolate the second dangerous panic inside the closure passed to `catch_unwind()`. The code in Listing 9-30 shows how this can be done.

Listing 9-30. Handling a Double Panic with `catch_unwind()`

```
use std::panic;

struct BadResource;
impl Drop for BadResource {
    fn drop(&mut self) {
        println!("Dropping BadResource");
        let result = panic::catch_unwind(|| {
            panic!("Panic in Drop");
        });

        match result {
            Ok(_) => println!("Closure completed successfully"),
            Err(e) => println!("Caught a panic but resource cleaned up"),
        }
    }
}
fn main() {
    let _br = BadResource;
    panic!("Main function panicked!");
}
```

The second panic occurs inside the closure passed to `std::panic::catch_unwind`, which establishes a panic boundary. When `panic!("Panic in Drop")` is triggered, the usual stack unwinding begins, but instead of propagating further, it is intercepted by `catch_unwind()` and converted into a `Result` value of type `Err`. This allows the program to regain control at the point of the `catch_unwind()` call. The returned `Result` is then matched, and since the closure panics, the `Err` branch is taken, printing a message that the panic was caught. In this way, the panic is handled gracefully within the `Drop` implementation, preventing it from escalating into a double panic and allowing the destructor to complete safely. If you were to execute this code, you might note that the statement corresponding to the `Err` arm in the `match` executes successfully. This means that, although the program panicked twice, the resource was cleared up cleanly.

A final note is that you should do your level best to make sure that drop implementations do not panic. However, if that is unavoidable, you can isolate the second dangerous panic using a `catch_unwind()`, as shown previously.

Summary

This chapter explained Rust's drop check mechanism and its role in memory safety. It showed how the `Drop` trait controls cleanup when values go out of scope. The compiler enforces drop check to prevent invalid memory access during destruction. Manual `Drop` implementations make the compiler more conservative about borrowing. Partial moves are restricted when a type implements `Drop`. The chapter explained how drop order works in different contexts. Local variables are dropped in reverse order of creation. Structs, tuples, and vectors follow source-code or insertion order. Self-referential types are not allowed due to safety risks. Techniques like `forget` and `ManuallyDrop` provide control over destruction. The chapter also discussed panic safety and stack unwinding behavior. Finally, you learned that `catch_unwind()` is used to safely handle panics and avoid double panic issues.

Index

A

Addition, 218
Assignment, 85–86

B

BadResource, 264
BankAccount struct, 96–99
Binding variable, 81
Borrowing rules, 96

C

Casting operations, 83–85
Chaining method
  BankAccount struct, 96–99
  borrowing rules, 96
  combinators, 145
    fallback options, 148–149
    fetch_user function, 146–147
    multiple fallible operations, 147–148
    transformation, 147
    transform-validate-fetch, 146
    validate/transform/fallback, 149
    value extraction, 148
  consecutive method, 96
  constructor function, 97
  debug iterator pipelines, 158–161
  immutable reference, 102
  mutable reference, 101–102
  owned type/self, 102–103
  returning method, 100
  types, 99
  withdraw method, 101
Chaining question mark operators
  complete_order method, 16
  concepts, 13–18
  main function, 17, 18
  OrderError enum, 14
  Order struct, 14
  process_payment method, 15
  ship_order method, 15
  validate method, 14, 16, 17
Coercions
  accepts_str function, 112
  concepts, 105
  deref method, 106–111
  email_notification function, 117
  execute_command function, 121
  function item, 117–119
  function pointer, 119
  generics, 122–124
  implicit transformation, 106
  layman terms, 106
  LUB (*see* Least upper bound (LUB) coercion)
  mut_ref/accepts_str functions, 114
  notify_user function, 118
  print_str function, 125
  references, 114–117
  returns_str function, 113
  return values, 113
  sms_notification function, 117

N. Azam, *Advanced Rust*, https://doi.org/10.1007/979-8-8688-2992-5

Coercions (*cont.*)
  source code, 112
  struct field initialization, 113
  trait object, 119–122
  transitivity, 124–127
  TurnOnLight and AdjustThermostat structs, 120
  types, 113
Combinators
  and_then method, 136–139
  cached_result method, 141
  chaining method, 145–149
  debug iterator pipelines, 158–161
  filter option, 143–145
  helper methods, 134
  key characteristics, 143, 144
  lazy evaluation, 141
  map function, 134–136
  or_else function, 140–141
  or function, 139–140
  println! statement, 136
  processing vectors, 154
    enumerate, 155–156
    fold, 156
    reduce, 157–158
    skip, 154
    take, 155
  refined version, 138
  unwrap_or/unwrap_or_else functions, 141–142
  vector transformations, 150
    cleaning option values, 152–153
    collections, 150–151
    filtering none values, 153–154
    iter method, 150
    mandatory value, 151–152
    option types, 153
    turbofish syntax, 151

D

Debugging techniques, 35
  dbg! macro
    expression, 39
    max_score, 37
    properties, 38–40
    return value, 39, 40
    source code, 40
    streams, 38
    working process, 36, 37
  Debug trait
    alternate() method, 50
    Color struct, 48
    deriving point, 45–46
    Display implementation, 51–52
    fmt method, 49
    fundamental tool, 44
    instances, 44
    line struct, 46
    manual implementation, 48–51
    point struct, 44
    pretty-print debug formatter, 47
    vector, 44
  definition, 36
  errors, 36
  iterator pipelines, 158–161
    approaches, 158
    incremental inspection, 158–160
    inspect, 160–161
    intermediate results, 160
  logging
    different modules, 68
    filtering level, 66, 67
    log and env_logger, 64–69
    logging messages, 65
    macros, 64, 65
    priority levels, 66
    rust_debugging module, 69

security module, 67
and tracing, 35
output streams, 41
panics, 52
backtracing records, 53–56
call stack, 54
downcast_ref method, 58
frame, 55
handling user login requests, 53
set_hook function, 56–59
rustfmt, 75, 76
standard output, 40–44
tracing/logging
authenticate function, 70
cargo.toml file, 69
log and env_logger, 69
output code, 73
process_request function, 71
process_request method, 70
save_to_DB function, 71
tracing_subscriber, 72
validate_order function, 70
VS Code, 59–64
Deref coercions
accept_str, 107
advantage, 109
custom defined type, 108–110
definition, 106
DerefMut implementation, 111
HtmlText implementation, 108, 109
standard library, 107, 111
strings, 107
types of, 110–111
Downcasting
&dyn Any, 229
&mut dyn, 230–231
Any trait, 226–227
as_any and as_mut_any methods, 232–234
as_any method, 227, 228
casting references, 232
check_type function, 239
concrete types, 239–240
definition, 225
event handling scenario, 234–236
identify_and_make_sound, 228, 229
immutable conversion, 227–230
mouse clicks/keyboard input, 234
mutable reference, 230–231
object conversions, 236–239
Drop check process, 243
benchmarking, 261–262
check constraints, 247–248
control cleanup, 262–263
data struct, 259–261
dropck_eyepatch function, 247
drop implementation, 245, 246
elapsed() method, 262
exception
containers, 252
order rules, 255
reverse order, 252
source-code order, 255
tuples, 253
vector containing references, 254
forget function, 261–262
mutable reference, 244–247
panic safety, 263
BadResource, 264
catch_unwind() function, 266–268
double situation, 265–266
handle double panics, 268–269
heap-allocated memory, 263–264
partial move, 248–250
print line statement, 246

Drop check process (*cont.*)
respective implementations, 250–252
self-referential type (*see* Self-referential type)
source code, 244

E, F

Error handling system
anyhow
AppError enum, 24
context method, 27
definition, 23
error conversions, 26
key characteristics, 29
read_and_parse_number function, 23–25
with_context method, 28
chaining question mark operators, 13–18
file opening function, 4
layered outcomes
control flows, 18
database connection function, 20
find_product function, 19, 20
handle_user_registration function, 21
option wrapping, 21–23
result wrapping option, 19–21
types, 18
match expression, 5
multiple error types
? operator, 9
celsius to fahrenheit function, 9
coordination function, 10
map_err method, 10–13
TemperatureError enum type, 11
temperature readings, 9
parse method, 5
propagation
definition, 6
enum option, 7
find method, 8
get method, 8
question mark operator, 6
read_number function, 6, 7
recoverable errors, 4–5
result and option, 1
thiserror
AppError enum, 29
comparison, 32
definition, 29
error attribute, 30
From implementations, 31
key advantage, 32
trait implementation, 30
unique and explicit approach, 2
unrecoverable error, 2–3
value-processing function, 3

G, H

Generic function, 122–124

I, J, K

identify_and_make_sound, 228–229
Immutable references
assignment, 85–86
binding variable, 81
casting, 85
chaining method, 102
coercions, 114–117
downcasting, 227–230
generic function, 123
tuple, 94

type inference, 89
updating process, 80
vectors, 96

L

Least upper bound (LUB) coercion
array elements, 131–132
control-flow branches, 127
if/else expressions, 127–130
JsonValue struct, 128
match expressions, 130–131
Lifetime relationships
bounds/subtyping
definition, 170
elision rules, 170–172
generics, 174
implied method, 172–175
updated function, 172
conceptual background, 163
concrete, 164–165
dangling reference, 165
elision rules, 169–170
generics, 166–167
non-lexical lifetimes, 165
return_str function, 169
static method, 167–169
string literal, 167
string slices, 168
contravariance
function signature, 179–180
intuitive mental model, 180–181
str_fn function, 179
subtype, 178
variables, 181
invariance
definition, 182
mutable references, 184–185
non_static_str, 182
non-static lifetime, 183
references, 183
source code, 182–184
variance, 175
accepts_str function, 175, 176
assignment, 178
contravariance, 178–181
covariance, 175–178
subtyping relationships, 176

M

make_sound, 226
ManuallyDrop, 262
Monomorphization, 123
Mutable references
assignment, 85–86
binding variable, 81
casting, 84
coercions, 114–117
downcasting, 230–231
invariance, 184
patterns, 87
reassignment, 80
returning method, 101–102
tuple, 94
vectors, 96

N

Non-lexical lifetimes (NLL), 115, 165

O

Orphan rule
addition trait, 218
library crate, 216, 218
line struct, 219

Orphan rule (*cont.*)
point struct/printable trait, 216
PointWrapper struct, 217
printable trait, 217
standard library, 220
wrapper struct, 217

P, Q

private_mod, 220

R

Recoverable errors, 4–5
References
&mut &String expression, 82
assignment, 85–86
binding variable, 80
casting, 83–85
coercion, 114–117
compound types
data types, 79, 94–96
function signature, 92
non-overlapping, 95
ref keyword, 91
simple/created using ref, 93
some_fn function, 93
tuple/struct, 91
vectors, 95
forms and types, 82
list summarization, 86
method chaining, 96–103
mutable and immutable, 80–83
pattern-based bindings
function signature, 91
heap allocation, 90
nested references, 89
non-copy types, 90
type inference, 88, 90
value assignment, 88–89
variable types, 87
reassignment, 80
SomeType, 86
syntactic forms, 87

S

Sealed traits
binary crate, 222
design pattern, 220
implementation, 220
main method, 222
parent module, 221
private_mod, 220
Self-referential types
definition, 256
SelfRef, 258
source code, 256, 257
stack-allocated types, 258–259
tuples, 257

T

TemperatureError, 10
Trait object coercion, 119
Trait object safety
associated types, 193–197
auto traits, 193
circle and square structs, 188, 189
compile time, 193
definition, 188
drawable and movable traits, 188
draw function, 195, 196, 203
draw method, 202
fundamental concepts, 188

generic methods, 197
    DrawbaleWithGenericFn, 197
    draw function, 200
    draw method, 198
    draw_with_generic method, 198
    modified definition, 197–198
    vtables, 198–201
move_and_draw function, 190, 191
orphan rule (*see* Orphan rule)
sealed traits, 220–223
self parameters, 204
    default methods, 205–206
    generic function, 209
    no_self function, 205–209
    sized/unsized, 207, 208
    SomeTrait method, 207
    source code, 204
    type-specific version, 208
size/unsized constraints, 209
    additional methods, 211, 212
    compilation time, 210
    drawable trait, 213
    error message, 211
    implications, 209–212
    main method, 211
    marking methods, 212–213
    partial object safety, 213–216
    single method, 210
    SomeTrait method, 210
SomeType, 194
specialized version, 201
static dispatch, 202
supertraits, 192
vtables, 191, 193, 204

U, V, W, X, Y, Z

Unrecoverable errors, 2–3

GPSR Compliance
The European Union's (EU) General Product Safety Regulation (GPSR) is a set of rules that requires consumer products to be safe and our obligations to ensure this.

If you have any concerns about our products, you can contact us on

ProductSafety@springernature.com

In case Publisher is established outside the EU, the EU authorized representative is:

Springer Nature Customer Service Center GmbH
Europaplatz 3
69115 Heidelberg, Germany

www.ingramcontent.com/pod-product-compliance
Lightning Source LLC
LaVergne TN
LVHW080033210926
848481LV00011B/3173

* 9 7 9 8 8 6 8 8 2 9 9 1 8 *